Moral Outrage
IN EDUCATION

Studies in the
Postmodern Theory of Education

Joe L. Kincheloe and Shirley R. Steinberg
General Editors

Vol. 102

PETER LANG
New York • Washington, D.C./Baltimore • Boston
Bern • Frankfurt am Main • Berlin • Vienna • Paris

David E. Purpel

Moral Outrage
IN EDUCATION

PETER LANG
New York • Washington, D.C./Baltimore • Boston
Bern • Frankfurt am Main • Berlin • Vienna • Paris

Library of Congress Cataloging-in-Publication Data

Purpel, David E.
Moral outrage in education / David E. Purpel.
p. cm. — (Counterpoints; vol. 102)
Includes bibliographical references.
1. Education—Social aspects—United States. 2. Social change—United States.
3. Moral education—United States. 4. Critical pedagogy—United States. 5. Purpel,
David E. I. Title. II. Series: Counterpoints (New York, N.Y.); vol. 102.
LC192.P87   370.11'5—dc21   98-37877
ISBN 0-8204-4169-4
ISSN 1058-1634

Die Deutsche Bibliothek-CIP-Einheitsaufnahme

Purpel, David E.:
Moral outrage in education / David E. Purpel.
–New York; Washington, D.C./Baltimore; Boston; Bern;
Frankfurt am Main; Berlin; Vienna; Paris: Lang.
(Counterpoints; Vol. 102)
ISBN 0-8204-4169-4

Cover design by Lisa Dillon

The paper in this book meets the guidelines for permanence and durability
of the Committee on Production Guidelines for Book Longevity
of the Council of Library Resources.

Printed in the United States of America

Table of Contents

Preface: A Mifgash

Shirley R. Steinberg

The first time I met David Purpel was "on the fly" in a corridor in the San Francisco Hilton. He was running up the stairs and I reached out and touched his arm, he stopped and realized he didn't know who I was . . . saved by the nametag on my jacket, he warmly shook my hand and said, "We have to talk . . ." as he continued his jog, he turned back to me and called: "*Mifgash*," a quick smile, shining eyes, he was gone. Marveling that indeed, I had *met* David Purpel, *the* moralist, *the* ethicist of education, I then queried what mifgash was. It was obviously a Hebrew word, and I obviously didn't know it. Embarrassed as I was, I needed to find the meaning without anyone knowing of my Hebraic shortcomings. Upon discrete inquiry, I found that the word, *mifgash*, could be understood as a word to signify *a gathering*. I liked the word. As I later found out from David, he was inviting me to an informal gathering of Jews in education who wanted to be together, talk, share and, most importantly, *gather*. By the end of that week, we did gather: David, Alan Block, and me. As we sat scrunched over a tiny table and cups of coffee, we talked about, well, we talked about everything. Why we were there, why we had a need to gather and how lucky we were to have found each other.

As an educator who has had my share of star sightings, I am always tentative about meeting the gurus of our field. Many are shy, many are rock stars, and many are pompous. David is not categorizable, he is David. A funky middle-aged man with dark hair and eyes, he looks best in turtlenecks and casual shabby chic. As I found quickly in my new friendship with David, he is a genuine, fine and sweet man. Genuine, fine and sweet in disposition and in scholarship. He is one of the best. I can go no further in my words for David. This is not a *festschrift*, and David is very much alive. I do not want to embarrass him by lauding him with words that are usually reserved for one's last *mifgash*. I would like to then, just introduce you to a collection of essays by David Purpel, an educator and a friend that I expect to have for many years. As you read this gathering of words, do not expect pedantic proclamations or patriarchal pandering. Expect human words that speak to each of us in the way we chose to receive them. *Shalom*.

Shirley R. Steinberg
Adelphi University

Introduction

When I was putting together this collection of essays, I found myself often thinking about the paradox involved in the necessity for expressing both affirmation and humility. As professionals, we are surely required to put forth our ideas for mutual examination, sharing, and criticism in the hope that the sum total of such efforts can contribute to valuable knowledge and insight. As human beings, we also delight in the pride and acclaim that often accompanies significant discovery and achievement. However, we are also very much aware of the problematics of speaking authoritatively, given the complexities of the search for truth. We, therefore, tend to be skeptical and wary in our research, because it is so difficult to be sure and so painful to be wrong.

We also have the opportunity and responsibility to support and affirm particular values, policies, platforms, and programs. Here again, we often struggle with the tension between having the confidence in and courage of our convictions and the vivid awareness of the dangers of dogmatism and authoritarianism. Surely there is danger in the wishy-washiness and timidity that can result from excessive caution, just as there is a peril in the oppression that is often the consequence of rigidity and arrogance. Striking the balance between useful knowledge and healthy skepticism, between affirmation and humility, knowing the difference between being open-minded and empty-minded, and being sensitive to the line between humility and self-effacement are vitally important challenges to us all. In this respect, Gordon Allport urged us to be "whole-hearted and half-sure" while Sharon Welsh suggests a formula of "absolute commitment and infinite suspicion."

An aphorism and an old story have helped me in the struggle to find this balance, each having its own message on the poignancy that comes from the difficulty of being able to act on the wisdom that we know so well.

The aphorism is attributed to André Gide and it goes something like this: "It is true that everything has already been said. However, it is also true that nobody was listening, and therefore, it is necessary to say it all over again."

The story is about the two professors walking across the campus of a prestigious university. One says proudly and excitedly, "My new book came out today!" The other professor replies, "Good for you, I'm very happy for you. My heartiest congratulations. So, by the way, what did you call it this time?"

In addition to confronting these lessons in responsibility and humility, the process of assembling this book has also given me an opportunity to reflect on the general nature of my work and to discern its themes and emphases. If indeed I have been repetitious, it was helpful to at least find out what I have been repeating! Moreover, it has allowed me the opportunity to review the path I have been taking and where I now find myself going.

Although I sort of stumbled into education as a profession, I had always wanted to change the world and began my career believing that this could be done, or at least seriously expedited, by reforming the schools. I basically bought into the premises of the late fifties and early sixties that educational problems could be resolved through hard-nosed social science research, imaginative curriculum development, and rigorous teacher training. In this view, social and cultural problems were rooted in ignorance and superficial thinking, and salvation lay in transforming a profession rooted in conventional thinking and mired in mediocrity into one energized by bold and critical thinking.

The naïveté and poignancy of this view was brought vividly home to us through the devastating critiques of the educational reforms of those times, perhaps best summed up as the rediscovery of the concept of the hidden curriculum. This research served to remind us not only of our blindness but of how saturated educational institutions had become with the consciousness and values of the dominant culture. It became clear that the problems extended far beyond the classroom, school system, and the profession, as weak and problematic as those institutions were and are. Surely there is still much to be done to improve the quality of classroom curriculum and instruction, to increase our understanding of the teaching-learning process, and to provide for more enlightened educational leadership. However, it has become painfully clear that school reform does not a Utopia make, and even more painful is the realization that school reform has often served to strengthen and perpetuate an unjust and oppressive status quo.

Like many of my colleagues, I continue to want to change the world (perhaps even more so given the state of the world and how much that impulse has come to be derided and dismissed). However, like many of my colleagues, I find it increasingly difficult to frame my concerns as "educational" issues. Rather, I see my work as focusing on social. cultural, political, economic, and moral issues as they get revealed and acted out in educational practices and policies. The notion of a science of education or of developing a corps of educators to provide objective and unbiased expertise seems at best inane, and at worst counterproductive. Our work is not primarily educational; it is primarily social, cultural, economic, political, and moral. Indeed, it is that emphasis that enables and validates those who focus this larger work within the comparatively narrower context of education.

I say this because I have come to a growing realization of the problematics of professionalism, that is, of the difficulties of identifying myself as an "educator" and doing my work in the field of "Education." This is not at all to suggest that the field is particularly intellectually inferior to or less socially important than other fields but rather to offer the distinction between work (as in vocation) and job (as in place of employment). I consider myself as one of the tens of millions of people who, at least implicitly, consider their struggle for social justice and personal meaning as their work, and one of the millions of people who have chosen to pursue this work in the context of their job as educators. To say that we are "professionals"or "educators" rather than people struggling for justice and meaning tends to deflect us from the profound significance of our task, and instead serves to trivialize and vulgarize our efforts as merely directed at generating expertise and increasing effectiveness.

Within this context and in retrospect, I can discern a number of broad hopes and purposes that seem to have generated and guided the writing of these essays. Although this book is permeated with a number of goals, it has become clear to me that what I have been largely involved in is an endeavor:

1. To frame education as primarily a moral, cultural, and social endeavor and to convince others to do likewise. The claim is certainly not that education does not have other dimensions (e.g. psychological, instructional, curricular) but that the continuing professional obsession with technical issues masks the fundamental reality that education is an expression of an elaborate cultural and societal agenda. Although this focus on technique has allowed the profession to opportunity to develop useful information and insight, it has also served to distract the public from its responsibility to critically examine the moral, political, and economic assumptions that provide the context for educational policies and practices.

2. To reduce unnecessary human suffering. This would seem to be the minimum task of any society that values the preciousness of life and that is committed to the principle that every person is to be afforded dignity. Every social institution and every political and economic policy should be informed by the principle that human agency is responsible for unnecessary human suffering and therefore is responsible for its amelioration, if not its elimination. Education would seem to be centrally involved in this task both as the focus of its policies and in its capacity to teach the skills appropriate to the task. Much of human misery—for example, poverty, hunger, homelessness—is the consequence of human failures—evil, greed, ignorance, or stupidity, all of which are proper concerns of the teaching-learning process.

3. To express outrage at the level of unnecessary human suffering and to deepen public and professional awareness of its depth. With all the enormous amount of information and data that is currently available, it is abundantly clear that there is an obscene degree of unnecessary human suffering in the United States. and in the rest of the world. In addition to the horror of this shocking reality, there is the equally scandalous reality that we do not as a culture or as a profession make this fact the central and overriding consideration in the determination of our policies and practices. Rather than rage at the injustice of needless suffering, the culture and the profession instead persists in avoiding its responsibilities through a thoroughgoing process of denial that includes blindness, self-absorption, and victim-blaming.

4. To speak to the limits of critical rationality as a mode of human liberation. It would be fatuous of me to express the singular and indispensable values of critical thinking and rigorous analysis. I see these processes as absolutely necessary, but clearly not sufficient for the struggle to create a just and loving community. We have all had to suffer the anguish of learning that virtue and decency are not necessarily correlated with intelligence and that creativity and imagination can and have been used for evil as well as for just purposes.

5. To affirm a moral credo that informs and energizes educational policies and practices and to urge other educators to do the same. Given that education is inherently and inevitably a moral endeavor, it would seem that candor and honesty should require that educators address their own attempts to explicitly examine the moral grounding of their work. This is certainly a complex and excruciatingly difficult task, as moral issues are not only notoriously elusive and ambiguous, but are also fraught with the potential for conflict, divisiveness, and polarization. Although this should compel us to proceed with humility, sensitivity, and caution, it does not make the task any less necessary.

6. To advocate a moral credo that affirms the dignity of each person and the preciousness of life that emerges from a dedication to a just and loving community. I surely do not see this affirmation as merely an expression of my own personal value system but rather as a reaffirmation of a moral vision that is deeply rooted in the culture's highest aspirations and deepest commitments. Indeed, I believe very strongly that however vague and ambiguous this vision may be, it nonetheless constitutes a solid and substantial basis for a broad moral consensus that can and should inform our policies and practices.

7. To speak out against the cruelty and injustice of hierarchy and competition. I believe that the root of all evil is the human compulsion to judge some people to be better and more deserving than others. The criteria may differ; it can be wealth or birth; it may be race, gender, or class; it may be ability, competence, or skill; but we persist in ranking people as to their worth. When we do this, we violate the premise of the inherent equality and dignity of all people by allocating social and cultural privileges according to these rankings. Particularly pernicious are those competitive practices that allocate these privileges at the expense of others, practices that are so integral to current educational policies and practices.

8. To integrate this social vision with a sense of the awe and mystery of the universe. This is clearly a daunting task, one that continues to challenge those of us who have not been able to rid themselves of the idea that there is more to life than skepticism and material existence. Such a task is particularly difficult for those who quest for a larger spiritual and cosmological framework, but who lack a compelling tradition within which to pursue this search. This personal search also reflects a larger cultural concern for larger meaning as represented in the extraordinary energy that is being directed to various religious and spiritual movements and projects, an event that educators must address as a very real and vital phenomenon.

The book is organized into four sections. Part One focuses on the general nature of my social and cultural critique of education. In these essays I examine the relationships between educational policies and practices and broader social and cultural concerns. I look at the social, political, cultural, and moral implications and consequences of a number of educational institutions, for example, higher education, the teaching profession, and the Goals 2000 program. At the center of my critique is the matter of the nature and quality of the field's responsiveness to the struggle for social justice and personal meaning.

Part Two deals with a number of curricular approaches designed as alternatives to the conventional and stultifying programs that currently pass for education in our schools. My efforts in these essays is to avoid both the pitfall of dismissing such innovations as merely palliative as well as the pitfall of an uncritical embrace of the "anything but what is going on now." More specifically, I offer critiques of moral education, character education, service learning, and holistic education.

Part Three is in the nature of a still deeper exploration into the possibilities of using religious and spiritual discourse in educational inquiry. The papers in this section represent my current focus of interest as well as the locus of my personal spiritual struggle. In that sense, it is still very much a work in progress as I wrestle with the enormity of cosmological matters and the limits of my own belief system. It has almost become a cliché to note the deep spiritual hunger that is so much of our current cultural condition, but clichés are not to be ignored, however displeasing their aesthetic may be. The essays in this section reflect that hunger and I hope will encourage others to address it in their work, for I have come to see that we must somehow account for the mysterious source of the energy that animates the quest for meaning.

Part Four consists of only one selection and it is an essay that is primarily autobiographical in nature. It was written for a book of collected essays (edited by my friend and colleague, Svi Shapiro) on how various academics have or have not integrated their Jewish origins with their scholarly work. I must confess that I remain unsure on the appropriateness of including this article for my own book of essays since it might easily be read as self-indulgent or parochial, or both. However, many of my colleagues have urged me to include it because it provides some of the personal and cultural context from which I write. So after considerable deliberation, I decided to include it with the hope that it will not bore readers or distract them from the larger educational issues with which the rest of the essays deal.

Although some of the essays are published for the first time in this book, others have appeared or will soon appear in other places. Two articles were originally published in *Holistic Education Review: Social Justice and Education*. *The Odd Couple* appeared in the Spring, 1993 issue, and *Social Transformation and Holistic Education* in the Summer, 1996 issue. This journal has since changed its name to *Encounter* and I am honored that they chose to publish *Service Learning: A Critique and Affirmation* in their Spring, 1998 edition.

Eyewitness to Higher Education: Confession and Indictment was originally published in the Spring, 1995 issue of *Taboo* while *The Politics of Character Education* first appeared in the 1996 *Yearbook of the National Society for the Study of Education*, titled "The Construction of Children's Character," edited by Alex Molnar. I am honored that two of my articles have appeared in books edited by Ron Miller: *Goals 2000: The Triumph of Vulgarity and the Legitimation of Social Injustice* originally appeared in his *Educational Freedom for a Democratic Society* published by the Resource Center for Redesigning Education in 1995. In addition, *Holistic Education in a Prophetic Voice* was included in *The Renewal of Meaning in Education* published in 1992 by Holistic Education Press.

The title essay, *Moral Outrage and Education* will appear in *Education, Information and Transformation* edited by Jeffrey Kane to be published by Prentice Hall in Fall, 1998. The autobiographical essay will be part of a book edited by Svi Shapiro and published by Lang Publications titled *Strangers in the Land*.

I am grateful to those concerned not only for granting their permission to reprint these pieces but for being so encouraging and facilitating in the process. Their generosity and graciousness are much appreciated.

It is also extremely important that I acknowledge the help, support, and criticism of any number of individuals who have influenced and helped shape this book even as I fear that I will likely fail to give proper due to these generous and gifted people. I certainly want to mention a few of these individuals, to thank them publicly, but to absolve them from the responsibility for how I have chosen to utilize their insight and knowledge. (For better or worse, such responsibility lies totally with me.) Among these folks are Chaim Dov Beliak, Jeff Kane, Svi Shapiro, Connie Krosney, Joe Kincheloe, Shirley Steinberg,

Ron Miller, Bill McLaurin, Roger Simon, and Alan Block. I also want to express my gratitude to the staff at Peter Lang Publishing, especially to Chris Myers for his support and patience and to Scott Gilliam for his astute and thorough editing.

When I began working on this book and in a moment of self-indulgent fantasy I determined that I should begin it with the sentence, "It *is* a dark and stormy night." We are indeed in a very difficult time, and the storms of injustice and oppression are intensified by the winds of individual indifference, political cynicism, economic exploitation, cultural vulgarity, and moral vacuity. Where we once hoped the dark could be illuminated by bursts of intellectual and creative energy, we see an educational system that has become increasingly controlling and vulgar. However, there are still those who remind us that the storm still rages, even as the official weather forecasters report blue skies, and there are many who insist that we in fact *do* something about the weather and not just talk about it. Perhaps then, a more accurate weather report would predict continuing storms with intermittent periods of sunshine.

We must take heart from the promise of sunshine and, at the same time, take leave of this metaphor. Like all metaphors, this one distorts as well as illumines for our social and cultural storms, darkness, and wind, unlike the real ones, are not uncontrollable events of Nature. It must be remembered, to our dismay, that much of the distress that we are experiencing is the result of human agency and cultural choice. It is also important to remind ourselves that we need to celebrate the equally powerful truth that human agency and cultural choice are also involved in the manifold and tireless efforts to create a just and loving community. My faith is that this mysterious impulse to make the world better continues and will continue to energize our hopes and vision. Furthermore, it is still my faith that these dreams can be realized with the help of an education that channels intellectual rigor and creative imagination to the fulfillment of our most cherished hopes.

Part One

A SOCIAL AND CULTURAL CRITIQUE OF EDUCATION

Social Justice and Education:
The Odd Couple

I have taken as my topic for this essay the relationship between social justice and formal education, and in so doing I wish to emphasize the mode as well as the substance of my discussion. First, I will begin with a discussion of social justice rather than education to underline my belief that the interests of social justice supersede those of what is called formal education. Second, I will limit the amount and quality of academic and scholarly analysis in order to emphasize my belief that such analysis often distracts us from our moral responsibilities.

Let me therefore begin with some notions of social responsibility. As I warned you, I will *not* present anything like a sophisticated analysis of the concept of "social" or of "justice," of the nature of reality, of what constitutes an ideal community, or of the nature of truth. The essential point is that I (and, I believe that most of us) accept as fact that there is an enormous amount of unnecessary human suffering in the world, in our own country, and in our own communities. By unnecessary human suffering I mean the horrors of poverty, disease, war, and bigotry whose origins and possibilities of resolution are basically human. It is in this sense that I use the first of two notions of responsibility—that is, that we as a people must accept responsibility for the creation and continuation of unnecessary human suffering. I am not speaking here of suffering that has its origins in nonhuman events,such as earthquakes and drought or in individual existentialist crises, such as unrequited love or the loss of loved ones. Rather I am speaking to the suffering that emerges from human greed, hostility, and/or stupidity as reflected in the cultural and social policies, practices, and traditions that have led us to our present human condition. This condition is one of intense and unbearable suffering for many and a life of comfort and ease for a few.

There is a second meaning of responsibility which pertains to the ability to respond—that is, to how we deal with human suffering including that which may not be rooted in human intentionality. Even though we are not responsible for earthquakes and *may* not be responsible for birth defects, we are responsible for how we deal with the consequent suffering and pain. Those responses have many human dimensions. In addition to the material ones, such as medical and relief care in times of disaster, there are matters of empathy, caring, and understanding of the pain, and the capacity to restore the wretched of the earth to a condition of dignity and autonomy.

Let me try to be clearer and more concrete by citing a very small number of statistics.

Forty thousand children in the United States and eleven-million children in the world die before their first birthday. In 1968 America ranked fifteenth among the world's nations on the infant mortality rate. Twenty years later, the ranking had fallen to nineteenth. Fourteen million children die of hunger-related causes per year. Four hundred and fifty million people suffer from hunger and malnutrition.

I have had over the years some fairly consistent reactions from other groups when I have presented such data. In fairness, the most common reactions are those of remembered anguish, suppressed outrage, and pained impotence. However, I also am often challenged on the validity and reliability of these statistics and accused of engaging in intellectual reductionism and rhetorical excess. Some people get irate because they've heard all this before, and so why am I wasting their time with the obvious? Some remind me of the limitations of a pedagogy of guilt induction, while others self-righteously insist that they are doing something constructive about these horrors. The most depressing reaction, however, is the shrugged shoulders, pursed lips, clenched mouths, and uplifted palms of powerlessness, futility, and despair.

I accept all of these (and others) as significant because they are at once authentically human and intellectually plausible. Beyond all the skepticism about the analysis and methodology and beyond all the interpersonal and intrapersonal pain, however, there is simply no doubt that there is a totally unacceptable amount of unnecessary suffering in our world, our nation, our community, and our neighborhood. This has been going on for a great many years, goes on as we speak, and will go on into the indefinite future UNLESS there are enormous changes in our culture. Indeed, this condition is so obscene, so heinous, and so evil that we find it too painful as a culture and society to confront it.

This apocalyptic pronouncement of our present human condition, of course, does not emerge from any kind of scholarly tradition and is not to be justified within the terms of a particular academic paradigm. I make this point partly to address the limitations of scholarly discourse, but more to set this out as the focus of my presentation. If this pronouncement is in any significant sense true, then we must face once again the most troubling questions of human history: Am I my brother's keeper? If not now, when? Who are we? Where are we going?

Indeed, if this pronouncement has validity, we must wrestle with the reality that most of us conduct our affairs *as if* it were *not* true. My challenge is to reflect on what we ought to do if it is true, and if we all believe it is true, will we make any changes in our lives?

Personally, and paradoxically in this case, I believe that the pursuit of truth is highly problematic and that we have to accept a life of continuous and profound uncertainty. In spite of this, I have no doubt about the general validity of my pronouncement since for me it is true enough and yet still lets me pay my respects to the awesome shadow of uncertainty. What, in this case, would it take to significantly reduce this shadow so that most of us could reach a useful conclusion? Will it ever be possible to do this? If so, when? If not, would it be better to assume that it is true, is false, or not knowable? Is further research necessary or expedient? What are the dangers of overestimating as well as underestimating the degree of human suffering? More to the point, what is *your own* assessment of the amount of unnecessary human suffering? How important is it to make such an assessment and how significant are its implications for how we live our lives?

My own view is that the magnitude of unnecessary human suffering is so vast and pervasive that it ought seriously to inform our personal and institutional projects. It ought to become our overriding and dominant concern and in so doing displace our obsessive concern with national pride, institutional glorification, and personal success. A commitment to a significant reduction of unnecessary personal suffering ought to supersede our present commitments to achievement, hierarchy, privilege, and domination. This requires a major shift in our thinking, but we are capable of such changes in consciousness. When there is a fire in someone's house or at a place of business, we typically show concern and sympathy for the victim, acknowledge the courage and skill of the firefighters, pray that we not ever have to experience a fire, and then go on with our work. On the other hand, in the event of a catastrophic earthquake or forest fire, we as a people are energized to take more dynamic steps—organize major relief efforts, examine the basic causes of the effects of the event, and push for major policy changes in such areas as building standards and land usage. Compare our reactions to the explosion in Saudi Arabia that killed American servicemen with those to the attack on Pearl Harbor. Contrast our research effort in atomic warfare and our commitment to research in solar energy. I share the view that we must come to see social injustice as more like a conflagration than a fire, more like a world war than a skirmish, more like an issue of cultural survival than one of social adaptation.

It is within this broad context, then, that I address the relationship between formal education and social injustice. In this analysis, it is extremely important that I affirm from the very beginning the enormous contribution that tens of thousands of educators personally have made by working for a world of justice and joy. These contributions involve the courage of commitment, the genius of research, and the energy of teaching and without them our condition clearly would be even more dire and dangerous. My criticisms of formal education become even more poignant and painful when one becomes aware of our extraordinary tradition of the struggle for social justice, for it highlights the power of the cultural and social forces that thwart even those heroic efforts. By the same token, it must be acknowledged that our profession contains its share of rogues, parasites, incompetents, and charlatans, though I doubt that we are significantly different in this regard from other professions. However, as serious as the problem of "bad apples" is, my focus is not on them, but rather on the policies and practices of our solid and respectable educational institutions—the ethos of the educational establishment—an ethos that at best shows relative indifference to unnecessary human suffering and at worst contributes to it.

What I want to examine are the official claims and goals of the champions of enlightenment education. The basic claims are twofold: one is for the profound contribution the pursuit of truth makes to the creation of a just world, the other is that the pursuit of truth is in itself the highest form of fulfillment. We are told that the truth shall make us free, that the unexamined life is not worth living; furthermore, that democracy requires a well-informed electorate, and that the life of the mind is one of exquisite sublimity.

As educators we claim that beyond the acquisition of certain basic skills lies the possibility of learning how to be thoughtful, interpretative, critical, analytical, and creative. These processes make up the core of our educational aspirations, for we for the most part believe we can forge a life of justice and joy through highly developed rational, analytical, and creative understanding. In addition, for educators getting there is at least half the fun because we not only have faith in the utility of these processes but in their inherent esthetic value.

The basic rhetoric that mainstream educators use is one in which knowledge, analysis, and understanding are keys to the solution of major human problems. The argument on the high plane is that a democratic society requires an informed electorate, that a life of meaning emerges primarily from a life of reflection, and that the highest aspirations of a culture are intertwined with the scholarly pursuit of knowledge. A corollary of these assumptions is that it is incumbent on a society to promote and nurture its academic traditions of free and open research for their own sake—that is, that the serious pursuit of knowledge is a good in and of itself. This rhetoric covers both bases—scholarship not only is to be treasured per se, but it's also good for us.

This highly developed rhetoric has become hallowed over the years by dint of an eloquent and persuasive discourse to the point of becoming hegemonic. Indeed, to challenge the validity of this dogma is to open oneself to charges of barbarism and anti-intellectualism. Of course, there are other reasons besides eloquence that explain the incredibly strong faith in formal education; for example, the political interests of those who benefit from the rhetoric of the nobility and grandeur of formal education. A great deal of money is spent to subsidize what for other people would be called hobbies or benign obsessions. Hundreds of thousands of jobs have been created by our reverence for formal education, and the public's willingness to offer sacrifices to the pagan gods of the academy seems boundless. We offer up our money, our commitment, even our children to appease and satisfy these idols.

More particularly, schools and colleges do deliver on a number of commitments, some of which are more profane than sacred. Formal education does indeed legitimate social and cultural hierarchy, it provides credentials (some of which are even appropriate), facilitates meritocracy, offers a pleasant environment for like-minded people, and supports a great deal of research, some of which is extremely important for a variety of purposes ranging from redemptive to destructive. Parents and students get a chance to get ahead, get well connected, and get cultured. The society gets disciplined and orderly workers, and, in many cases, shrewd and creative leaders and artists. The culture gets transmitted and preserved; the power structure is stabilized and the social class system maintained, having somehow survived the keen and thorough criticism of academic analysis. Professors get stuff published and thereby become virtuous, students get certain grades thereby earning honor, and universities receive the grants that enable them to become national treasures. Degrees are given, tenure is granted, friendships are bonded, truth is pursued, privilege is mystified, and credentials are stamped amid the pomp and pride of re-created vows of poverty and service.

The scorn and anger that I am expressing emerges from my own deep ambivalence towards our profession. Indeed, I do not offer myself as someone who has been able to rise above the contradictions, failures, and corruption that attend formal education. Rather, I offer myself to witness and confess. What I want to witness and confess is not, however, abject evil, but something less dramatic and perhaps more troubling, and that is the degree to which we may have been overzealous and pretentious in our claims for enlightenment, and for the efficacy of analysis, reason, and science. I have seen stunning statistics from a study designed to give some measure of progress since the Enlightenment, capital E. According to this study 100 million people have been killed in wars since the eighteenth century, 90 percent of them in the twentieth century.

We surely know that well-educated people (whether more or less than uneducated people is still not clear to me) are capable of cruelty, destructiveness, insensitivity, moral callousness, and cynical manipulation. Yet it would be the height of absurdist reductionism to dismiss reason and scholarship as being handmaidens of the self-serving or another path to hubris or both. What we need is to sort out genuine possibility from pious hope and to discriminate between what is parochially interesting and societally important.

I share our culture's commitment to freedom—to the right to pursue our own interests and inclinations insofar as they do not significantly interfere with those of others. This freedom surely includes the freedom of artists, poets, musicians, writers, and scholars to explore and deepen their private imaginations. It surely includes the right to celebrate those pursuits as well as those that involve inquiry into the natural and social order. There are, however, two major sticking points to this kind of freedom. First, only a very small number of people have this kind of freedom to any appreciable degree. Of course, some very well may choose not to define their lives through such pursuits but the reality is that many others are in no position to make such a choice because of poverty, ignorance, and other forms of preventable and remedial oppression. Surely our moral traditions do not allow us to assume that such a freedom can be divisible. In other words, we accept the dictum that *we cannot endure half free and half slave*, that we cannot rest till freedom is available to all of us.

Even more noxious, of course, is the reality that the freedom of some comes at the expense of the oppression of the many. Hence, our moral task has been and will continue to relentlessly and constantly enlarge the benefit of freedom for an ever-greater number of human beings.

The second hitch with this freedom emerges from the first one, and this is the relationship between the cluster of artistic and scholarly pursuits that constitutes the core of our educational establishment and the struggle to enlarge the boundaries of those who are free. Aye, and there's the rub. It is one thing to say that scholarship is valuable unto itself and that people ought to be free to engage in it. It is quite another thing to say that this same scholarship is necessary for the liberation of the oppressed. What a wonderful world it would be if what academics studied and taught was not only personally interesting but also socially important. What an incredible synchrony it would be if what promoted social injustice was aesthetically satisfying. How joyous it would be if the intense energy directed at individual pursuits contributed equally to the alleviation of unnecessary human suffering. How wonderful, how joyous, how naïve—and how blind. I believe that we put an unnecessary burden on our profession when we make such a preposterous claim and that it prevents us from confronting the limits of our present notions of education. I believe that it is accurate, *and* liberating, to acknowledge that the basic educational processes of analysis, critical thinking, and reasoned inquiry are necessary but not sufficient conditions for the creation of a socially just order. Surely they are necessary, for it is research that helps us become aware of the human suffering, and it is critical thinking that enables us to see much of it as unnecessary. It is through analysis and imagination that we penetrate the ignorance and blindness that surround social inequities and find ways to alleviate human misery. But this is not true of *all* scholarship or of *all* research. The particular percentage is not crucial; what is crucial is to recognize that the pursuit of truths and flights of imagination are not inevitably linked to issues of social injustice.

In a time of catastrophic human suffering, we must ask ourselves if we are or are not directly contributing to its alleviation and to what degree. Why in the name of heaven would we do that which does not alleviate such suffering? Why are we not, as we would in a state of emergency, directing *all* of our energies towards what is urgently needed rather than to what is at best of marginal value? I go back to the issue of whether or not you and I believe that we are now in such an emergency. Elie Wiesel has said that "we live in biblical times," and if by that he means that we are engaged in a titanic struggle over our ability to meet our highest aspirations to create a just world, then I am in agreement. If there are stakes, how could they be any higher than they now are? If there is a tenuous struggle for human dignity and survival, is it going well enough to allow for the luxury of education as usual? Will a few publish while we all perish?

Furthermore, we must confront the reality that however necessary knowledge and critical thinking are, they have been used for a variety of political and moral purposes. We live, after all, in a world where decisions are made by people who typically have a lot of formal education. Wars are declared and organized more times than not by people who know and think a lot. Our economy, our social policies, and our cultural affairs are for the most part not in the hands of the unschooled, but in the hands of multidegreed and multihonored graduates of our educational institutions. Indeed, as I look around the world in which we live I worry more about the schooled than about the unschooled. Do we realize the significance of advocating the extension and deepening of the kind of education that has informed our current political and social leaders? Have they done so well that we need to emulate them? What all this adds up to is something our grandparents keep telling us, and that is that it's not enough to be smart. If only we were smart enough to know that.

Why is it that highly creative people use their imagination and artistry to persuade children to buy toy weapons? Why is it that brilliant chemists would help create real weapons and why is it that people with a sophisticated understanding of politics would order their use! It took genius to develop both penicillin and napalm; sophisticated demographic research is used both to help alleviate poverty and to sell shoddy products to the poor. We need not only to respect knowledge but also to be wary of it because it has enormous potential for good and evil. What we need to focus on, therefore, is the "not sufficient" aspect of my belief that traditional education is a necessary but not sufficient condition for the creation of a just society, or even for the reduction of unnecessary human suffering.

What would make traditional education sufficient is its integration, with wisdom, with a moral vision that informs and directs the insights, reflections, and findings of serious inquiry towards a just world. The pursuit of knowledge, the delights of analysis, and the fun of building models—what one wit has called "the leisure of the theory class"—is not what the suffering hope for. What they hope for is compassion and wisdom. Buckminster Fuller challenged our society twenty years ago with his assertion that with existing knowledge and existing technology we could sufficiently clothe, feed, and shelter the world's population. He claimed this could be done even if we were to shut down immediately every university, every school, and every research institution. What is needed to reduce unnecessary human suffering is not more knowledge but the will to follow through on our most profound commitments.

In addition to knowledge and critical reflection, then, there must be compassion, wisdom, moral commitment, and political will. Are these aspirations and goals appropriate to universities, colleges, and schools? Is it fair or even logical to ask teachers and students to be committed to serving justice, to dedicate their lives to the struggle to alleviate unnecessary human suffering? Is the language of moral vision and wisdom congruent with the language of dispassionate scholarship? It seems to me that the responses to these troubling questions can help us see more clearly the odd coupling of traditional education emphasizing the pursuit of knowledge with critical reflection with the social goal of creating a just world. Let me make some suggestions about how we educators might address more constructively the dilemma that reflects our passion for both education and social justice.

First, it would seem particularly appropriate for us to re-member and re-cognize the humility inherent in our vocation. Whenever we look at our work honestly and seriously we are almost always knocked off our feet by the complexity and perplexities of the topic. It usually doesn't take a great deal of prodding to be humbled by the mysteries and enigmas that attend efforts to make sense of the world. It is a cliché among academics to say that the more we study the less we know, that every answer seems to beget more questions, and that more research is needed. Why then should we presume to claim that the truth shall positively make us free, that an unexamined life is surely not worth living, that we really know what critical thinking is, that there is such a thing as basic education without bothering to describe what it is the basis of, or that truth and progress are going steady? Would it not be more seemly for us to accept a role other than the last great hope for Western Civilization?

If we are truly unwilling to transform our notions of what constitutes the essentials of education, then the least (or perhaps the most) we can do is to accept a more limited role in the process of social transformation. Perhaps, as I've indicated, we can acknowledge that critical reflection is a necessary but not sufficient condition for creating a just society. We might even go further and release the aesthetes and pure scholars from the hostage of relevance and even admit that social justice is at best an unintended consequence of scholarship and inquiry. This would be more honest, and would clarify the role of formal education, reduce guilt and confusion, and, most importantly, recognize the development of other vital processes that are more directly concerned with reducing unnecessary human suffering. It would be a very great act of generosity (although clearly one involving great risk) if educators would focus neither on what their country can do for their specialty nor on what their specialty can do for the country. Since both of the formulations are essentially self-serving, it would be much more responsible to ask what our country, community, and planet most need at this moment and to prepare to deal with the results of an honest assessment of these needs. When there is an earthquake or a forest fire, there is surely more need for medical and rescue personnel than for tap dancers and tattooists. Surely our society is enriched by tap dancers and tattooists, but we need not stretch our sense of what is urgently needed in order to accommodate them. No doubt the tap dancers and their colleagues can make some personal contribution to easing the horrors of our earthquake, but it is unlikely that it will take the form of tap dancing. No doubt the members of the National Association of Tap Dancers are fuming and likely to suggest that tap dancers can lighten the misery of the survivors through sparkling performance or therapeutic tap dancing. As for me, I have no difficulty in insisting that on the whole what's needed most are medical personnel and rescue workers. Is there some role for tap dancing and tattooing in such situation? Probably, but it surely is a marginal and modest one.

There is a second major contribution that educators can make to the serious reduction of unnecessary human suffering, and that is to offer leadership by raising public consciousness. Russell Jacoby in his book, *The Last Intellectuals*, describes what he believes to be a dying tradition in America, that of public intellectuals. It is Jacoby's point that whereas America once was enriched by the contributions of a number of very creative and brilliant intellectuals who made it a point to address a public rather than an academic community, our younger generation of intellectuals does not seem to accept the responsibility. There is great irony in this situation since, according to Jacoby, our current crop of intellectuals are not only talented but strongly ideological. At the heart of Jacoby's interpretation is his belief that intellectuals have, by and large, accepted university positions rather than trying to make it as freelance writers, as did intellectuals in the 1920s and 1930s. This, according to Jacoby, has meant that these intellectuals, ideological as they still are, tend to be preoccupied with the life of the academy and tend to write for each other rather than for the public at large, preferring academic collegiality to public involvement. As he says: "To put it sharply: the habitat, manners, and idiom of intellectuals have been transformed within the past fifty years. Younger intellectuals no longer need or want a larger public; they are almost exclusively professors. Campuses are their homes; colleges their audiences; monographs and specialized journals their media. Unlike past intellectuals they situate themselves within fields and disciplines—for good reason. Their jobs, advancement, and salaries depend on the evaluation of specialists, and this dependence affects the issues broached and the language employed" (Jacoby, 1987, p. 6).

This has contributed to the impoverishment of what Hannah Arendt has called "the public space," a place for well-informed dialogue and debate on community and public issues. In a culture that celebrates couch-potatoes, in a society where political campaigns take on the qualities of slick cynicism, and in a culture of happy-talk news, the erosion of the role of the public intellectual is an extremely serious event. Surely, teachers and educators can and should participate in efforts to raise public awareness and understanding of the immense unnecessary human suffering that surrounds us. We as concerned educators and citizens can contribute not only our insights and understanding, but our moral energies and our share of outrage, compassion, and commitment. As educators we have a significant amount of respect from the larger public and considerable access to our students and colleagues. It is wise to remember the adage that silence can be consent and to be alert to the consequences of our *not* speaking out on the obscenities of social injustice.

In addition to offering up the gifts of humility and leadership, educators also have the opportunity and responsibility to engage in the ongoing process of reconceptualizing education. Ours is not only an era of untold human suffering. It also is an era of extraordinary intellectual ferment; a time when paradigms are shifting; and a time when virtually every professional and academic area is locked in heavy duty soul-searching and methodological debate. Among the dominant themes of this ferment are renewed concern for a religious sensitivity, the rediscovering of human subjectivity, and a re-energized reliance on the imagination. Our language is becoming increasingly constructivist and our faith in science is beginning to wane. We have heard that epistemology is dead, that patriarchal images in religion must be replaced, and that power precedes knowledge. Scientific certainty is getting as quaint as religious dogma even as it is difficult to tell the difference between some scientists and some theologians without an ontological score card.

This ferment is sure to spread to notions of what constitutes a valid education. Even now we can envision a shift in emphasis from mastery to mystery, from objectivity to subjectivity, from departmental studies to holistic inquiries. Most importantly, we must come to grips with the growing realization that knowledge cannot legitimately be separated from its historical and moral contexts, that we must construct a curriculum that takes into account the intensely relational nature of knowledge. As educators determined to direct our energies toward the horrors of unnecessary human suffering, we must be particularly concerned with the task of consciously infusing our scholarly traditions with moral visions.

This task is surely as important as it is perilous, for it is fraught with the dangers of self-righteousness and zealotry. Thankfully, there are people who are sensitively engaged in this process, especially theologians and most particularly feminist theologians. Sallie McFague (1987) has provided us with startling new religious metaphors that complement her very helpful analysis of the significance of metaphors. Sharon Welch (1985), another feminist theologian who, in courageously addressing her own conflict between a growing intellectual uncertainty and her strong moral convictions, urges us to have both "absolute commitments" and "infinite suspicions."

It is Cornel West (1987) who has provided me with the best clue as to how this process might best proceed. His analysis of the problematics of locating the preparation of ministers in a university has clear parallels with other professions, particularly in the education of teachers. Let me quote from this fascinating and provocative article.

"An appropriate starting point for reform in theological education is seminary professors creating for themselves a sense of vocation and purpose that revels in the life of the mind—always in conversation with the best that is being thought and written regarding their intellectual concerns—yet puts this at the service of the people of God. Seminary professors first and foremost must view themselves as servants of the Kingdom of God and thereby resist the lucrative temptations of a flaccid careerism and a flagrant demoninationalism."

It is clear that not all educators can or will want to consider themselves as servants of the people of God. However, in a time of moral emergency and human catastrophe, educators must with others respond in good faith. I see no reason why we have to choose between a life of moral responsibility and a life of the mind. Another theologian, Matthew Fox (1979), has said:

"Just as there can be no justice without ideas and an intellectual life, so there can be no compassion without an intellectual life, for compassion involves the whole person in quest for justice and a mind with ideas is an obviously significant portion of any of us."

Fox is not unaware of barriers in the academy, however, as he goes on to say: "Compassion, being so closely allied with justice-making, requires a critical consciousness, one *that resists all kinds of Keptness, including that of Kept academics and Kept intellectuals*" [emphasis added].

We are in yet another era of "the best of times, the worst of times," in a moment of both tremendous danger and extraordinary opportunity. It is clearly a time, as Reinhold Niebuhr once urged us, "to avoid both despair and sentimentality." We must not flinch at the harsh realities of unnecessary human misery either through avoidance *or* paralysis. There are indeed hopes and possibilities embodied in the energies and imaginations of tens of thousands of our sisters and brothers committed to creating a more just world.

We must regard this moment as a time of utmost crisis, and, therefore, must respond . . . with all our energy and imagination. We cannot disregard the horrors of misery, starvation, poverty for millions of people, nor the possibility of nuclear destruction of billions of people. Not to act or not to respond fully are acts of enormous consequence. As educator-prophets we can be guided by [Rabbi] Heschel's precept that "it is an act of evil to accept the state of evil as either inevitable or final". . . Nor can we disregard the immense human capacity and interest in continuing the struggle for a world of love and joy. We must confront our enormous capacities for both good *and* evil: What we have broken we can surely mend, what we have yet to create we can surely construct.

References

Fox, Matthew. 1979. *A Spirituality Named Compassion*. Minneapolis: Winston Press.

Jacoby, Russell. 1987. *The Last Intellectuals*. New York: Farrar, Straus, and Giroux.

McFague, Sallie. 1987. *Models of God*. Philadelphia: Fortress Press.

Sivard, Ruth. 1985. *World Military and Social Experience (1985)*. World Priorities.

Welch, Sharon. 1985. *Communities of Resistance and Solidarity*. Maryknoll, N.Y.: Orbis Books.

West, Cornell. 1988. *Prophetic Fragments*. Grand Rapids, MI: Eerdmans Publishing.

Social Responsibility and Educational Scholars

In addressing this topic, I will first need to clarify what I mean by educational scholars and why I choose to use this term. I am first of all addressing you and your colleagues as people who focus your energies on research, scholarship, and inquiry, as opposed to other educators who focus on the clinical concerns of application and practice. I surely do not intend to raise the issue of the complex relationship between these areas but only to sharpen the point I wish to make about the dilemma stemming from the conflict between detachment and affirmation. A theme of this paper is that this dilemma has special significance and poignancy for those of us who are in the field of capital E Education.

There are of course scholars in many traditional disciplines (e.g. history, philosophy, psychology, and sociology) who focus their disciplinary attention on education. Such people are likely to describe themselves as historians, philosophers, psychologists, or sociologists who study educational issues. This is in contrast to those who identify themselves as being in the field of Education, who rely on traditional disciplines to support their work. Of course, these distinctions are often a function of organizational and political vagaries more than they are of significant intellectual differences. However, because of the power of acculturation, there clearly is a difference in the consciousness and ethos of these two broad groups notwithstanding the significant degree of commonality in methodology.

What I want to center on particularly in this paper are the problematics of intellectual detachment for scholars of education who identify themselves as being in capital E Education. The problematics I will address include epistemological difficulties, ideological hazards, and, most importantly, concerns about our responsibilities as citizens and educators. My analysis is in part guided by Gramsci's concept of organic intellectuals. According to Henry Giroux, Gramsci "criticizes those theorists who decontextualized the intellectual by suggesting that he or she exist independently of issues of class, culture, power, and politics. Such a view [holds] that the intellectual is obligated to engage in value free discourse, one that necessitates refusal to make a commitment" (Aronowitz and Giroux, 1985, p. 35).

In discussing the problematics of intellectual detachment, let me, however, first, briefly, and at the risk of over-simplification, refer to the recent research on the limitations of objectivity and dangers of neutrality. I am certainly not the person nor is this the occasion to present a thorough and sophisticated summary of this extraordinary and complex work, but suffice to say that it has seriously undermined confidence in certainty, objectivity, and universal truth. Scientists, ironically enough, have led the way in demonstrating the futility of seeking final answers as they not only offer us the uncertainty principle but they also emphasize the significance of constructed and relational notions of knowledge. Deconstructionists have hammered home the historical and cultural contingencies of belief systems, work that resonates with the research in such fields as the sociology of knowledge and cultural anthropology. Philosophical disputes have reached the point where prominent philosophers have announced the death not only of God but of epistemology. Logical positivists are in retreat, analytical philosophers are on the defensive, scientists write books on cosmology, and art is becoming the new root metaphor of our era.

A related intellectual movement has also attacked the myth of neutrality and objectivity from the perspectives of ideological analysis. In a remarkable confluence of Left and Right thinking, we have come to see how our beliefs and knowledge are inevitably imprinted with ideological markings. It appears that behind the bland mask of objectivity and neutrality are sculpted faces. These faces look out at the world with lenses formed by such forces as race, class, gender, and culture. Marxists have of course been saying this for years, but it has taken the New Right to make this concept acceptable and legitimate. Indeed, it was Ronald Reagan himself who repeatedly said that the schools could not be neutral. It was indeed breath-taking to have the Great Communicator become the spokesman for the concept of the hidden curriculum.

Indeed, one of the most frustrating aspects of educational discourse in America is its failure to resonate with the intimate relationships between culture and education. I realize, of course, that our work is

essentially that—i.e.,—the study of that immensely important interpenetration of society, culture, and education. However, we also realize that the main currents of educational discourse flow from the gentle
and untroubled seas of the non-political and non-ideological psychological and social sciences. The dominant educational discourse dis-
tances and distracts us from some very important but surely disturbing and unsettling issues.

Perhaps we now know *too* much about the complexities, limitations, and problematics of gaining understanding, if not truth. Socrates
said that the unexamined life is not worth living, but someone else has
said that the examined life is not worth bearing. We have come to this
intensified crisis in authority and certainty at the worst possible time,
a time when we are still existentially reeling from our basic alienation
and spiritual drift. The late Michael Harrington in his wonderfully titled
book *The Politics of God's Funeral* captured the dilemma of the
skeptical intellectual in search of moral and spiritual grounding in this
quotation:

"I, like religious people, feel a sense of awe on the communion of
the universal, but without a religious interpretation of the origin of
that communion. . . . The serious atheistic humanist and the serious
religious humanist are, I suspect, talking about the same reality. That
these languages differ is not a minor detail by reducing antagonistic
philosophies to a vague emotion. Such a promiscuous ecumenism is,
of course, empty of content. But that common emotion does offer a
common point of departure" (Harrington, 1983, p. 77).

These intellectual crises, tragically enough, aggravate the more immediate political, social, and economic crises of our era. We live in a
time of immense dangers—our planet, indeed our existence is at risk
from the possibilities of ecological disaster and/or nuclear devastation. We are polluted not only by pesticides and poisons but by the
obscenities of structured and persistent poverty, hunger, malnutrition,
and disease on a gigantic scale. Indeed, we are enduring the unendur-
able and thinking the unthinkable—we live and operate in a world of
immense suffering. Most of the suffering is unnecessary; its origins
and solutions both emerge from human will. We are an amazing
people—we have created soaring covenants and aspirations and also
created antithetical modes of violating the most essential dimensions
of those visions.

In a word, we find ourselves in a situation in which it is intellectually difficult to adopt an objective stance toward our research; politically naïve to believe that we can be neutral about our professional

concerns; and morally questionable to be detached from our social responsibilities. This professional, intellectual, and moral crisis is, of course, significantly exacerbated by the particular ethos of the Academy, an ethos that Russell Jacoby's book *The Last of the Intellectuals* has helped illumine.

In this analysis, Jacoby points to the disappearance of a vital fixture in American culture, what he called the "public intellectual." Public intellectual is defined as "writers and thinkers who address a general and educated audience" (Jacoby, 1987, 5). Jacoby's basic point is that even though many brilliant intellectuals with strong ideological commitments have entered the University since the 1960s their voices are muted. His position is that this vital force has been taken over by the specialized and truncated requirements of full membership in the academic and professional elite.

I believe this condition pertains to the field of Education as well as other fields but I believe also that there are more specific and perhaps more poignant dimensions of this general analysis to our field. As a profession committed to disciplined study and informed practice, we must necessarily be concerned not only with what is interesting but also with what is important. In addition, we are both scholars and practitioners; intellectuals and citizens; and, ironically enough, because of the nature of our work know a great deal about the relationship between ideas and practice.

Cornel West's very stimulating and provocative essay on issues involving the preparation of Christian ministers has provided me with some very useful insights into these matters. Obviously, there are very important differences between educating ministers and preparing educators and West's analysis can only be partially extended to issues of professional education. However, as we need to be mindful of the limitations of his critique we also need to be open to its heuristic possibilities. At the very least, it is interesting to note the parallels between the concerns expressed about a field which is simultaneously very different and very similar to education, i.e. the ministry. For example, West's essay *The Crisis in Theological Education* begins with this comment:

> "Our seminaries and divinity schools are not simply in intellectual disarray and existential disorientation; our very conceptions of what they should be doing are in shambles. For example, students come ill-equipped for and unaware of what they will encounter in our theological schools; faculty often are uninterested in and unrewarded for meeting the *practical* demands of edu-

cating refined and relevant Christian ministers; and administrators usually have little vision of or capacity for guiding theological schools in a prophetic (as opposed to a cost-benefit) manner" (West, 1988, 273).

Surely, such a statement would not require a great deal of change to make it relevant to our teacher training programs and graduate schools of education. He goes on to say that these problems are rooted in the confusion of the role of a Christian minister in our present historical moment. This confusion emerges, according to West, from three broad phenomena. First, "they initially derive from . . . the institutional matrices in which preparation for the Christian ministry takes place . . . in the grip of either a debilitating ethos of professionalization and specialization and/or a parochial atmosphere of denominationalism and dogmatism" (273).

The second crisis has to do with what he calls the "decentering of Europe, the demystifying of European cultural hegemony, the deconstruction of European philosophical edifices, and the decolonization of the third world" (274). To West, this has meant the erosion of what had been a reliable, stable, consensual, and recognizable knowledge base. The third development is the dramatic rise of liberation movements from the marginalized and oppressed as reflected, for example, in the explosion of liberationist and feminist theologies.

Clearly, such an analysis has also only partial relevance to the profession of Education. Yet, there are parallels—there surely is a confusion over broad goals, the loss of a clear vision, and the growing recognition that our education is not equally responsive to all American subcultures. Furthermore, the essential underlying structural forces that West describes are cultural and social conditions that have influenced all social institutions and if they are compelling for theological educators they are likely to have at least some significance for Education.

What I want to focus on in this paper, however, is the first of West's points, i.e. the tension involved in the problematics of the orientations of the preparing institutions. Professor West's analysis of these issues appropriately include mention not only of the institution and its faculty but also its students and the churches that lure them:

"Students are, like all of us, products of culture. Advanced capitalist culture—with its consumer sensibilities, flashing images, and quick information—simply does not provide the kind of exposure to and appreciation for the spiritual discipline, biblical grounding, and church ritualistic practices requisite for a vital and vibrant Christian ministry" (West, 1987, 278).

Again, this analysis is clearly rooted in a particular religious framework with language quite alien to public education. However, it seems fair to conclude that students entering education not only emerge from the same culture that West describes but exhibit a parallel lack of discipline and commitment.

West speaks also to the churches' bewilderment with the graduates of these programs: for what he considers good reasons:

> "For instance the historical–critical methods of reading the biblical texts add little to the religious sustenance of most Christians, and few biblical professors at seminaries provide the interpretative tools required to contribute to this sustenance for congregations. This tremendous task often falls upon the shoulders of students. . . . [Most] of the professors have little or no experience in (and few have little or no appreciation for) the Christian pastoral ministry. Hence many fine prospective ministers are seduced into graduate work principally on grounds of prestige and status. This is a loss for the church—and in no way a gain for the Academy" (276).

Surely schools are not churches and teachers are not pastors but there clearly are tensions between schools and universities and between the demands of school practices and the canons of academic research. It is also clear that the road to status, privilege, and fame is not the gravel country road of school teaching but the slickly engineered Interstate highway of the Academy.

West's efforts to respond constructively to the crises he describes begin with some ideas on the role and consciousness of the seminary professor—the analogue to those of us involved with the preparation of educators. His orientation is quite clear: ". . . seminary professors [need to create] . . . for themselves a sense of vocation and purpose that revels in the life the mind,—always in conversation with the best that is being thought and written regarding their intellectual concerns— yet puts this at the service of the people of God. Seminary professors first and foremost must view themselves as servants of the Kingdom of God and thereby resist the lucrative temptations of a flaccid careerism and a flagrant denominationalism" (277).

I want to briefly explore the possibilities that this provocative and eloquent statement might have for informing our concern for our role as scholars in or of education. We can easily identify and affirm West's notions of a vocation that revels in the mind and that allows us to be in conversation with intellectuals, but the difficulty is in finding an analogue to his insistence that this be within the context of "service to the people of God." It is perhaps relatively easy to rule out the appropriateness of the term "people of God" to our profession, given its constituency and makeup. However the idea of scholars/professors being of service is not so easy to elude.

In what sense is our vocation a service profession? Whom do we or should we serve? We can and have been able to respond to such questions without a great deal of perplexity. We can and do say that we serve the teaching profession and the university by offering our insights, energies, and scholarship as ways to promote understanding of our society and education. Our assumption is that the understanding can illumine wise and prudent thinking processes that will guide educational policies and practices. We can and often also say that we serve the principles and traditions of scholarship itself—that the rigorous, critical, and thorough search for Truth is in itself a high vocation.

Fair but not quite far enough! Perhaps such a response may be adequate for those who accept, if not celebrate, a role of detachment—and the possibility of neutral scholarship. However, the dilemma is still quite severe for those of us who accept the serious moral and intellectual problematics of disinterestedness and detachment. Are we only interested in *analyzing* the dimensions, history, and implications of educational policies and practices? Are we not also interested in what these policies and practices ought to be? Indeed, it would seem to be very difficult, if not impossible, to offer a critical analysis of educational issues without some frame of reference. I accept the political principle that academic work, like all other human activities, willy-nilly serves some interests. As scholars and professionals we must then ask ourselves the ancient and still vital question of whose interests are served when we claim objectivity, celebrate detachment, and affirm neutrality. My own sense is that such an orientation helps to strengthen the status quo since it draws energy away from concerted efforts at significant change. Such an orientation blunts the force of moral suasion by its claims that serious cultural issues are ultimately amenable to technical and logical processes alone.

Moreover, since universities and colleges greatly depend upon resources provided by the dominant social and cultural institutions, they are very reluctant to become agencies of transformation. The effect on faculty who want to succeed, or at least stay, in the university is to channel scholarship to the safer currents of detached investigation. In the case of capital e Education, there is the additional influence of the expectation of the public school system, institutions not known for their love of criticism or for their devotion to social transformation.

This is a skeleton of my own notions of the moral and political implications of a stance of objectivity and detachment by educational scholars. My challenge is not so much to persuade you to accept the one I have chosen but rather to urge you and other colleagues to offer your own analysis of whose interests are served by this orientation. At the very least, the profession has the responsibility to address the issues candidly and thoroughly in the name of our deepest scholarly traditions of honest and relentless self-examination.

Beyond the nature of reflecting on the appropriateness of the concept of service and the question of whose interests are, in fact, being served, there is the matter of, if we should serve, then, whom should we serve? Are our loyalties to a discipline—do we offer homage to History, Philosophy, Sociology? This, of course, begs the question of whether the disciplines are ends in themselves, thus raising the possibility of reification if not idolatry.

Are we to serve the University in its effort to sustain and maintain itself as an autonomous and productive institution? Or are we to serve the State, at least in ways in which we believe are appropriate? Perhaps we are to serve the schools, or the educational profession, or serve the children or parents. Perhaps a combination of these constituencies or perhaps none of the above. Perhaps we work to serve our own personal impulses to read, write, and teach with a minimum of interference and to regard our work not in political but in aesthetic terms.

Let me at this point speak briefly to how some of our colleagues have responded to these important and perplexing questions. Some urge on us the responsibility for increased self-awareness to heed the admonition "Know thyself." As intellectuals we are very much aware of the ways in which historical and biographical contingencies impinge on research and policy making. Therefore, we have a special responsibility to be more scrupulous in examining our own critiques and to urge our students to engage in this process so vital to honest communication and a consciousness of trust.

Furthermore, as people in the field of Education, we need to be more sensitive to the particular requirements of the profession especially of practioners. Presumably, we are all to some extent involved with the preparation of practioners and presumably we are united by a commitment *to* and faith *in* improving practice through informed reflection.

Practice, as has been often said, is messy, but practice also requires decisions in the face of the mess of complexity, uncertainty, and inadequate information. It is surely wise to maintain a critical posture toward the reasoning that leads to such decisions, but it does not help to assume that practioners should keep at it till they get it right. Perhaps scholars can share in the anguish of practioners by engaging more directly in their own messy praxis—that of the dialectic between rational analysis and moral commitment.

Clearly, academics often affirm particular elements of scholarly ethics such as civility, fairness, honesty, and openness. In addition, researchers frequently focus on ethical, political, and moral dimensions of their topics. Such issues are also dealt with institutionally when major curriculum changes in the University are suggested. The continuing debate on the centrality of the study of Western civilization has certainly served to stimulate reflection and discussion on what constitutes the society's and the university's central value system. However, many, if not most, faculty remain chary if not anxious about how their own moral and political convictions are related to their professional and scholarly work. Some still insist that the concerns of objectivity and neutrality offer, if not attainable, then reasonable and proper guidelines. Others, particularly junior faculty, are very reluctant to risk promotion and tenure by going against the grain of the conventional academic ethos. Many faculty believe that it is possible, if not desirable, to separate their personal lives from their work and to choose to exercise their social responsibilities beyond the gates of academia.

I in no way wish to minimize the complexities or dilemmas involved in these issues, but by the same token, it is also vital that we not minimize their importance. We must address these matters not as problems to be solved or as hypotheses to test but as fundamental dimensions of the human struggle. I believe that we ought to deal with these issues more directly and explicitly in our articles, books, monographs, and discussions. I believe that the existing dialogue on these matters would be greatly enriched by individual accounts by researchers of their own struggles and difficulties in reconciling their own social views with scholarly demands. In a word, I am suggesting the old—fashioned remedy of increased awareness, dialogue and reflection, or in the words of our most honored cliché—further research is required.

However, I do not wish to leave the matter there and I want to make two far-less-benign suggestions. The first has to do with the question of the nature of the context in which this further research and increased reflection ought to be conducted. I believe it is time for academics to confront important elements of their own subculture with particular reference to its rampant competitiveness and hostility. It is an open secret that academics vie with each other for status, privilege, and reputation. Moreover, it is also clear that one mode of achieving academic renown is to savage the work of other scholars, always of course in the name of critical rationality. These rivalries and conflicts can exacerbate existing dilemmas, paradoxes, and differences by polarizing them into dualisms and turn intellectual problems into issues of ideological and personal loyalties. When this happens, the conditions for honest dialogue and reflection become much more difficult, for another set of more personal, more self-serving items are placed on the agenda. This is an extremely sensitive area for academics because it involves many concerns crucial to scholarship—critical consciousness, candor, passion, debate, and dialogue. We must also find ways to affirm other dimensions necessary for the struggle to understand ourselves and our world, particularly those of compassion, humility, and community. Compassion in the sense of "suffering with," i.e. a consciousness in which we can share the difficulties and struggles that we and our colleagues face when we confront our work. By humility, I do not mean abasement but rather the awe that emerges when we confront the enormity and complexity of what we study. We also need to do a lot more about establishing true collegiality as we work for a greater sense of intellectual and professional community. I believe that a necessary condition for these values to be nurtured is a significant reduction in the guerrilla warfare, intellectual sniping, and self-serving careerism that stain our traditions.

Let me make one final suggestion, and that is that we affirm affirmation. I accept as a given the difficulties, complexities, and paradoxes, the tragic history of other noble causes and lofty principles, and the high risks involved. But I also insist that there are greater risks in avoiding affirmation and indeed, to go further and suggest that the tasks may not be so impossible. For one thing, we can all agree that the long run is here, and we do not need or cannot wait for further research. Enough data is in—100 million people have been killed in wars in the twentieth century, 2 billion live in abject poverty, 450 million people suffer from hunger and malnutrition, 1 in 5 American children currently lives in poverty. Buckminister Fuller wrote 20 years ago that there was existing technology and resources available to provide sufficient food, shelter, and clothing to every person on earth.

Surely, we can express our outrage and intolerance of this immense, unnecessary human suffering, and express our rejection of the human policies and institutions that have created this catastrophe. Surely, we can affirm our commitment, more directly, cogently, and specifically to social justice, peace, community, and freedom. Indeed, it is perhaps vital that we consider the relationship between *our* work and human suffering and misery. If we say that there is little or no relationship, then we must ask ourselves why we are bothering with it and if we claim that there is some relationship, then we need to make that relationship clear and explicit.

It is hard for me to accept the notion that some of our ablest and most thoughtful citizens should be exempt from the struggle to reduce unnecessary human suffering. Indeed, a value that we can all affirm is to live in a society where all people can pursue their own interests in safety. However, we live in a world where only a few people can do this and often at the expense of a great many who cannot. In this time of unparalleled crises, we must see ourselves at the service of reducing human pain, anguish, misery and in meeting such responsibilities.

We are not at all without powerful ideas, traditions, and images in the service of promoting a world of peace, justice, and community. Cornel West summed up his notion of the challenge of theological education this way:

> This process can be served when the "tension—generated principally by the ineluctability of historical consciousness, that inescapable hermeneutical character of our Christian perspectives—and the inexpungible partiality and partisanship of our scholarship become a virtue" (280).

Centuries ago Rabbi Hillel urged that we address our responsibilities by confronting these question:

"If I am not for myself, who will be for me? And if only for myself, what am I? And if not now—when?"

What is to be our response?

References

Aronowitz, Stanley and Henry Giroux. 1985. *Education Under Siege.* South Hadley, MA: Bergin and Garvey.

Harrington, Michael. 1983. *The Politics of God's Funeral.* New York: Holt, Rinehart and Winston.

Jacoby, Russell. 1987. *The Last Intellectuals.* New York: Farrar, Straus and Giroux.

West, Cornel. 1988. *Prophetic Fragments.* Grand Rapids, MI: Eerdmans Publishing.

Eyewitness to Higher Education: Confession and Indictment

Background

My effort in this paper will be to examine the condition of higher education on the basis of my sense of where we are as a culture and a society. Let me then present some assumptions of where we are as a culture and a society and then speak to the situation of higher education from that perspective.

I share the view that ours is a time of enormous suffering and pain fraught with the dangers of even greater suffering and pain. We live in a time of immense poverty and great luxury for far too many; a time of intense rivalry, division, rage, hatred among too many groups; a time when there is concern for the survival not only of particular groups, nations, and races but indeed of humanity and the planet. It is yet another best of times/worst of times era for we are also witnessing an ever—increasing burst of imagination, brilliance, and creativity, testifying once again to untold human capacities to extend the boundaries of possibility. It is clear for example, that human genius has developed the capacity to provide for extraordinarily rapid transportation and communication, for unbelievably efficient modes of storing and disseminating information, and that we have made enormous strides in responding to the human necessities of food, shelter, and health. I believe, with Buckminster Fuller and others, that we indeed now possess the technological wherewithal to provide the basic necessities of food, medical care, and shelter for every person in the world. Yet alas, although the flesh is able, the spirit is not willing. Yes, we have developed our material power to undreamed of levels, but our spiritual powers lag far behind. Our impulse to be a caring, joyous, loving people is being sapped by the impulse to succeed, achieve, compete, win, and dominate. Gandhi has said that there are enough resources to meet human need, but there is not enough to meet the demands of human greed. These difficulties are, of course, deeply rooted in historical events, cultural phenomena, and social forces: the devastation of world-wide wars—of Auschwitz, Hiroshima; the dread and horror of ecological, nuclear disasters; the shock of corruption and the tragedy of cynicism—an era of Watergate, insider trading, Whitewater, and the savings and loan debacle. In addition, we are in the midst of an ongoing spiritual crisis. While many asked where God was at Auschwitz and declared God dead, many more sought solace in fundamentalism and fierce zealotry. Those shaken by their inability to find spiritual meaning have had to confront the parallel declaration by many intellectuals of the death of certainty and objectivity. At the same time, many, many more struggle to find and clear obscured and barely familiar spiritual paths in order to ground their work in hope and meaning.

In America, we have come to an economy that produces homelessness and a consciousness that is increasingly tolerant of it. We have a politics of sound bites, spin doctors, and panderers, and with all that an electorate that is ever more captured and intrigued by them. We have a culture of ever-increasing diversity and richness and a consciousness dangerously intolerant of it. However, in the face of a politics of divisiveness, rancor, and rage and an economy of greed and callousness we yearn for meaning, community, and love.

It is an age where we are coming to see the follies and horrors of a moral consciousness that is dominated by a concern for self—what passes for self-understanding and self-esteem often turns out to be self-advancement and self-gratification. In our search for community, we find ourselves in a time when our global economy renders the nation as too small and our remembered cultural identifies render the nation as too large. The cross currents of simultaneous worldwide struggles for common markets and separatist communities find expression in the United States as well as in other parts of the world. America faces increasing tensions as a function of the renewed interest among several so-called minority groups—African-Americans, Hispanic-Americans, Asian-Americans, women, gays, lesbians—in affirming their identities. Part of the struggle has been conducted in the intense but relatively removed battlefields of academia, as reflected in the curricular debate over the so-called canon. Some of this struggle has been conducted in bitter legislative and judicial battles over multicultural education, the English-only movement, the abortion issue, and the extension of civil rights. We also continue to suffer ugly and horrifying increases in violence as well as periodic eruptions of serious rioting.

There is profoundly painful suffering about in the land—racism, violence, rage, child abuse, wife abuse, homophobia, and cultural cancers like prostitution and teenage suicide seem to be ever more present. As a nation founded on strong spiritual and moral traditions, we have good reason to be ashamed and contrite. As a nation founded on the hope and energy of those traditions, we also continue in our determination to overcome and transcend these horrors.

What then do I see as the part higher education plays in all of this? First, and at the risk of being gratuitous, I believe it important to affirm the extraordinary contributions that higher education has made to our well-being. Colleges and universities have provided a relatively safe and supportive environment in which enriching and nourishing dialogues and relationships have developed and been sustained. The enormous strides that have been made in science, technology, medicine, food production, public health, communications, and transportation, are directly and vitally connected to the scholarship and research that is so avidly promoted and supported in institutions of higher education. Not only students and faculty but the larger community have been stimulated, charmed, enlarged, and enchanted by the wit, erudition, and wisdom of critics, artists, healers, scholars, teachers given haven in the university. I believe that more people know more than ever and that there is more knowledge, more sophisticated research and more insight available than ever before. For this, institutions of higher education are largely responsible. I very much hope that this judgment will not be trivialized or marginalized by the rest of my analysis, for to do so would be to fail to affirm the achievements as well as the struggles of those who have so valiantly worked to meet our highest aspirations. It would also serve to mitigate the tragedy of our situation.

Complicity

I begin the more painful part of this analysis with a concern for which higher education might additionally and reasonably take responsibility. The harsh reality is that the most important decisions that have resulted in our present crises have been made mostly by people who are the products of higher education and indeed many of society's

movers and shakers are honored graduates of some of our most prestigious and distinguished universities. The pivotal and far-reaching
policies and practices in foreign policy, investment strategies, budget
priorities, city planning, architecture, housing, and transportation are,
after all, not made by illiterates, dropouts, and the great unwashed but
by those who have learned to read, reason, analyze, interpret, and
integrate very well, or at least at the college level. These informed
decisions have produced the situation I have described—a world of
danger, suffering, and anguish—a situation largely the result of human
agency.

Perhaps universities can deplore what some of their graduates have
done with their education, or perhaps universities can be more humble
in their claims of what they can accomplish. It is even possible that in
the wake of the depth of our present crises that we consider the possibility, if not necessity, for profound cultural transformation rather
than major reform in higher education. However, in the real world,
universities are ecstatic when their graduates take on powerful and
influential positions, and the more power and influence the more ec-
stacy. It is unheard of for a university to mourn when one of its community becomes an influential member of another community dedicated to preserving policies of privilege and exploitation. It is also rare
for those in higher education to suggest that the education that they
offer has little, if any, effect on the broad direction of social and cultural policies or to admit that they really are at a loss to know how to
effect them.

Within the academy, we tend to be more sanguine about the capacity of our students to resist our best educational efforts and more
cynical about the achievements of our graduates. We tend to excul-
pate ourselves by claiming incompetence, ineffectiveness, and powerlessness (ours, theirs, or both). I will not deny the availability of all
these capacities to any of us as individuals but this analysis will simply
not wash for the institution. It would be comforting to believe that
Newt Gingrich and Bill Clinton have betrayed their university legacy
or that the media moguls, advertising executives, and Wall Street fin-
anciers did not learn their lessons when they were going to school. It
would be reassuring to believe that history would be dramatically different if the university were to support teaching more than research or
if there had been many more classroom discussions and much smaller
classes, we would not have had the savings and loans scandal nor
continue to have homelessness. On the contrary, for my view is that

the social and cultural policies and practices that have proved to be so ruinous emerge from beliefs and values that are integral to and cherished by institutions of higher education. Indeed, colleges and universities not only serve to embody and promote these beliefs and values, but to rationalize and legitimate them.

Chief among these values and beliefs are those that cluster around the legitimation of hierarchy and privilege, and in so doing colleges and universities have made a major contribution to the proliferation of the sin of confusing human worth with personal achievement. This phenomenon is as devastating as it has become virtually totally taken for granted, beyond criticism if not awareness. Indeed, many of the most sacred of cows of higher education attempt to validate what is at base an effort to establish a kind of Platonic hierarchy that is charitable to the lesser of us and generous to the greater of us. Among these icons are such revered practices as selective admissions, honors programs, graduating with honor, merit pay, honor societies, class ranking, the professorial ranks, the status given to refereed journals, and countless other policies that claim to be directed at raising standards but serve instead to provide differential rewards and status for a few and to deny them to most others.

As presently constituted, institutions of higher education could not operate without distributing their rewards by ranking, grading, and discriminating among its faculty, staff, and students. Of course, the dirty little secret of higher education is that it is the major social instrument for getting an edge, for moving ahead in the serious game of making it in America, in a word of gaining privilege through access to the better jobs and the better-placed networks. It can hardly be said that these are frail and vulnerable institutions being coerced against their will into being used or misused in this way, since most colleges and universities present themselves as having this very purpose and effect and indeed pride themselves on their ability to deliver on this promise. Moreover, these institutions are themselves proudly and blatantly hierarchical, replete with elaborate systems of inclusion and exclusion, ranks, pecking orders, castes, classes, and differential rewards and privileges. To a degree beyond other closed or secret societies, institutions of higher education have been able to mask this system of privilege as a process essential to maintaining the integrity of the scholarly process if not the very essence of the culture itself. In this way, colleges and universities mirror as well as legitimate the culture's determination to maintain a class system and a hierarchy of winners and losers, in spite of this being in stark violation of our commitment to the ideal of a just community in which all are to be afforded equal dignity. However, institutions of higher education are not only an important instrument in an apparatus of allocating and rationing dignity but also the prime source of the ideology that justifies it.

The very metaphor "higher" education reveals the deep-seated hierarchical nature of the institution and of our culture, and the demand for expanding the system testifies to its critical role in social and cultural advancement. At the moral base of a system of social hierarchy is the danger of a consciousness in which some people are deemed more deserving than others, or worse, that some people are better than others, or at its extreme that some people are expendable. Such a consciousness not only is contrary to our deepest moral and spiritual convictions but has also demonstrated that it can lead and has led to disastrous consequences in the form of divisiveness, polarization, gross inequities, and even genocide.

Not only does higher education embody a social vision of harsh competition for differential dignity, status, and standard of living, and not only does it furnish the culture with the justification and validation of this ideology, but it also provides the training of those who operate the other major institutions grounded in this vision. A substantial burden of the responsibility for this training is borne by professional schools and departments, although I by no means want to exclude liberal arts colleges nor graduate programs in the disciplines from consideration of their role in this process. As an instance of this area of responsibility, I will rely on my own experience as a member of the faculty of a School of Education and address how we in this field tend to respond to the task of preparing people to work in other educational institutions. Although I really am not sure about this, I suspect that the problematics of this responsibility are similar to those faced by other training programs including Ph.D. programs in the academic disciplines.

For purposes of clarity I will focus my discussion on the example of teacher training programs, since these programs constitute the basic raison d'être for schools and departments of education. Although there surely are differences among these programs, there is constant pressure to reduce these differences except in certain superficial and cosmetic regards. The prime and most limiting operational principle that teacher training programs must accept at their peril is that when the trainees are finished, they must be able to perform the task of teacher *as it is presently defined and practiced in the public schools.* This pressure comes from three principal sources—the schools who want more of what they have, the students who want to be hired, and the university which wants FTEs (full time equivalent students) and the gratitude of the community for responding to the needs of public education. The pressure gets expressed in such shibboleths as "we have very good, close, working relationships with the local public schools"; "it is vital that the process of teacher training be a cooperative effort between the Colleges of Arts and Sciences and Schools of Education and between universities, school systems, the state department of education (and increasingly, the business community)"; and "it is important that universities provide teachers with the practical skills of teaching in the real world of schools instead of focusing on fanciful theories." This operating principle is enforced through a variety of procedures: practice-teaching in which the local schools have a crucial role; certification requirements which reflect a strongly professional orientation; professional and state accreditation processes which are the teeth of the certification apparatus; and ultimately by the twin consumers-the schools who do the hiring and the students who seek the jobs. (The press for even greater uniformity is reflected in the intense pressure for the national licensing of teachers and for a national K–12 curriculum.)

The role of the higher education in this area becomes primarily one of reproducing the prevailing educational orientation and indeed colleges and universities take great pride in this as a powerful indication of their dedication to the public good. What is important to note here is what is left out of this formulation is the independent and critical role of the university. For what higher education is specifically asked, if not forced, to do is to suspend this tradition in the name of "cooperation." Moreover, we are asked to be partners with an established bureaucracy and the deeply entrenched apparatchiks of that system. So reified has education become that we are hardly able to distinguish it from the public schools. In effect we are asked to collaborate with (and thereby legitimate) a very particular special interest group with a very specific agenda and orientation rather than maintain critical distance from it. I have tried to argue (with little effect I might add) that as a professional educator, my responsibility is not to the *state* of North Carolina nor to the state and local school organizations, but rather to the *people* of the state, and to the highest aspirations of the nation and the culture.

In fact, I would go further and argue that we should avoid close working relationships with any established institution lest we lose our critical perspective and independent status. Alas, this argument is like whistling in the graveyard since the battle for independence, at least in this realm, is lost. In part, this is a matter of marketing in that teacher education is often one of the cash cows that sustains the college budget, and in the present economy, faculty and students tend to want jobs more than critical distance. In addition, this situation also reflects an active and deliberate willingness to collaborate with and endorse the basic thrust of the educational establishment or, even more disheartening, it might represent an unexamined affirmation more by default than by reflection. Whatever the motivation or explanation may be, the consequences are clear—teacher education programs continue to prepare teachers to work in schools as they are rather than as they ought or might be, and in so doing they are an important force in their perpetuation and validation. Moreover, this is not a situation into which the University or the Education departments have been dragged, kicking and screaming, but on the contrary have accepted with embarrassing, if not shortsighted, enthusiasm. This surely is not in the tradition of the University as a place for independent and fearless criticism nor is it in the University tradition of detached and contemplative reflection but rather it is in the tradition of the University actively, if not cynically, colluding with institutions of established power in order to maintain the status quo and its piece of the action. It further represents the craven and unprincipled ways in which the University continues to cave in to the demands of accrediting agencies and state bureaucracies. The issue is not limited to the implicit support of existing public school practices and policies, since this capitulation extends to what had been the fiercely defended University prerogatives of determining its curriculum and standards as the content and substance of teacher education programs and courses take on an ever more uniform quality as they conform to relentless external pressures and unabating internal toadying.

On the Other Hand . . .

Lest I be labeled a hopeless Jeremiah and in a spirit of fairness, I want to testify to the importance of a balanced presentation. I would note first of all the heroic efforts of many, many individual faculty members to resist this consciousness and who have offered vital and telling critiques of the culture, the society, and of higher education as well as thoughtful suggestions for reform. In addition, we must take note of the enormous difficulties inherent in the awesome, if not ultimately futile and arrogant, task of creating a just and loving society and with that soberness, perhaps we might adopt a somewhat more humble attitude towards the power of education, at least as customarily defined in the academy. We need also to remind ourselves that for all its difficulties, higher education is a place where freedom of expression, creativity, and inquiry are cherished and nourished perhaps more than in any other institution. Last in this chain of cautions, we need to be mindful of the dangers of reductionism and of despair that are inherent in analyses such as this one and be reminded of the Talmud's teaching: "The work is not for us to finish, but neither are we free to take no part in it."

Nevertheless, these times of very clear and present peril and unbearable human suffering call more for candor than caution, more for commitment than balance, more for outrage than civility. We need to face up to the University's (and sadly, that includes the good guys and gals) complicity and implication in a morally bankrupt and spiritually empty culture. It would be painful enough to simply face up to the realization that our inability to overcome our crises reflects an intellectual failure to develop the ideas, knowledge, and imagination necessary for the creation of a significantly more just and loving community. With all our knowledge and all our vaunted brilliance, we are still not able to invent an economy without unemployment and poverty, and with all our learned sophistication and all our delicate sensibilities, nations still rely on the obscenities of torture, war, and terror to enforce their will. Perhaps then, the research is simply not deep enough, the knowledge too skimpy, the poetry not powerful enough, the music not stirring enough, the essays and criticism not penetrating enough. In any case, whatever it is the University has to offer, it doesn't seem to be anywhere near enough to sufficiently resist the rampant madness, cruelty, and destructiveness.

Indictment

When I use terms like "higher education" and "the University" I am, of course, using them as metaphors of an aggregate consciousness, as the sum of all the varied and diverse efforts of hundreds of thousands of individuals and thousands of programs and activities. In so doing I face the risk of overgeneralization and paranoia, but perhaps it can help to avoid the risk of tunnel vision and denial. As I have already indicated before, I recognize the courageous and invaluable struggles of many of our colleagues. Yet there is the harsh and anguishing reality that they and the rest of us derive special and substantial benefits from our affiliation with higher education and that the vast majority of us participate in those activities that promote privilege, hierarchy, and elitism both within and outside the University. We all to a greater or lesser degree participate and legitimate high-stakes competition for more money, more status, more power, more recognition, the kind of competition in which there are winners and losers, in which some benefit at the expense of others, the kind that I believe will likely destroy us. We do this sometimes in the name of high standards, often persuasively, cogently, and compassionately. Sometimes we do so carelessly and mindlessly, either assuming or taking for granted that such practices are inevitable, if not benign. Rarely, if ever, is the moral and spiritual significance of such policies and practices examined, never mind discussed and debated in the academy. It is far more likely that the official rhetoric of higher education involves a reverence and exultation of "high standards," "selectivity," and "careful screening."

Surely, there are differences among us, and clearly some are far more competent than others, and surely we ought to demand that people in responsible positions be talented and able. The moral challenge that we face is how to recognize these realities and necessities in such a way as to afford dignity and worth to all and without affording privilege for some at the expense of others. It is a challenge that attracts the energies of only a very small part of those in higher education and even in those instances, mainly as an object of study. For not only has the University largely failed to teach us how we might mitigate the bitter consequences of ruthless competition; it has encouraged and supported this value system within its own community as manifested, for example in its increasingly obsessive rituals involved in the promotion and tenure process, a kind of in-house ethnic cleansing done cruelly but fairly.

Another important dimension of this cruel and harsh competition is the widely accepted and admired practice of academic bashing, often done with devastating wit and demoralizing effect. To outsiders, the ferocity of internecine warfare in the academy seems oddly incommensurate to the issues involved—why on earth are sane and civilized people so exercised over this or that theory? It is perfectly understandable, of course, that academics would be passionate about their ideas, but that would not seem to be enough to account for the practice of deliberately trying to discredit, discount, and diminish others. The reality in academia is that reputations can be and are made at the expense of others'. Indeed when academics are asked to assume the basic position, they are very likely to get into a consciousness of search and destroy. What would be considered untoward jealousy, hostility, and cruelty in most environments is considered to be simply part of what comes with the territory of higher education. It is a fiercely contested territory in which very skillful and talented people from time to time use their verbal abilities to score points by deriding and verbally abusing their colleagues. In fact, this practice has become not only an effective competitive technique but a culturally approved spectator sport in which the object is to make the most derogatory but plausible criticism in the wittiest manner possible. This practice is sometimes referred to as the zest and excitement of searching for truth in the free market place of ideas.

What we seem to have here, then, is a system fully in league and congruence with some of the most destructive and despicable dimensions of our culture—the ruthless pursuit of success, privilege, and personal advantage; the legitimation and rationalization of this consciousness, which is not only self-serving but serves to perpetuate a life-threatening status quo; and all of this done by the very people who are probably most aware of the consequences of this consciousness. My indictment of higher education thus involves three counts: its active complicity with destructive elements of the culture; its failure to confess this collaboration and its failure to provide a morally compelling alternative vision. The thread that connects these counts is a wicked spirit which animates and inhabits our work environment with the animus of mean-spirited aggressiveness and the sins of excessive pride, institutional idolatry, and moral numbness.

Guilt and Responsibility

I want to make it very clear that I do not present myself as being free of this complicity or responsibility or as someone who is somewhat purer or more saintly than others in the field. I am to some extent aware of the contradictions, irony, and anguish of those like me who can make a career out of pointing out the injustices of our system. Whether I am a hypocrite or a confessing sinner, or both, however, does not gainsay the reality or the significance of our crises which extend beyond concerns for preserving an individual's integrity or providing for individual comfort.

I accept Reinhold Niebuhr's notion in *Moral Man and Immoral Society* that we must face the consequences of our being born into a well-developed, highly determined world of corruption as we ponder our social responsibilities. I am also guided and deeply moved by his crystallization of the prophetic response to this condition: "the great insight of the Biblical prophets is that they said that life is good in spite of its evil and that it is evil in spite of good. In such faith both sentimentality and despair are avoided."

I am also mindful of certain traditions of higher education that run directly counter to the terms and foci of my indictment, traditions that speak to independence, contemplativeness, distance, reverence, and the selfless pursuit of truth and wisdom. It is my experience, however, that there is little real interest in reducing higher education's colonization by and of the culture or in significantly reducing our commitment to the secularization of the university. However, there does seem to be a fairly strong and persistent voice that calls on the university to return to a focus on study and scholarship and to restrict its membership to those who have a deep "love of learning" or with the potential to develop such a devotion. Many of us find this approach to be very satisfying personally, and it has the further advantage of providing the possibility of disassociating the university from complicity in social injustices and cultural injuries. It would, however, be a lot more acceptable to me if I believed that all this could be done without enhancing elitism and privileged hierarchy and in a way that such an opportunity could be afforded to those so inclined regardless of income, class, gender, race, or any other needlessly restrictive category. I confess and affirm, moreover, that such an enterprise seems relatively frivolous in the present context of immense unnecessary human suffering, and perhaps one index of a just society would be the persuasive absence of such a reservation. It is imperative that we always consider the social context of any proposed reforms in higher education and at the same time to continue to insist that they be considered within a moral context in which peace, freedom, and justice are indivisible, and where there is strong determination not to gain at the expense of others as well as a solid commitment to the liberation of *all* people.

What also must be seriously considered is the accumulated force of the various pressures, demands, and expectations that significantly limit whatever impulses there are, great or small, to resist and transform. There is the reality that in the present economy for many people, higher education provides one of the very few, if not the only source of the possibility of a decent and meaningful job. We have already mentioned the immense power of entrenched interest groups, and it goes without saying that this includes the force of internal university politics, whether active or inert. What has not been mentioned is the public's very strong and totally unambiguous expectation and demand that higher education provide access to the existing system by training them for the better jobs and providing the cultural capital necessary for social advancement. Government, business, the professions, and for that matter, all social and cultural institutions take it very much for granted that higher education will happily and gratefully keep on doing the research and instruction that will allow them to continue and thrive. Nor is there, to my knowledge, any significant public political base or cultural movement that could support and sustain a serious effort at profound transformation of higher education. What then are we to do if there is some semblance of truth in this analysis and if we are of a mind to change direction?

Higher Education as a Spiritual Activity

I certainly believe it critically important that ongoing efforts at serious institutional reform and the transformative work of individual faculty be strongly affirmed, supported,and sustained, even if, as I believe, such efforts are unlikely to produce genuine cultural transformation. What is required for people to persevere in such clearly important (though likely futile) work is the courage and conviction that emerges from a vision or spirit or energy that gives them meaning and the possibility of redemption. Such visions and spirits are quite rare in academia, having been banished and excommunicated by its most prominent citizens. The major exception to the general expulsion of spirits has, of course, been the increasingly less tacit veneration of the spirits of personal achievement, material success, conquest, pride, and power. It is these spirits that give such enormous energy and vitality to the work of the culture and higher education even as our enlightenment ontology denies spirits and our moral posture scorns our materialist ethic. I believe, however, that there are important countercurrents working against the mainstream consciousness of personalism, materialism, and secularism that provide for redemptive hope and possibility.

One of the most exciting cultural and intellectual movements now at work is the emergence of moral and spiritual discourses as influential and possibly decisive elements in the construction of more vital and meaningful social theory. Unfortunately, far too much attention has been placed on the resurgence of religious fundamentalism and its connections with the Far Right and not enough on the broader dramatic increase in the development of a variety of spiritual sensibilities including a significant religious Left. Such movements as liberation theology, feminist theology, and "conservadox" Judaism have greatly affected my thinking and, I am sure, the thinking of a great many others.

Among the most helpful contributions being made by contemporary theorists and activists using religious images and theological insights have been those concerned with the destructive problem of deepening despair, powerlessness, and pessimism and with, in the words of that deeply religious politician Jesse Jackson, "keeping hope alive." These writers, thinkers, and activists not only remind us of the central political importance of hope but they also provide us both with a language of sustaining hope in the face of empirically valid reasons for despair and some direction as to what we might and should hope for. To put it more bluntly, they offer us visions and spirits.

I am intrigued by the relevance of the religious concepts of confession and witness to our struggle to do our work, given the social context, the human condition, and our particular circumstances. It would seem to be more honest and more morally responsible, if not psychologically healing, if we in the academy were to publicly own up to and confess and witness the moral contradictions, incongruities, and offenses that mark our work, not as sensational narratives of individual guilt and perversity but as instances of shared responsibility, pain, and bewilderment. This is not to be seen as directed at catharsis (although that might be a very salutary consequence) but primarily as part of the educative process of seeking broader and communal understanding of who we are, where we are, and where we might go. It would also legitimately serve to involve the larger community in a dialogue regarding the culture's vision in general and, in particular, its relationship to education. If we cannot deliver on our promise that the truth will make us free, then we owe several words of explanation. If we have no intention of working for liberty and justice for all, then the least we can do is to admit it. There is, as we all know, a great deal of controversy over what constitutes the most sacred element of the

University canon. My nomination would be that having been entrusted as teachers to participate in the process of determining, elaborating, preserving, and enriching the culture's highest aspirations and deepest commitments, we have a solemn responsibility to be honest and forthright about what we are really doing and not doing. I do not think that it is a sin to be incompetent, however valuable and desired competence might be, but I have to say that our institutional and professional disingenuousness has led me to wonder again about the difference between sin and evil and to marvel at the human capacity to deny and rationalize with such genius.

I want to reiterate any disclaimer that I am not party to this terrible and dangerous charade. I know that I am guilty of most, if not all, of the charges that I have made. I say this even as I feel that neither I nor my colleagues are really trying to emulate a wicked, cruel, and hard-hearted Pharaoh. What does haunt me, however, is why you and I are not really trying to emulate a far more likable and attractive figure like Moses, a human being with recognizable limitations who rather reluctantly responded to a seemingly impossible demand to work for cultural transformation on the basis of a revealed and dazzling moral vision. His major resources were a spirit of transcendent hope, an extraordinary ability to image and to convey (teach) these fantastic images to those who had never before been able to see what they were now imagining, and the courage to overcome his own doubts and history. Moses was, as we know, not quite a Super-Hero—he made many serious mistakes and miscalculations and was beset with various rebellions, disasters, and setbacks and ultimately failed in his quest to reach the Promised Land. However, his constant struggle to reconcile an inspiring spiritual vision that was so vivid to him with the disheartening human activity that was just as vivid to him remains an abiding and accessible image for those who falter in their hope and aspiration to "do good."

Education as Grief

What I have come to in my own struggle is a growing awareness of the significance of what Walter Brueggemann refers to as the necessity for grief as a precondition for engaging in the pursuit of transformation. Moses would not have been able to fully see or act on the vision had he not experienced and felt the pain, cruelty, and agony of tyranny and suffering, experiences that he was later able to integrate with his spiritual vision and which became part of the metaphor of his political and educational project. I believe that neither I nor the vast majority of my colleagues or fellow citizens sufficiently mourn the stark and horrible tragedies that are consequences of our cultural and social policies and practices, and I agree with Brueggemann that this failure to grieve, as painful as it would be, only prolongs the suffering for all of us. In lieu of grief, we offer explanation, analysis, and sometimes blame; instead of mourning we complain and berate; and rather than sharing the pain and the responsibility we intellectualize them. Indeed, we are often told that our judgment can be adversely affected by intense emotional involvement and perhaps we need to be mindful of that danger and of the corollary danger that our judgment may be adversely affected by intense intellectual detachment.

Brueggemann says in *The Prophetic Imagination* that: "Real criticism begins in the capacity to grieve because that is the most visceral announcement that things are not right. Only in the empire are we pressed and urged and invited to pretend that things are all right-either in the dean's office or in our marriage or in the hospital room. And as long as the empire can keep the pretense alive that things are all right, there will be no real grieving and no real criticism" (1978, 163).

Let me make it clear that even as I quote theologians and use religious metaphors, what I am *not* advocating here is more research and instruction in theology and religious studies, even though that might be a reasonable idea in some other context. What I am suggesting is the possibility that professional and scholarly work could be greatly enriched if it were to be significantly grounded in matters of the spirit and in a moral vision. More particularly, we could provide ourselves with a lot more integrity and the larger community with a lot more service if we were to add generous doses of witnessing, confessing, and grieving as well as large amounts of humility to our research, scholarship, and teaching.

I have come to believe that if by some miraculous course of events everyone in the world had an IQ of at least 147, that if every person had scored a minimum of 1478 on the GREs, that if all the world's people were critically literate enough to satisfy Mortimer Adler, and had sufficient mathematical and scientific understanding to allow Admiral Rickover to rest in peace—that even all this would not be sufficient unto the day. As we have come to know, our crises are not precipitated by ignorance alone, and solutions to them will not emerge from knowledge alone. What is required, on one hand, is no real mystery—we need to have profound faith that there is meaning in our life on earth. We need to be able to affirm a vision of that meaningful life and to trust that our work has the potential for redemptive consequence. On the other hand, the source of such a consciousness remains stubbornly and tragically elusive for most of us, and in that sense its origins and accessibility represent genuine Mystery. I am convinced that we must not give up the quest for an energizing spirit that can provide us with life-sustaining comfort, meaning, direction, and courage. I am further convinced that we are very unlikely to find significant clues to the whereabouts of that spirit in the contemporary counting house, academy, or, for that matter, church.

It is this quest that can connect us to those who have preceded and who will follow us in the work of creating a more just, loving, joyous community, for it is clear that the pursuit of larger meaning is a deep and persistent part of human experience. We need to ponder why this ubiquitous dimension of life is so alien to the University and to consider the consequences of its continuing marginality to work in the academy. I am persuaded that only a vital and compelling spiritual and moral grounding will be able to prevent higher education from becoming at best, irrelevant and at worst, pathogenic.

References

Brueggemann, Walter. 1978. *The Prophetic Imagination*. Philadelphia: Fortress Press.

Brueggemann, Walter. 1987. *Hope within History*. Atlanta: John Knox Press.

Heschel, Abraham Joshua. 1962. *The Prophets*. New York: Harper and Row.

Niebuhr, Reinhold. (1932, reprinted 1960). *Moral Man and Immoral Society*. New York: Charles Scribner.

Goals 2000, The Triumph of Vulgarity, and The Legitimation of Social Injustice

Preface

I believe that the policies, procedures, and programs represented in the Goals 2000 legislation represent a significant crystallization of recent trends in educational thought so much so that they can be used as a telling if not chilling index of a quite clear social and cultural consensus on a number of critically important professional and public issues. This legislation, its support, and the nature of the critical response to it tell us a great deal about the present state of the continuous debate on the basic direction of American society and the role of public education in the determination and shaping of the direction. In this essay, I want to comment on those aspects of the legislation that seem to have provoked the least negative response, as it is my assumption that these are the aspects that represent the greatest amount of consensus by the public and the profession. Like the dog in the Sherlock Holmes story, what is significant here is the absence of barking and howling, or more precisely, the particular rhythms and qualities of the barking and the silences.

It is quite clear that the passage of the law was not a matter of great public interest. It received little attention in the media, and it certainly was not highlighted as one of the major political battles of the Clinton administration as were health care and welfare reform. It is premature to fully gauge mainstream professional reactions but my impression is that it has been relatively tepid and that the criticisms tend to focus on the meagerness of the funds involved and the high degree of federal

involvement in curriculum decisions. Time will tell whether this relative indifference represents a shrewd insight into what might turn out
to be toothless legislation with marginal consequences, or a gross
miscalculation of the far-reaching consequences of landmark educational policy making. However, the debate and eventual passage of
this program is a permanent record of what seems to constitute a
clear current consensus (public and professional) on what ought to be
both the purposes of education and the basic curriculum orientation.

What is particularly revealing about this legislation is that it represents an effort to integrate educational policy into a clear, unambiguous, and coherent social, economic, political, and cultural agenda. This
is not a program directed at education "for its own sake" but is openly
and proudly presented as an instrument of a particular set of government policies. Indeed, there is little indication that those who proposed the legislation make *any* distinction between education and socioeconomic policy, although there is no ample evidence of a close
analysis of the relationship between proposed curriculum policies and
economic goals.

Curriculum Theory

Although the legislation does not obviously attempt to delve into serious curriculum theorizing, it does deal quite decisively, if rather heavy-
handedly, with what we have come to believe is a complex and perplexing issue, namely the question about what should be taught. After
all the debates and struggles and all the painstaking and heated debates on the nature of knowledge, on what knowledge is of most worth,
on whether we should strive to be child-centered or subject-centered,
on whether we can integrate critical pedagogy with eco-feminism, on
the place of the arts, on the balance of the body, mind, and spirit, and
all the other countless and important controversies, proposals, projects,
and critiques, finally the President and the Congress have cut through
all these knots and conundrums and have decided. One clear winner
is the ever popular and remarkably resilient gaggle of conventional
disciplines—"English, mathematics, science, foreign languages, civics
and government, arts, history, and geography." Another winner is the
much unloved and critically abused "mastery and competence" approach to learning which says something about the comparative influence of Madeline Hunter and Paulo Freire on American consciousness. The losers include many of the areas that progressive and

humanistic educators have emphasized over the years: interdiscipli-
nary studies, critical thinking, constructivism, service learning, education for democracy, education for personal expression, education for
social responsibility, esthetics education, moral education, multicultural
education, environmental education, physical education, health education, and sexuality education, to mention a few prominent ones.
This is not to say that these areas are dead and buried but the legislation makes its priorities crystal clear and one doesn't have to be clair-
voyant to figure out how the United States Government sees the difference between the truly important and the merely interesting
components of the curriculum. The harsh reality is that there is now
official sanction and anointment for a particular curriculum perspective, a reality made poignant if not tragic given that this perspective is
culturally narrow and intellectually shallow.

This poignancy is magnified when we consider what seems to be
the utter irrelevance and futility of the sum total of the profession's
efforts to sophisticate the public dialogue on these issues. After decades of articles, books, experiments, debates, investigations, and
critiques, and with a heritage of brilliant and imaginative pedagogical
theories we are told that the best we can do is to turn to a dreary
collection of depressing clichés and anachronisms. Apart from the
ideological concerns, this legislation surely must be seen as totally
devoid of any kind of semi-serious educational theorizing or reasoning
or to put in another way, it is written as if there is *no* tradition of
educational discourse. In this regard, we in the profession must confront what appears to be our humiliating and shameful failure to penetrate the consciousness of mainstream American intellectual and
political thought. How do we as a profession account for the failure to
at least ameliorate the effects of political cynicism and public naïveté?
To what degree is the profession complicit by dint of those who pan-
der to the powerful? To what degree is the profession incompetent by
dint of its failure to establish a framework of a sophisticated public
discourse of education? To what degree is the profession derelict in its
responsibility to engage the public in genuine dialogue on the social,
political, economic, cultural, and moral dimensions of educational policy
and practice? Ultimately, as we have seen in the case of Goals 2000,
educational policy is determined by those in power, but the ease by
which vulgar and shallow educational thought has triumphed tells us
that we must work a great deal harder and smarter to insist that such
decisions be made with full knowledge of the complexities involved. In

this way we can maintain hope in the educability of the public and re-energize our sense of the purpose and importance of our work.

Socio-economic Policy

Not much ambiguity here. The words "productive" and "competitive" reappear with amazing regularity as if to reassure everyone that this piece of educational legislation is for real, that is, it is specifically designed for the very real and heavily competitive world of the global economy. The political and economic contexts for the significance of the legislation had been long established and astonishingly enough largely accepted. We are to believe that America is in a desperate struggle for economic dominance, if not survival with other more disciplined and hard-working nations. We are in this predicament and in danger of losing even more ground in part because of slackness and mediocrity in our schools, as it is clear that our competitor nations are outdistancing us in intellectual achievements, particularly in the crucial areas of science, technology, and mathematics. What is urgently needed then, is to stiffen our will, increase standards, demand more work from our students and teachers, and to carefully scrutinize and monitor educational achievement. The problem is a lack of sufficiently trained cadres of hardworking, productive, technologically savvy workers, and the solution is for the schools to cull out those with promise and motivate, train, test, and produce them. The cry became: "The nation is at risk—fix the schools."

This readily accepted myth represents policies that serve a number of purposes. First, it co-opts the public schools to accept their primary task to be that of feeding and sustaining the interests of international capitalists who require a lot of hardworking, productive, technologically savvy workers, and a great number of people who believe that this is the only right and proper purpose of education. Secondly, it distracts us into believing that our social and economic problems are rooted in our schools rather than in our social and economic policies and institutions, thereby avoiding rather messy and troubling questions on what constitutes a just and equitable system of distributing wealth and privilege. Thirdly, it provides a convenient justification to impose more control, uniformity, and orthodoxy in a culture very unsure and uneasy about dissent, difference, and pluralism. The "nation at risk" myth suggests that we simply can't afford 1960s style experimentation and counter-culturalism in a period of economic crisis. In addition, the myth encourages the best friends of those who want to maintain their power, namely, fear and anxiety and their companions, suspicion and divisiveness. The message is clear—the future belongs to the willing and the talented and for them it holds fame and fortune. Such people need only follow directions. For those who insist on slovenliness, laziness, and surliness the future is bleak and threatening, and they are advised to get out of the way and be prepared to take their just deserts. For those who are willing but who have limited talents the future is extremely uncertain, and such people are well advised to be obedient, work harder, lay low, be alert and stay on guard.

It is by now clear that we are immersed in a more virulent form of capitalism in which national boundaries, social contracts, and moral frameworks become increasingly irrelevant. It is a time of downsizing, bottom-line thinking, mergers, intense competition, and an era when greed is masked as freedom, and hustling becomes a creative activity. The effects on our community have been staggering—persistent unemployment and underemployment; an ever-widening gap between have and have-not nations; greater pollution and erosion of natural resources; increasing disparities in income; a shortage of meaningful jobs; intense pressures on families to earn a living wage; homelessness; poverty; welfare bashing; the rationing of medical care; and many other manifestations of a cruel and relentless economic order. This triumphant and unchallenged order must be seen as the driving force of not only Goals 2000 but of virtually all current official efforts at school reform, and indeed, we are well advised to examine the substance of this economic grounding rather than focusing only on the procedural and curricular dimensions of this legislation. This legislation is not primarily about advancing knowledge, or expanding intellectual and creative horizons, nor is it about the pursuit of meaning and the nurturing of the soul; it is, instead, concerned with the deployment of human resources into immense struggles for economic dominance, privilege, and hegemony. Goals 2000 is not directed at individual empowerment or social democracy but is instead designed to supply the arsenal of human resources needed for the bloody economic wars being fought by transnational corporations, national economies, and financial entrepreneurs.

President Clinton summed up this point rather well in his 1994 State of the Union speech in which he endorsed public school choice and chartering, "as long as we measure every school by one high standard: Are our children learning what they need to know to compete and win in the global economy?" What a commentary on our society when the President, in a major policy address to the nation, enunciates our basic educational policy as one that reduces the purposes of education to the promotion of material success and the intensification of international economic competition.

Moral Vision

The kind of economic policy which drives the Goals 2000 program has had an enormous influence not only on material issues, as I have already indicated, but also on our relationships with each other and on our basic human values. It is a time when meritocracy has shifted from being a term of accusation and dread to one of approbation and celebration, a time of a re-energized and revalidated social Darwinism. Our new post-industrial society and post-modern culture require highly skilled, tough-minded, highly sophisticated people who can and do change intellectual, cultural, and moral loyalties easily and joyfully. All bets are off, traditional loyalties and allegiances are suspect, communities and credos are all problematic, it's all flow and go. Presumably, the good news is that what will or, at least should, count is not family or social connections or previous conditions of mastery but sheer talent, and for that reason we must not discriminate by the outmoded cultural categories of race, class, and gender but by the more democratic and hip ones of cybernetic literacy, language fluency, and entrepreneurial chutzpa. This consciousness is well expressed in the well-nigh universally accepted shibboleth of "leveling the playing field," that is, the importance of reducing socially artificial barriers to achievement. Indeed, this concept is reflected in the Goals 2000 legislation with its references to the development of "opportunity standards," defined in the act as "the criteria for, and the basis of, assessing the sufficiency or quality of the resources, practices, and conditions necessary at each level of the education system . . . to provide all students with an opportunity to learn the material in voluntary national content standards or State content standards." (Goals 2000, 1994) Presumably, once we have established and controlled for the independent variables (e.g., quality and quantity of educational resources) we can get on with judging children on the critical dependent variable of achievement. The metaphor of a playing field is very likely used to evoke images of enjoyable contests among willing, fair-minded folks who relish the opportunity to display and hone their skills with other evenly matched and motivated folks. Everyone is expected to play by the rules, to try hard, to be fair, and to accept the outcome with grace. Leveling the playing field is about removing irrelevant, unfair and preventable barriers to fair competition. So, what is wrong with this picture?

Let's take a closer look at this metaphor and examine the consequences of games played on a level playing field under the assumption that miraculously there is a political will to do this leveling and that we are successful at achieving the goal. Such games still involve competition, contestants of enormously varied interests, abilities, and competitiveness, winners and losers, ranking,and differential rewards which in this case have enormous consequences. The spoils go to the victor and this is to be celebrated because the victory is "fair," that is, based on the inherent and demonstrable superiority of the winner. The major moral tragedy here is that such a contest requires and structures losers, for indeed the game cannot be played without losers and its primary purpose is to identify them as part of the process of distributing the wealth. What we have here is a variation of the age-old process of powerful groups imposing a system of hierarchy and privilege and simultaneously providing a discourse of pragmatic justification and social inevitability for what is at base a cruel and callous policy of calculated legitimated inequality. Presumably the myth of equality of *opportunity* allows us to believe that both the victors and the losers deserve their fate and that the community has fulfilled its responsibilities by removing "artificial" barriers to "genuine" competition. What, in fact, the community has done is to mask a system in which human beings are required to compete even if they are averse to competing and to compete in contests even if it requires them to display skills in which they are uninterested, lacking, or both. The penalty for not engaging in these compulsory contests is the same, if not worse, as coming in dead last in the games themselves. The consequences are *intended* to be very serious, namely, one's socioeconomic standing in the community. Put another way, they involve the matter of whether you will be rich or poor, hungry or well fed, and whether you will have a home or not.

One of the major technological problems of our society, therefore, becomes how to develop a "fair" system of affording privilege, legitimating inequality, and evading the Golden Rule. As usual, the intellectual and professional classes have been eager to stoop to the task and have developed a stunning array of sophisticated modes of judging people's worth which goes under more euphemistic terms like measurement and assessment. Accountability and evaluation become indispensable dimensions of a cruel but fair meritocracy in which our compelling moral responsibility is shifted from creating a more just and loving community to the moral imperative of providing reliable and valid techniques to maintain an inherently unfair society. If nothing else, Goals 2000 is an epiphany to the evaluation and sorting process, an official enshrinement of valid and reliable rituals of ultimate judgment, and an iconization of testing. So much for the traditions of education for play, creativity, and growth; so much for nurturing respect and compassion for each other; so much for the notion of public education as an instrument for nourishing a democratic community with liberty and justice for all.

Goals 2000 is an apt metaphor for a cultural vision of personal achievement, materialism, individuality, survival of the fittest, ruthless competition, political realism, and detached technology. It is a vision that discourages solidarity among peoples, since people are not seen as family members but as competitors. It is a vision that is so powerful that educators find themselves having to work very hard to make convincing and persuasive arguments on the importance of caring and compassion. The fact that nourishing the impulse to care is seen as an intriguing and interesting educational innovation and that the presence of guns is now accepted as commonplace in the school is powerful testimony to the desperation and divisiveness in our culture. The response of Goals 2000 to our social and cultural crises is to define the major educational problem to be that of low productivity and to locate the solution in raising educational achievement and to formalize and institutionalize a national policy of even more testing, sorting, discriminating, classifying, allocating, and channeling of children in order that we might "compete and win in the global economy."

So What's New?

As I've already mentioned, the public response to Goals 2000 has been something less than heated, and indeed, seems to have been one of the major non-events of 1994. I believe that this in part represents a "so what?" reaction to what is by now the emergent and familiar public consensus on what constitutes the essential process and purpose of education. This consensus has now been formally ratified by the President and Congress. There has been some professional and public criticism, most of which has centered on the issues of federal control and the imposition of uniform educational standards. What is truly extraordinary in the reaction, however, is the explicit and implicit acclaim with which the public and profession have lavished on the broad goals themselves, even in criticizing them as unrealistic and romantic.

A typical form of criticism begins with a disclaimer on criticizing the goals themselves and then proceeds to take the legislation to task for not providing sufficient funds for these well-intentioned goals or for not recognizing the structural problems that are barriers to achieving these lofty aspirations. Writing as guest editor of a special issue of the *Phi Delta Kappan* mostly devoted to a critical symposium on Goals 2000, Evans Clinchy describes the contributors to the symposium as "transformationists" and clearly their articles are thoughtful and insightful critiques of major elements of the legislation. However, in the very beginning of his lead article, Clinchy has this to say: ". . . this new national mission may at first glance appear to be *no more than a list of obviously desirable goals and generally non-controversial aims* . . . Indeed, the question here is not whether these . . . goals are worth pursuing but whether the Clinton Administration and the Congress understand what the goals imply and thus what it will take to actually achieve them" [emphasis added] (Clinchy, 1995).

What Clinchy characterizes as "transformationist" critique for the most part turns out to be essentially grounded in serious concerns about pedagogical, curricular, and organizational issues, with only occasional references to fundamental social and cultural concerns and none to economic ones. Therefore, what is not new here is the endorsement of an educational policy thoroughly folded into the interests of the dominant industrial, financial, and business interests and totally integrated into the ideology of the free market system (i.e., capitalism). Moreover, what is also constant in the reactions, both pro and con, is the implicit ratification of the existing social, political, and economic paradigm, at least by default, by the vast majority of the profession.

To the extent that there is strong criticism from the profession, my impression is that it tends to focus on the issues of an unimaginative curriculum, an overdetermined degree of testing, and on the matter of the federal imposition of educational uniformity. I have already made reference to the dreariness of the curricular orientation represented in

Goals 2000, and, as depressing as it may be, there is the reality that it is an orientation that has persisted and prevailed both in the schools and in the public consciousness as virtually inevitable, if not incomparable. The status of the sacred five subjects (English, science, history, mathematics, and foreign languages) has reached a level of near permanence and has remained basically unchallenged as the starting point of curricular discussions for several decades. Again, Goals 2000 does not represent an abrupt change in what constitutes the prevailing views on curriculum but has simply affirmed a political reality: namely, that the struggles for serious and fundamental reexamination of the curriculum have had little or no impact on broad educational policy. And surely the emphasis on testing and accountability is hardly a surprise in an era when we are supposed to cheer "authentic assessment" and "portfolios" as progressive ways of rendering to Caesar his insistence on ranking and judging children.

What does appear to be new and ominous is the rather large foot of the federal government in the door of educational regulation, not withstanding the clearly disingenuous and promiscuous use of the term "voluntary" in the legislation. I agree with those who see this as a dangerous and potentially devastating blow to our vital principles and traditions of teacher autonomy, community involvement, and student participation, and as an important aspect of an irresistible tide of centralized rigidity, uniformity, and control. The dangers here are very real and involve the possibility of the total politicization of education by the federal government, the erosion of pluralism, diversity, and experimentation, and an escalation of bureaucratic interference, harassment, meddling, and Mickey Mousing. As dreadful as these policies may be, they basically represent a continuation, perhaps at a somewhat more intense level, of well-established, basically uncontested, and generally accepted educational policies and practices. Through a combination of various factors and forces—for example, the homogenization of American culture, the near uniformity in college admissions requirements, the enormous mobility of American workers and families, the existence of a de facto national curriculum (see above), accreditation and certification requirements, the textbook and testing industry, and so on, to all intents and purposes the public schools in the United States are virtually uniform in all the most important respects. One very important exception to this uniformity, however, is the area of allocated resources. Indeed, because we as a society have wanted to be able to move from school to school easily, we have arranged an organization, curriculum, and culture of public education of easily recognizable, and assembled interchangeable parts. There surely are vigorous programs in many communities that allow for significant parental and/or teacher involvement, but they, for the most part, still work within the framework of these interchangeable parts. The enthusiasm for state mandated accountability as a mode of imposing uniform standards is as real as it is depressing, and the striking similarity of these standards across the states should not be in the least surprising.

What's Going on Here?

For me, the main issue here is not so much about clarifying the new dangers to public education that Goals 2000 poses but rather to be alert to the old dangers of public education to our vision of a just and loving community. What Goals 2000 represents, extends, magnifies, and cements is an essentially unchallenged educational paradigm that mirrors and seeks to extend a cruel and unjust cultural vision. I believe that critics are right to point out that the legislation seriously erodes the vitality of grass roots, local involvement in the public schools, surely an extremely important dimension of a democratic society. I also agree with the critics who lament the rather crude emphasis on test results that seriously undermines efforts at stimulating critical thinking, individual expression, and human creativity. And, as I've indicated, Goals 2000 accentuates an extremely unwise and self-defeating growth in uniformity, rigidity, and overregulation. However, as important and vital as these criticisms are, they do not go nearly far enough in interpreting the social, political, and cultural significance of the meaning of this latest round of educational reform. We get more insight into the bedrock issues from the critics who correctly point out that our political leaders are very reluctant to confront the real financial and political cost of actually trying seriously to meet the goals, for example, by failing to discuss the impact that programs directed at the virtual elimination of drugs and violence would have on federal and state budgets or by avoiding discussion of what it really takes to reduce poverty, so necessary even for the relatively modest goal of equal opportunity.

Disingenuousness, however, is not the exclusive prerogative of politicians. It is also very much in evidence among educators who seek to distance schooling from the social, cultural, economic, and political visions in which they are embedded. The operative present visions (educational and otherwise) actually require, structure, and ensure inequality and poverty in their insistence on hierarchy, competition, and meritocracy. Key to the understanding of why education is such a hotly debated issue is the well-understood tenet that it is a critically important mode of attaining an edge in achieving privilege in a society that embraces and legitimates an unequal distribution of wealth. It seems to me that this is *the* critical axis that our educational institutions turn on, and astonishingly enough, the least questioned and resisted. I certainly prefer that teachers and parents work at the local and school levels to improve educational programs but not if the programs maintain and accentuate the present system of structured inequality and poverty. I also love to support imaginative, child-centered, developmentally appropriate, and thought provoking curricula but my concern for an education that fosters a just and loving community is far greater. Perhaps we do not have to choose between local control and justice or between a humane curriculum and equality, but we must make the connection very, very clear because the reality is that our dominant public and professional discourse is very muddy on these relationships. Actually, the politicians (as in Goals 2000) tend to be much more up front in their insistence on connecting education to the needs of business, government, and the military. It seems that many professionals are invested in reifying education such that it can be separated from ideological concerns, operating from the myth that good education is good education, good teaching is good teaching,and good schools are good schools regardless of the political and economic contexts.

What Should We Do?

There are, as I see it, three major problems here: (1) the triumphalism of the reactionary educational reform movement as reflected in the ho-hum reaction to the passage of the Goals 2000 project; (2) the timidity and modesty of oppositional forces as reflected in the mildness of the criticisms of Goals 2000; and (3) the sense of futility and despair as reflected in the near absence of alternative social, economic, and cultural visions to the one represented in Goals 2000. The energy that is created from the interaction of triumphalism, timidity, and despair is surely entropic and hence can only magnify our crises of poverty, inequity, and polarization. What needs to be done is, therefore, quite clear and very difficult: to reinstill our visions, dreams, and hopes for creating a loving and just world and to recover our confidence in the human capacity to overcome the obstacles to them. This is not the time to be timid precisely because there is so much timidity. This is not the time to be despairing especially because there is so little hope out there. This is not the time to preserve the status-quo particularly because there is so little effort to work for social and cultural transformation.

Let's put it another way—we don't need professional and intellectual classes to ratify and legitimate policies that engender and sustain social injustice, poverty, and privilege or to add to the sense of their inevitability and immutability. If there ever was a time for those who aspire to leadership and responsibility to speak out with passion and conviction on our shared vision of an end to poverty, unnecessary human suffering, to homelessness, to humiliation, to authoritarianism, and to anything else standing in the way of a life of meaning and dignity for all people, this is surely it. There is an extraordinary vacuum in the public sphere needing to be filled with a greater understanding of the moral, social, and cultural consequences of our educational policies and with an educational vision that is grounded in a commitment to a world of peace, love, and community. As educators our responsibility is surely not to carry out current educational policies and practices, however oppressive they may be, but to uphold and nourish the cherished principles that inform our deepest dreams and highest aspirations. As responsible professionals, we are uniquely positioned to affirm the capacity of education to contribute to a consciousness of compassion and justice. However, this is a time when we need to talk less about our educational goals and more about our moral aspirations, less about our professional role as educators and more about ethical responsibilities as citizens. We need to stop accommodating to the forces of institutional control and instead renew our commitment to the spirit of joyous community. To paraphrase Rabbi Hillel, if we as a profession do not support education, who will? If we are only for our profession, what are we? If not now, when?

References

Goals 2000: Educate America Act. Public Law 103-227—March 31, 1994.

Clinchy, Evans. "Sustaining and Expanding the Educational Conversation" in *Phi Delta Kappan*, March 20, 1995.

The Vocation of Teaching

I had the privilege in 1994 of spending a semester teaching at Seattle University, a distinguished Jesuit university noted for its vitality, diversity, and commitment to principle. While I was there, I was asked to give a talk to a group of Catholic school principals on my views on teaching, which is the basis of the following essay.

One of the frequent phrases that I have come across in my recent and ongoing exposure to Jesuit education is a reference to the importance of perceiving teaching not as a career but as a vocation, not so much a job as a calling. In this essay, I will discuss the implications of this challenging if not ambiguous notion, particularly focusing on the questions regarding what it exactly is we are called upon to do and what it is we find ourselves actually doing. This is clearly a complex and controversial project and one that allows for any number of interpretations and analyses. However, I would insist that as educators, we all have the obligation to respond to this challenge, even as we have the right to different and varying responses. I therefore offer my views in the spirit of a colleague struggling with you to bring moral and spiritual meaning to a professional life that is often chaotic and frustrating at best, and pointless if not counter productive, at worst.

Let me begin with a number of my basic assumptions: First, I think of education as a social and cultural phenomenon, inextricably enmeshed and interconnected with a society's political, economic, and social structures, beliefs, values, and concerns. Indeed, I often tell my students that there are no such things as "educational issues"; there are instead, any number of moral, political, economic, philosophic, and cultural issues that get acted out in educational settings. One of the tragic and unforeseen consequences of the professionalization of education has been its diversion, if not trivialization, into relatively narrow and technical concerns. *The* most important questions for education are really not about what materials or teaching approach to use; not about the length of the school year; nor about testing or financing or teacher salaries. The most important educational questions are the same as the most important questions we have of life itself; questions such as: Who are we? Where did we come from? Where are we going? Is there meaning to life? If so, what is it? How are we to live with each other?

The old cliché that education is about life may be old and tired, but it does have the virtue of having a great deal of validity to it. The continuing tendency to separate and reify education into an autonomous and independent entity is intellectually unsound, politically naive, and professionally irresponsible. Education, as John Dewey put it so well, "is about the making of a world." All of us as citizens, family members, workers, professionals, neighbors, friends, and acquaintances are continuously called upon to participate in the creation, recreation, and the maintenance of our culture, society, and community. In this sense we all participate, to one degree or another, and in varying degrees of awareness, in this extraordinary, awesome, and complex task of determining what kind of world we want to make, what kind we are actually making, and what kind of world it is possible to make.

As professional educators, we have, of course, particular and specialized roles to play in this supremely important task of making meaning out of our existence. I do not share the view that institutional education is the only or even chief agent in the determination of our social structures and cultural consciousness, but I certainly affirm its vital and central relationship. As educational professionals we, at the very least, need to be aware of the explicit and implicit social and cultural aspirations with which our educational theories and practices are congruent and contributory. Beyond that, I would argue that we also have the responsibility to have our own critical and affirmative positions, that is, to adopt a moral perspective that allows us to know right from wrong, to morally discriminate among social and cultural forms and directions, and to be able to discern the moral consequences of particular educational policies and practices. As educators, we are *ipso facto*, for better or worse, part of the process of making a world and we must be willing to be accountable, not only for so-called educational effects but for our contribution to the construction of the world that has been and is being made. We do not have the option to be ignorant, to be unaware, or uninterested in the social, cultural, moral, and spiritual significance of what we do in the name of education; nor do we have the right to claim that we are merely servants of the social order, that we are only following orders. It is precisely this dimension of our work that makes it so profoundly important, so exhilarating, so risky, so terrifying, *and* what qualifies it for being a vocation rather than a job or a career.

What is clearly required of us, then, is an accounting of our moral vision, of what constitutes our notion of an ideal society, of a direction and path that we should follow, and a confession of the spirit that guides us on that path. I, of course, do not mean this to be expressed as an occasional and honorific exercise (i.e., as an empty and perfunctory flourish of piety and platitude), but as an ongoing commitment to integrating educational policy and practice with moral and spiritual vision such that they are not easily separated. It must also be pointed out that it is both possible and necessary to discern the moral vision(s) inherent in educational policies and practices and to examine the moral claims of varying educational orientations. Indeed, the entire notion of separating the moral from the educational is patently absurd; as if it were possible to have education without moral effect, implication, or meaning. Make no mistake about it—we are all and at all times, whether we like it or not, moral educators. To paraphrase Martin Luther King, we need to be judged not by the texture of our resumés but by the quality of our character, and by the same token, the quality of our educational programs need to be judged not by test scores or famous alumni but by the moral character of the community it has participated in fashioning.

Let us then examine, briefly, something of the moral visions contained in some educational formulations, something of the character of the world we are making and reproducing, and some educational implications of alternative moral visions. My own sense of this examination is that a charitable view would be that as a people we are mightily confused; a less charitable interpretation would be that we live a life of industrial strength contradiction verging on hypocrisy, if not madness. In a nation founded on a belief that all people are created equal, we have created a social structure that requires and legitimates inequality; in a culture rooted in a passion for life and a commitment to dignity for all, we have produced a discourse of hierarchy, privilege, and elitism. Tragically, we find ourselves engaged in maintaining and revitalizing a social structure in the form of a social triage in which some flourish, many struggle, and far too many perish. In a civilization energized by a spirit of love and justice, we are captured by a spirit of competition, achievement, success, mastery that pits people against people, group against group, nation against nation, culture against culture. We enjoin each other to love our neighbor, but we are very selective about where we live, never mind the kind of neighbor we choose to tolerate. We read that the poor are blessed and that the meek will inherit the earth, yet we as a culture find ourselves increasingly indignant, impatient, and inconvenienced by the presence and persistence of the homeless and altogether disgusted at those on welfare.

We live in a time of increasing racial tensions and divisiveness, of cultural polarization, escalating violence, of increasing suicide and prostitution among teenagers, of pollution, environmental catastrophes, of enormous alienation, despair, and cynicism. As a culture, it can be said that we have a crisis of faith—we are rapidly losing our faith in our political system. Our faith in the capacity of science and technology to solve our problems has surely been shaken; we indeed have very serious doubts about every social and cultural institution, including religious and educational ones. In the face of such loss of connection and meaning, much of the culture finds itself mired in the self-indulgence of personal or institutional narcissism or both.

What you may and, I hope, *do* ask is, "What does all of this have to do with education?" One certainly hopes that there is some significant relationship for it would be extremely depressing if we did what we did without effect on the culture. It might relieve our guilt, but it surely would diminish our sense of the significance of our work. We cannot, however, have it both ways, i.e., to proclaim the importance of education without accepting the responsibility for its impact, for better or worse, on the way we live together. It is clear to me that, on the whole, institutionalized education is, unfortunately, in very sharp and clear congruence with the culture and society. Indeed, educators almost always proudly affirm this resonance as not only real but desirable, and it is in this sense that organized education helps to validate and legitimate the status quo. Beyond that, schools and universities function in ways that enable and facilitate the social system—schools and universities help to sort out students through its elaborate evaluation, grading, honor awarding processes, thereby both validating and institutionalizing a class and caste system that allocates privilege and rations dignity. Schools also embody and legitimate the major cultural values of our society—stress on achievement and success, individuality, materialism, pride, ambition, power, competition, and domination. To be sure, there are many places where individual and groups of educators strive to offer experiences that often run counter to the dominant culture and their courage and energy must always be registered and affirmed. Surely there are teachers who work mightily to establish strong bonds of connection with students not as a mode of instruction but as a way of being; we know that there are educators out there who resist the emphasis on testing and grading; that there are serious efforts to promote social justice and a community of love and joy through the educative process. Alas, we also know that such efforts go against the grain of the dominant cultural and educational consciousness of competition, success, self-advancement, and hyperindividuality.

The dominant theme of current educational discourse was never better articulated in all its brutal linearity and poignant contradiction than in President Clinton's recent [1994] State of the Union speech in which he spoke eloquently of "our better angels" and where he rather movingly urged us "to stand strong against the forces of despair and evil." In this same speech the President strongly recommended that we embrace a policy of educational diversity and choice with a very significant proviso, namely (and I quote), "as long as we measure every school by one high standard." What is that ultimate standard that is so vital, so critical, so clear that it makes issues of educational approach of marginal significance? Is it the preservation of democracy? No! Is it the development of an ethos of justice, love and community? No! Is it then perhaps, the preservation of Western civilization? No, not even that! It is, in the President's words, "Are our children learning what they need to know to compete and win in the global economy."

Is it truly our vocation to immerse ourselves passionately and energetically in an intense struggle to establish the United States as the most powerful economic force in the world? Is this the ultimate goal for which we are asked to sacrifice and commit our lives? Is it in this struggle that we are to find meaning and purpose in life? Is this to be the path to spiritual and cosmic fulfillment? Does such a course represent the way of the "better angels"?

Perhaps you may believe that I am being unfair, even unkind, if not simplistic and sardonic. I see the President's understandably terse metaphor of educational purpose not surely as his definitive views on education but I do see it as representative of the broad perspective in which most educational discourse is framed. It is an orientation that goes basically unchallenged except in a few and remote circles of grumpy discontent. More importantly, it is an orientation that significantly informs our day to day and month to month thinking and practices. Of course, the most appalling thing of all is that such thinking is, I believe, not only politically and socially problematic, it is morally and spiritually bankrupt, bereft of redemptive or transcendent meaning. It is, in fact, still another exemplification of the triumph of materialism in our society, in our culture, and in our education; or put another way, it represents further evidence of the erosion of our commitment to center our education in the struggle to create a world immersed in a vision of love, justice, meaning, and joy.

As educators we are required to respond—responsibility is about the ability to respond—and whatever the nature of that response, it will be important. In this case, silence amounts to consent, so no response speaks volumes. Are we to acquiesce? If so, should we do so gleefully? Sullenly? With fingers crossed? With resignation? Or with mischief in mind? Or should we resist and if so should we resist passively or aggressively? Self-righteously or apologetically? How are we to know what to do? How is it we don't know what to do?

It seems to me that the only way for educators to come to grips with such questions is to see them within a larger context, i.e., within a particular framework that offers a compelling critique *of* and alternative *to* the dominant culture. Where are such frameworks to be found? One very valuable resource is in our religious and spiritual traditions, particularly those that attempt to connect human experience with larger meaning. Peter Berger has defined religion as "the audacious attempt to conceive of the entire universe as being humanly significant." Religious traditions often arise in part as critical reactions to perceived deficiencies in the social and cultural institutions of the time and attempt to offer criteria by which to judge the validity of existing policies and arrangements as well as provide principles to guide us to more ideal ones. As Robert Ackerman puts it, "Religion is a perennial source of social critique, but religion in general is not equivalent to social critique. . . . [But] the major religions always retain the potential of developing pungent social critique, no matter how accommodating a form they have assumed in particular institutional contexts. If religion is to provide the possibility of social critique, it can never be reduced to a set of mechanically understood dogmata, for in that focus it would necessarily lose touch with changing social reality. . . . Critique does not exhaust religion, but religion that cannot critique is already dead."

To put matters bluntly, the vocation of educators is not about improving instruction, or about developing an integrated curriculum, or even providing for a smooth and orderly school organization, but rather it is to participate in the struggle for a just and loving community. Educators are moral leaders who work in educational institutions, not pedagogues who occasionally have to deal with ethical problems. The major question that we need ask educators is not "What is your philosophy of education?" but "What is your philosophy of life and what are its ramifications for education?"

What our culture and society desperately need are genuine alternatives, not merely more acceptable and palatable variations of the same themes of education for privilege, domination, and competition. Religious and spiritual traditions certainly provide us with alternative social visions, and we look to educators who affirm these visions to develop policies and practices that are congruent with these alternative visions. It is very hard for me to believe that educational policies designed to reproduce our materialistic and hierarchical society can be used, even in modified form, to nurture a community of justice and love. What would seem to be especially dangerous is to delude ourselves into thinking that we are doing God's work with the techniques and consciousness of a competitive and materialistic culture. Such formulations offer the possibility of misguided, if not disingenuous, rationalization and denial.

Let me put the point to you very directly. If one believes, as I do, that there is a mysterious force that impels us to create loving and just communities, then one is literally crazy not to infuse such ideas into their views on education. If one believes, as I do, that our present culture and society promote policies that do not honor the sacred qualities of life, then one is irresponsible not to say so. If you believe, as I do, that the human spirit is being crushed by a culture and an education that values success, materialism, and individual achievement, then for us not to actively resist these policies is to be sinful. To witness hunger, poverty, and homelessness is to witness a morally corrupt and spiritually bankrupt culture *and* education.

Each of us has a compelling responsibility to continually witness, confess, and discern. By this I mean that we are required to be fully aware of the human condition and our part in it—that we are required to affirm our deepest convictions and highest aspirations and be prepared to confront our failures to meet them. I mean that we need to continually engage in the dialectical process of examining our deepest beliefs in the context of day- to-day events in order that we may have greater insight into our beliefs and increase our ability to act in greater accordance with them.

Personally, I am profoundly moved by the teachings of Jesus and am extremely interested in infusing them into educational discourse. How are we to interpret the Sermon on the Mount in the context of our existing educational orientation? Are we actually asked to love our neighbors and students? All of them? How is a teacher to love a child who does not achieve? What is the relationship between unconditional love and a hierarchical society? Shouldn't a Christian school be profoundly different than a secular school? What is the ultimate source of knowledge? To what ultimate service is knowledge to be used or is knowledge itself to be worshipped? I would truly love to be in dialogue with you on such questions.

Our social and cultural dangers are of an immense and critical nature and as educators we ought to be responding in kind. Yet the field has reacted with incredible timidity, blindness, and blandness to these terrifying dangers. In the face of spiritual alienation, political despair, and unbearable human suffering our profession responds with new texts, new technologies, and new slogans. The world cries out for meaning and the profession offers accountability as a response; the people perish for a lack of vision, and the profession suggests more elaborate lesson plans. Our responsibility in this historical moment is to engage in the search for meaning, vision, and spirit to our efforts. Unfortunately, we are tragically distracted from this task by the extraordinary vulgarization and trivialization of the teaching process. Are we really to have schools serve as an arena in which people are required to earn their dignity? Where honor is rationed out? Where people learn to achieve and to get ahead of each other? Are we to establish schools in order to legitimate and facilitate the process of determining the winners and losers of the race to attain material achievement and personal success? Was it for this that Moses led his people to Sinai? Was it for this that Jesus gave his life? Was it for this that great religious leaders gave of their energies, wisdom, and often their lives? Will our redemption be based on our ability to help some people to become rich and famous?

As a profession we are obliged to be models and to affirm models for ourselves. The greatest models of teachers have been religious figures—people like Moses, Jesus, Buddha, Dietrich Bonhoeffer, Martin Luther King, and Mohandas Gandhi—who have inspired millions upon millions to be guided in their lives by a vision that provides light, warmth, and transcendence. It is to participate in this task, however humbly, however inadequately, that enables our work to be worthy of being considered sacred. To paraphrase the words of Rabbi Heschel, "When you seek to teach, take off your shoes, for you are indeed on sacred ground."

Part Two

AN EXAMINATION OF ALTERNATIVE APPROACHES TO EDUCATION

The Politics of Character Education

Background

The current debate on moral and character education is one of the few instances where there is as much, if not more, public as professional debate and discussion. Indeed, the public discussion of character education has come to the point where it has become an overtly partisan political issue, serving as metaphor and code for those interested in pursuing the neoconservative social and cultural agenda. Part of the strategy of neoconservatives is to create a discourse in which the schools are blamed for not "teaching values" and families are blamed for teaching the wrong ones. Implicit in such a discourse is the assumption that our social problems are *not* so much rooted in the failures of our social, economic, and political structures as they are in the personal attitudes and behaviors of individuals. The thrust of this approach is to move the discussion away from the extremely controversial realm of ideological dispute toward the safer and presumably more consensual realm of desirable personal traits, to convert social and political issues into educational and pedagogical ones, and to focus on stability rather than transformation.

We would all be better served by recognizing that the current so-called Character Education Movement essentially represents an *ideological and political* movement rather than a debate about curricular and instructional matters. My basic criticisms of this approach are elaborated in this paper and briefly, have to do with the naivete and/ or disingenuousness of the discourse and of the inadequacies of its political and social assumptions. I will also try to show how this movement, far from being innovative and reforming, represents instead a long-standing tradition of using schools as agents of social stability, political stasis, and cultural preservation. It is also my hope that this analysis will shed light on the more general issues of moral education and the moral nature of education.

The Politics of the Discourse: An Historical Perspective

The matter of deliberately intervening into the behavior and character of students is a central if not dominating theme in the history of public schooling in the United States. Indeed, our early colonial experience with formal education not only foreshadows this emphasis, but much of its agenda and orientation continues to have an important influence on current views, policies, and practices. We can speculate further and posit the claim that basic to the entire colonization project were two obsessions that are fundamental to the subsequent and continuing development of American culture (and hence a critical dimension of public education)—the drive to make the community morally good and the individual materially rich. The attempts to reconcile these two projects with Christianity and, later, with democracy has led to a highly complex, ingenious, and compelling, if not contradictory, ambiguous, and controversial social and cultural system, or, if you will, mythos. This mythos represents an attempt to create a vision of America which seemingly integrates moral, religious, political, economic, social, and cultural perspectives seamlessly. The broad effort involved in creating, promoting, enforcing, and sustaining this vision has, of course, a very important *political* dimension, i.e., issues regarding who is to be involved in this process, who is privileged by this process, and who benefits from the substance of the vision.

It is clear that public schooling has always been considered an important resource in this political task from colonial times (Bailyn 1962) to the Common School movement (Kaestle 1983) to the present (Purpel 1995). The establishment of the early Puritan schools was in response to fears that families were increasingly unable or unwilling to adequately inculcate their children with the spiritual beliefs and moral virtues of the Puritan Commonwealth. The battle for compulsory education in the nineteenth century was led by members of the establishment who strongly believed that a system of schools with a common curriculum was the answer to the worries over national solidarity, social stability, and cultural purity. The current revival of interest in character education represents merely a revival of awareness of issues and concerns that have been a constant in our educational discourse, which should not be especially surprising given the essentially moral character of education. However, what is surprising about this revival is that, in its present discourse, character education is characterized as innovative and/or controversial. What is also surprising is how little the political and ideological substance of this particular discourse has changed over the past 300 years.

One of the important changes in the current broader educational discourse relates to the matter of explicitness; whereas the language of colonial and nineteenth century education is overtly and aggressively moral in content, contemporary educational discourse tends to be circumspect and wary when it comes to moral issues. This is partly a function of a politics of legal fairness and impartiality that emerges from the constitutional separation of Church and State and a politics of accommodation that reflects the realities of a pluralistic society. Another dimension of the coyness about the moral aspects of education is intellectual, i.e., the dominant position of positivism has produced a consciousness of the primacy and necessity of objectivity and neutrality in which moral issues are seen as necessarily "subjective" and hence irrelevant and distracting. The confluence of constitutional limits, political expediency, and positivistic paradigm has produced an orientation in which education becomes a process of learning information and gaining intellectual insights that are presumed to be independent of moral and political consideration. This has allowed the phenomenon of a "new" field of moral or character education, which has been able to transform what used to be assumed as inevitable and inherent aspects of educational dialogue into a problematic and controversial agenda issue. The question changed over time from, "What should be the moral orientation of education?" to "Should education have a moral orientation?" thereby allowing the notion of moral education to be seen as a possibility rather than an inevitability.

However, one of the anomalies of much recent literature in moral education is that many of the writers easily and quickly accept and postulate that moral education *is* always present, inevitably and inherently *and yet* go on to urge that the schools develop moral/character education programs! Thomas Lickona titles a section of his book *Educating for Character*, "The Case for Values Education" (1991), a title that suggests that we have a choice of whether or not there needs to be values education. He goes on to list "at least ten good reasons why schools should be making a clearheaded and wholehearted commitment to teaching moral values and developing good character"(p. 20). On the very same page, good reason number 6 turns out to be,

"There is no such thing as value-free education." Lickona sums up this view this way: "In short, the relevant issue is never 'Should schools teach values?' but rather 'Which values will they teach?' and 'How well will they teach them?'"(21).

There are some troublesome issues here. If the schools are already engaged in values education, then why a discourse (as so much of the Character Education literature stresses strongly) on the necessity of schools doing what they are already doing. Much of the discourse in both the political and educational realms has been framed in such a way that values, morality, and ethics are seen as notoriously absent from the schools and must be reintroduced, as represented by the theme "Our nation needs to return to family values." If as Lickona puts it so acutely, "the relevant issue is never' Should schools teach values," then why does he begin his book with a whole chapter titled, "The Case for Values Education" (Lickona, 1991)?

The effect of such a discourse is to mischievously polarize education (and other social and cultural institutions) into those which are concerned with moral issues and those which are not. Furthermore, this absurdity has a way of giving aid and comfort to those educators and theorists who are extremely wary and nervous about concepts like *moral* and *character* and who are loathe to get involved in such a discourse. It is difficult to attribute naïveté to those in Character Education who actually affirm the inevitability of moral education but perhaps easier to interpret their coyness as an attempt to seize the territory as their own. The political issue at hand then has to do with who is to control the current discourse on the moral and ethical dimensions of education? I believe, regrettably, that the answer to this question has to be that it is controlled largely by those who have been able to reify the concept of moral/character education into something distinct and separable from the broader curriculum and social-cultural context. This control is especially troublesome when this is exercised by those who seem to have a particularly sophisticated understanding of how values impinge powerfully and pervasively on all aspects of schooling.

This separation has allowed some politicians (and educators) to claim a monopoly on a concern for the moral character of society and individuals. When such people call for putting values "back" into the classroom, we might get some satisfaction from knowing that this is tautological and absurd thinking. However, such rhetoric has been used effectively in the public arena and has enhanced the political and literary ambitions of many. More importantly, in the wake of serving the narrow political interests of the Right it has also blurred and distorted the extraordinarily important issues involved. The reality that this reductive and misleading discourse has gone almost unchallenged only adds to the tragedy of the near impossibility of engaging the public in serious and thoughtful debate and dialogue on such complex, sensitive, and vital matters. If the question before the House becomes "Should we or should we not have values education in the schools?" then it seems to me that the appropriate response ought to be either (politely) "Yes"; or (impertinently) "That's a silly question." How then can we account for the persistence of such silly questions?

One explanation that is persuasive to me is that there is a code operating here and that the masked issue is really not a demand for raising public awareness and moral sensitivity nor an attempt to promote the development of ethical consciousness. Rather, it is that the call for moral/character education that comes from the Character Education movement and, by its parallels in the political arena, turns out to be a call on behalf of a *particular and specific moral and ethical system*. It is one thing to advocate that educators and the public seriously address the moral and ethical implications of educational policies and practices and to urge us to ground our education in a moral framework; it is altogether different to urge that we buy into a distinct and particular moral orientation. Either one or both of these discourses is to me perfectly valid; but what I find irresponsible is to blur them in such a way that to favor moral discourse on education equates to having a particular moral point of view and cultural vision.

Not only is such an approach disingenuous but it serves to further alienate those who have always suspected that discussion of moral issues is, at best, the equivalent to Sunday school and at worst, to sectarian indoctrination. Furthermore, such a discourse can serve to create an artificial and destructive distinction between those who are pure of heart and those who are not, which, of course, tends to exacerbate existing suspicion, divisiveness, and distrust. Unfortunately, much of the professional discourse in this area mirrors the political rhetoric of those who seek to claim for themselves the mantle of moral righteousness in distinction to those whose morals are of an uncertain if not dubious nature. Again, Lickona has put it trenchantly: "The relevant question is . . . which values will they [the schools] teach and how well will they teach them?" (1991). In other words, let us end this absurdity of framing the debate over whether or not schools should be involved in moral/character issues and get on with the much more compelling questions regarding the question of what moral orientation(s) ought to ground our educational policies and principles (Purpel, 1991). It is also time that those educators who have had the courage to engage in the often thankless task of addressing these challenging and daunting issues—but who have insisted on blurring the questions with the answers—acknowledge that these are public issues requiring very wide participation by the public and the profession. Hence, they have a responsibility to frame the issues in such a way as to invite and promote the reluctant, the confused, the conflicted, and the squeamish to become involved in the dialogue. By the same token, those who have luxuriated in their detachment and non-commitment must not leave the struggle to those who have particular if not narrow moral orientations and therefore need to give up their ennui and extend their responsibility beyond claiming that dialogue on the moral dimensions of education amounts to the return of the Spanish Inquisition. We owe the moral educators our gratitude for their questions; we need to be thankful to the skeptical for their criticality; and we should respect the reluctant and uncommitted for their hesitation. Yet we must all be mindful of the insufficiency of separating criticality and affirmation from each other. Criticism without affirmation can easily lead us to the emptiness and despair of cynicism, while affirmation without criticism can just as easily lead us to the distracting and self-serving blandness of sentimentality.

Character Education and Ideology

Let us then indeed move to the question of which values are actually being taught in the public schools. We can perhaps illumine this issue (as well as reiterate the prior point of the inevitability of moral education) by offering examples of values that are more or less uniformly imparted by way of general public and professional consensus on what constitutes good values and proper character. Schools teach that work and effort are good; that learning as well as imagination and creativity are valuable. Students are urged to be polite, respectful, and obedient to adults in general and school personnel in particular. They are taught that achievement is extremely important and that competition is inevitable if not salubrious; that those who do well in school merit certain advantages and that those who flout the rules and expectations deserve to be punished. Generally speaking, students are expected to talk, write, move, and go to the bathroom when they are given permission. Schools teach that time is valuable—tardiness, absences, and missed deadlines are considered offenses that require forgiveness. Students are required to do things they may not wish to do and are taught that this is a good thing.

Even though I basically agree with Herbert Kliebard's (1986) thesis that the public school curriculum represents a mélange of conflicting orientations, I am able to perceive some recognizable ideological shape to such moral emphases. My sense is that the values taught in the schools are very much in the line of Puritan traditions of obedience, hierarchy, and hard work, values which overlap nicely with the requirements of an economic system that values a compliant and industrious work force, and a social system that demands stability and order. There is an ideology here that puts very strong emphasis on control—adult control of children is mandated and legitimated and children's self-control of their bodies and minds are demanded. Moreover, the state, acting as surrogate for the economic and cultural systems, exercises its power to impose this ideology by requiring children to attend institutions that the state establishes and controls and which are financed by mandatory taxation.

This cursory interpretation is not meant in any way to pass for a complete ideological analysis of the curriculum but only to indicate that it is possible (and valuable) to discern larger political and cultural meaning in school practice and to emphasize the ideological nature of moral\character education. Clearly, one can find other, sometimes conflicting ideological forces at work in the public schools (e.g., concerns for democracy and/or individualism), for the point is that schools are important public arenas of ideological debate and struggle. The concerns I want to raise here have to do with the ideological nature of moral/character education proposals and with my assumption that any such program is necessarily embedded in some larger social, political, cultural, economic vision. Moral issues are by definition socially and culturally situated and any dialogue on proper character is based on some communal notion of propriety.

Unfortunately, one of the characteristics of the recent professional literature in this area has been the near absence of ideological analysis, never mind ideological affirmation. This again seems extraordinarily anomalous, particularly for those who write in a context of responding to a sense of cultural and moral crisis, since it would seem that a thoughtful response to crisis inevitably requires some interpretation of its etiology and nature. It is interesting that virtually all of the recent researchers in this field tend to provide some social and cultural perspective to their work but their programs are largely, if not entirely, psychologically oriented—the problems are acknowledged to be largely social but the proposed solutions are largely personal! The anomaly is a discourse that seemingly recognizes the interpenetration of social, historical, cultural, economic, and personal forces, yet which fails to acknowledge its own ideological assumptions and tends consequently to focus only on personal intervention.

This anomaly is especially apparent in the work of those who are closely identified with the current Character Education Movement (e.g., Lickona 1991; Wynne and Ryan 1993). These writers identify a series of serious social and cultural problems that they characterize as reflecting moral and character deterioration. Included in these phenomena are such matters as the rates of divorce, unwed parents, teenage pregnancies, substance abuse, crime, school violence, classroom cheating, and child abuse. There tends to be very little in the way of close examination of the data used to substantiate their claim that we are in the midst of moral degeneration, and about the only interpretation that they offer for this state of affairs is a rise in a consciousness of personalism and individualistic hedonism. There is no serious effort, for example, to examine the complex issues regarding teenage pregnancies—first of all there is data that suggests that the rate of teen-age pregnancies tends to fluctuate and that current rates are not unprecedented (Rhode and Lawson 1993). Even if there has been a significant increase, there still is a question of why this is considered to be a moral transgression? Is it wrong because the parents will be economically or psychologically unable to provide appropriate child care? If the problems are economic in origin then we have to ask why we have an economy that makes it so difficult to raise children at times that Nature seems to indicate are close to optimal? Or is the problem here one of morality? Do the writers believe that teenagers simply shouldn't be sexually active at this age. What is the grounding for such a morality? community convention? Part of a larger religious framework? Personal opinion? Moreover, why is this issue lumped together with certain other issues like substance abuse and school violence and not with others like social inequality and multinational capitalism? Surely these writers ought to have some reasonably comprehensive framework that gives order and meaning to their critique and program, but alas, what they offer is skimpy and thin.

The reluctance or inability of the Character Education Movement to elaborate and clarify its larger worldview is unfortunate for at least two reasons. First of all, it represents a truncated dialogue which deprives us of a chance to recognize the way in which educational and social/cultural/political issues are interrelated and thus significantly weakens the opportunity for a more thorough and comprehensive public discussion. Secondly, it allows others (like me) to attempt to fill in the missing links, which may or may not do justice to their orientation. However, this is a vacuum that needs to be filled as long as those in the movement fail to fully own up to their prior political, spiritual, and theoretical assumptions.

As it stands, the Character Education movement seems to me to have an uncanny resemblance to certain historical traditions as well as to particular strains of contemporary political ideology. Historically, the emphasis on the maintenance of the status quo, order, hard work, obedience, sexual restraint, stability, and hierarchy represent the continuation of the Puritan tradition, minus the explicit affirmation of Christianity. Its rhetoric of fear and trembling of rapid moral and social deterioration, and its insistence on a return to an ethic of communal responsibility, sobriety, delay of gratification, respect for authority, industriousness, and conventional morality can hardly be differentiated from the pietistic language of nineteenth century advocates of the common school.

Carl Kaestle, in his book *Pillars of the Republic* (1983), has interpreted the common school movement as a triumph of an "ideology centered on republicanism, Protestantism, and capitalism, three sources of social belief that were intertwined and mutually supporting." He goes on to delineate several of what he terms to be "major propositions of native Protestant ideology" (76). The presence as well the absence of these themes in the current Character Education movement is revealing and instructive. Briefly these themes are a concern for the "fragility of the republican polity"; the importance of individual character in maintaining social morality; the critical importance of "personal industry" as determinants of merit; a respected but limited domestic role for women; the critical importance of a strong and appropriate family and social environment (in contrast to those of certain ethnic and racial groups) to character building; the superiority of white American Protestant culture; the equality and abundance of economic opportunity; the grandeur of American destiny; and the "necessity of a determined public effort to unify America's polyglot population, chiefly through education.'" (76–77).

This nineteenth century ideology clearly bears striking resemblance to the rhetoric and program of the neoconservative movement of the past two decades, as exemplified currently in the political arena by the likes of Newt Gingrich and Pat Buchanan and culturally by people like William Bennett and Pat Robertson. It is surely not the same—the conditions are very different and the language has very different resonance with present historical circumstances. However, it is also clear (and reasonable to expect) that the culture continues to passionately engage in issues that confronted the nation in its early history. It is also apparent that the orientation towards these issues that Kaestle describes as the native Protestant ideology of the mid-nineteenth century overlaps substantially with perhaps the dominant political ideology of the 1990s, and more to the point, has significant resonance with the Character Education movement.

I want to make it clear that I am not suggesting that there is collusion and conspiracy between the professional and political figures of the Character Education Movement or even that the professional movement is totally congruent with the agenda of the political Right. I am saying, however, that at the very least there is an implicit, fairly consistent and coherent political orientation embedded within the message of Character Education and that the message has strong and vital resonance with the neoconservative political and cultural program.

Edward Wynne, for example, in advocating schools promoting "traditional values," which he defines as "the panoply of virtues connoted by phrases such as the work ethic and obedience to legitimate authority and by the important nonreligious themes articulated by the Ten Commandments" (Wynne 1989, 19). Note the attempt to define the concept of "traditional values" as unproblematic and to focus on work and obedience. He goes on to make a case for the close connection between character development and academic performance, claiming, "Academics and character are coincident, since persons with character are, by definition, industrious"(31). In a discussion of teacher-student relations, he asserts that, "Adults who routinely deal with children and adolescents are gradually driven to recognize that adult-child relations in schools cannot and should not be governed by so-called democratic theories"(34). This is hardly an affirmation of the traditional values of democracy and autonomy.

Another major figure in Character Education, Thomas Lickona, lists ten current "signs of a moral decline" to be "violence and vandalism, stealing, cheating, disrespect for authority, peer cruelty, bigotry, bad language, sexual precocity and abuse, increasing self-centeredness and declining civic responsibility, and self-destructive behavior" (Lickona, 1991, 12–18). This is hardly distinguishable from what would come in a Dan Quayle speech in its focus on individual behavior and its absence of structural criticism.

We also can gain further insight into Character Education's ideology by reflecting on what is not considered, that is, by what is presumably not a "sign of moral decline." There is, for example and in this case in sharp contrast to the nineteenth century ideology, only token mention of the importance of sustaining a democratic consciousness. The references seem to be mostly concerned with procedural issues like voting rather than notions of social democracy, and there certainly is no sense of a crisis in the vitality of democratic institutions. Clearly, there is no mention or even an implied affirmation of the American tradition of revolutionary democracy as an expression of resistance to authoritarianism nor of the spiritual traditions that command us to afford human dignity to all as an expression of divine will.

Nor is there a concern for the harshness and cruelty of an increasingly unbridled free market economy, of growing economic inequality, of the systemic nature of poverty, of the enormous disparity in the quality of medical care, of ecological devastation, of the ever-increasing desperation of have-not nations, or of the continuing dangers of international conflicts. The basic theory the Character Education Movement offers for moral decline is a psychological one, that the problems are rooted in an inflated sense of personalism and self-centeredness rather than rooted in social economic, and cultural institutions. The Character Education Movement therefore, takes on, at least implicitly, the ideology of the struggle to preserve the social and political status quo; there are serious problems out there and what we have to do is not make structural changes (the economic system, the social class structure, the political hierarchy) but instead insist that individuals change. In this ideology, society is being victimized by unvirtuous (lazy, selfish, indulgent, and indolent) individuals rather than an ideology which posits individuals as being victimized by an unvirtuous (rapacious, callous, competitive, and heartless) society.

The politics of the preservation of the status quo involves the privileging of those already in positions of power, influence, and advantage and maintaining the barriers to those who are relatively powerless and disadvantaged. In our present social reality we find ourselves in a particularly divisive situation in which virtually all the major social, political, and cultural institutions and traditions have been seriously challenged, if not threatened, by dramatic changes in consciousness. The most visible of these changes can be seen not only in such phenomena as the civil rights, anti-war, multiculturalism, women's liberation, gay rights movements but also in the more pervasive mood of growing alienation, disenchantment, and frustration. Much of the energy behind the conservative movement is in counterreaction to the challenge to and disaffection with the status quo and it is in this context that the Character Education movement can best be understood. The context is like the one in which an army that is winning but has not yet won the war, calls for peace, i.e., the conservative call for an increase in such admirable qualities as civility, deference to the community, stability, and orderliness also serves to consolidate the gains and authority of those already in power. It also serves to distract attention from the potentially disruptive substantive critique of established social institutions to the more emotionally charged issues of personal morality and conduct. Better to discuss poverty in terms of personal laziness and moral flabbiness than as an inevitable and structured consequence of our economic system; better to discuss the alienation of youth in terms of school violence than as aspects of a culture drowning in dispiriting materialism and consumerism. This is not to say that we should ignore the real dangers inherent in a doctrine of social and cultural determinism or forget that individuals have important responsibilities and opportunities for agency. It strikes me however, that we would be better served by an analysis that accepts a dynamic dialectic between the social and the individual, between the forces of social realities and the possibilities of individual responsiveness, and between individual rights and social responsibility.

It is also extremely important to point out that this body of work does not exhaust by any means the literature on moral/character education, and by the same token to note that all other such orientations require political and ideological examination, analysis, and interpretation. For example, my work has focused on the necessity to ground education in a commitment to pursue a vision of a just and loving community within a consciousness of moral outrage and personal responsibility (Purpel 1989). In addition, there are other major orientations such as the program for democratic schools, reflected in the work of Ralph Mosher (1994), and the notions of teaching for compassion, nurturance, and caring, as reflected in the work of Nel Noddings (1992) and Jane Roland Martin (1992), which carry with them quite different but equally strong ideological. political, and cultural assumptions in varying degrees of explicitness. We simply cannot allow those in the Character Education movement to monopolize and control the moral discourse of education. Conservatives, like any other political group, not only have the right but have the responsibility to lay out the educational implications of their ideology, but they, like other groups, have a corresponding responsibility to engage in good faith dialogue on the realities of divergent viewpoints.

It is also vital to remember that this realm is not exhausted by those who write explicitly about moral/character education, for we must also examine work that impinges directly and indirectly on efforts to develop particular moral values and behaviors, such as material on school discipline, instructional theory, school counseling, attendance policies, curriculum development, and just about everything else. In a word, to talk of education is to inevitably talk of personal character and a moral community, and to talk of personal character and a moral community is inevitably to speak of political, social, cultural, and economic structures.

Problematics of the Field

I believe very strongly that the most important aspects of education are moral and that the term moral education is largely redundant. Because of this, I have argued that we would be better off without a field of moral/character education (Purpel 1991) on the basis that such a discourse is distracting and misleading. As I have maintained above, this discourse tends toward reification as it ignores and separates itself from the moral aspects of the larger school and social settings. A major anomaly in much of this field is its tendency to base its program on broad diagnosis and narrow treatment, on locating the problems in the society and culture and the responses to be located in schools and classrooms. Those who work in this field have made a very important contribution by drawing our attention to these problems and issues, for the reality is that mainstream educators have allowed moral discourse to atrophy, perhaps out of a naive faith in the possibility of so-called value-free education. In addition, they have provided a much needed balance to the theories of social and economic determinists in stressing the importance and possibilities of individual responsibility. Moral/character educators also provide much needed energy and hope, and, perhaps most importantly, remind us of our responsibility to honor our moral commitments. Our quest for the morally good society and for becoming good persons cannot be limited to compiling lists of attractive characteristics but must be extended to a serious examination of the conditions under which these contradictions continue to persist. Our task as educators is not limited to striving for morally sound schools and to improving the character of its students but also involves participation in the broader task of creating a just and loving society and a culture of joy and fulfillment for all. This task requires that we embrace a politics that does not privilege, exclude, or demean but rather one that includes, affirms, and empowers everyone. Whatever advances that vision is sound moral/character education.

References

Bailyn, Bernard. 1962. *Education in the Forming of American Society: Needs and Opportunities for Study*. New York: W.W. Norton.

Educational Freedom for a Democratic Society: A Critique of *National Goals, Standards, and Curriculum* (Brandon, VT: Resource Center for Redesigning Education.

Kaestle, Carl. 1983. *Pillars of the Republic: Common Schools and American Society*. New York: Hill and Wang.

Kliebard, Herbert. 1986. *The Struggle for the American Curriculum 1893–1958*. Boston: Routledge and Kegan Paul.

Lickona, Thomas. 1991. *Educating for Character: How Our School Can Teach Respect and Responsibility*. New York: Bantam.

Mosher, Ralph and Robert A. Kenny. 1994. *Preparing for Citizenship: Teaching Youth to Live Democratically*. Westport: Praeger.

Noddings, Nel, 1992. *The Challenge to Care in Schools: An Alternative to Education*. New York: Teachers College Press.

Purpel, David E. "Goals 2000, The Triumph of Vulgarity and The Legitimation of Social Justice" in Ron Miller (ed.), 1995.

Purpel, David E. "Moral Education: An Idea Whose Time Has Gone," *Clearing House*, 64, (May/June 1991): 309–312.

Purpel, David E. 1989. *The Moral and Spiritual Crisis in Education*. Granby, MA.: Bergin and Garvey.

Rhode, Deborah and Annette Lawson. *The Politics of Pregnancy: Adolescent Sexuality and Public Policy*. New.Haven: Yale University Press.

Roland Martin, Jane. 1992. *The Schoolhome: Rethinking Schools for Changing Families* Cambridge: Harvard University Press.

Wynne, Edward A. "Transmitting Traditional Values in Contemporary Schools" in Larry B. Nucci (ed.), *Moral Development and Character Education: A Dialogue*. Berkeley: McCutchan.

Wynne, Edward A. and Kevin Ryan. *Reclaiming Our Schools: A Handbook on Teaching Character, Academics, and Discipline*. N.Y., N.Y.: Merrill.

Service Learning:
A Critique and Affirmation

I want in this paper to look first at service learning critically, and then at the problematics of the criticism of service learning, that is, to carefully examine the nature of these criticisms. In this way I hope to shed some light not only on the particularities of service learning but also on some general issues involving efforts for educational reform and cultural change. I very much accept the vital importance of maintaining a wary and skeptical posture towards so-called new ideas and embrace the tradition of critical analysis as a necessary component of an education directed at human liberation. However, I want to add two qualifications to this affirmation: first, that if it makes sense to be critical of an idea then it makes sense to be critical of the ideas contained in the criticism; and second, that however necessary critical rationality may be for human liberation, it is not sufficient. In other words, thoroughgoing intellectual criticism is both vital *and* inadequate. There is the grim reality that those intent on evil rely on critical thinking and imagination as much as the angelic do to pursue their goals. Put another way, critical thinking without a moral vision becomes only a powerful and useful tool kit that has contributed as much to what is shameful as to what is exalting in human experience.

Critique

Among the broad criticisms of service learning that have been made are those that focus on: the likelihood of insensitivity to cultural differences and relevant history; the misuse and abuse of power; the dangers of implicit elitism; its instrumental orientation; and the futility of such projects. Let me try to summarize briefly the essence of these concerns, all of which I share. First, there is the probability that those who seek to serve will be asked to work with the unfamiliar and the marginal, with the mores, sensibilities, and expectations of particular cultures and subcultures. In such a situation the possibility for miscommunication and cultural misunderstanding, if not bewilderment, is quite high. The task of gaining sufficient sensitivity to the proclivities of these groups and to their historical and experiential commonalities would seem to be quite daunting. This is an especially acute difficulty for those who have little awareness of their own cultural identity and history, never mind those of remote and marginal groups.

On the related issue of the abuse of power, there is implicit in the concept of "service" the notion that there are those who need help and there are those prepared to help, thus setting up a duality and hierarchy between the needy and the providers, the helpless and the helpful, the powerless and the powerful, the takers and the givers. Such a duality allows for the possibility that this distinction, if not already in place, can easily be turned into a relationship of dependence in which the weak become the oppressed and the strong become the oppressors. Furthermore, such a posture lends itself to a consciousness of paternalism and colonialism which can readily foster a sense of arrogance and condescension on the part of those who presume to know, and act to intervene for what is best for other people. Lurking in the background of such relationships is the very real possibility of enhanced resentment, guilt, humiliation, and alienation for all involved, which can culminate in the pain of embittered polarization. Who gives us the right to tell others what to eat, think, believe, wear, take, read, or appreciate? By what authority do we claim to know what is best for those we do not really know? Who really benefits from our solutions and programs? Who should decide what the "real" problems are? What is the essential difference between those who provide service and those who are the receivers? Is it need? Awareness? Education? Class? Or is it power? If it truly is better to give than to receive, then why have we structured a relationship in which many receive and a few give?

In addition, there is a way in which service learning is not presented so as much as a virtue but more as a necessity, i.e,. as an effective technique and means to some other presumably more important goal. In such a formulation, the act of providing service is seen as facilitating understanding and learning, such as in "By spending time in a soup kitchen you'll be able to get more insight into the problems of the poor" or "Working in a medical clinic for the homeless will provide you with very valuable clinical experiences." This would seem to undercut the notion of these experiences as less acts of altruism and compassion than of self-serving expedience.

Even if all these doubts could be overcome, there remains the question of the efficacy of service learning, that is what impact such activities will actually have on social problems. Given the enormity of our ills, is it not pretentious, if not disingenuous, to foster the notion that at best such efforts could have anything except the most marginal and tenuous effect on the deeply structured inequities of our society? Is there not a danger of a backlash of disillusionment and disenchantment emerging from unrealistic and romantic expectations? Even more troubling is the real possibility that relatively modest successes can actually exacerbate problems through the process of cooptation, in which amelioration serves to prop up the very structures that created the problems in the first place. It is bad enough to believe that service activities may have little positive effect on social problems but the notion that they may actually serve to strengthen an unacceptable status quo is almost unbearable to sustain. Yet, however painful, that possibility exists, and, indeed, the cliché with perhaps the most staying power across recorded history is the one about the materials used in the construction of the paths to hell.

How then are we to respond to the critics and the naysayers, those who are so skeptical, so wary, so cautious, and, alas, so perceptive? Although I am operating on the assumption that these criticisms are acute and valuable insights that require our attention, I want also to insist that this attention should not become a trip to the land of inertia and paralysis. The best criticism ought not to disarm and neutralize but instead should serve to rearm and energize. In that sense those of us committed to whatever it is that is represented by the metaphor "service learning" need to be as clear as is humanly possible about what vital and compelling concerns are truly involved. This process involves the necessity of locating our ideas in conceptual frameworks that do justice to our best impulses, since criticism is more often than not an attempt to frame ideas in the realm of our worst impulses. Surely, it is absolutely necessary that we be constantly reminded of our human capacity to be self-serving, self-aggrandizing, and self-righteous; and by the same token, it is vital to remember that we also have the capacity as humans to be generous, caring, compassionate, and loving. What becomes crucial then is how we come to frame our impulses, what metaphors we use, what discourse we utilize or, to put it in the vernacular, what spin we put on our work.

Let me offer a number of spins by returning to some of the criticisms of service learning, with particular reference to the issues of the two extremes: one in which there is the danger of accomplishing too much, as in service learning that could easily be used to further enhance the dominant culture; or, on the other hand, the difficulty of accomplishing too little, as in the futility of all well-meaning but marginal and modest programs of reform. It is actually quite possible to see these seemingly dissimilar criticisms as perfectly compatible, in that one can say that at best, service learning will have little positive effect. I want to make it very clear that I strongly believe that these criticisms are essentially valid, and the source of this conviction for me lies in our history. For purposes of my analysis, I have decided to proclaim the coming of the Long Run—It is here, it has arrived, and the news is not good. After all that has been said and done, more has been said than done and what has been done has for the most part made lots of very important things worse. I probably do not need to repeat the litany of serious social and cultural crises that confront us— poverty, homelessness, racism, sexism, polarization, violence, alienation, despair, ecological devastation, international instability. Perhaps I do need to offer the observation that in spite of (or more gloomily, because of) a quantum increase in educational research and constant and intense efforts directed at educational reform, the schools are by and large less lively, less imaginative, less playful, less stimulating places than they were even 10 or 15 years ago. Among other things this tells me that the establishment has been able to ward off those social and educational changes and innovations that would have produced significant transformation and adopted or co-opted those that worked to preserve the status quo. There is nothing in my examination of long-run effects to indicate that the establishment will be any less willing or less competent to continue in their (should I not say our?) successful resistance to social, cultural, educational transformation. Nor do I see any reason at all that programs in service learning would somehow be immune from that fate and indeed I am thoroughly convinced that they will not.

Affirmation, Hope, and Despair

Having said all that, I also want very much to support, encourage, and be part of the service learning movement. What is involved here is of central concern to my present research focus, which has to do with the question of what can be done to significantly improve our schools and transform our society, or, at the very least, what can we do as professionals that will not contribute to our growing crises? As educators, we inevitably share to one degree or another in the cultural malaise of pessimism, frustration, and despair, if not cynicism, about the possibility of fundamental positive change. However, as educators we are very reluctant to add to the problem by spreading the contagion of hopelessness and helplessness for we know that this surely contributes to a self-fulfilling prophecy of doom and disaster. We as professionals are continuously asked to walk the thin line between the responsibilities of providing both sobering criticism and intoxicating hope, and in so doing we invite the possibility of losing our balance and falling into the bottomless pit of paralysis or the velvet trap of complacency.

For me personally, it has been a real struggle to find hope and possibility in the many efforts by colleagues who work for concrete constructive changes, since my orientation has been heavy on the critical, pessimistic, and skeptical side and very, very light on the support of those who are optimistic and enthusiastic about the possibility of real and substantive change. I therefore see my current challenge as finding some balance in my continuing work, which has focused on the delineation of the major deficiencies in our social, cultural, and educational institutions and on offering alternative theoretical and ideological models to our present consciousness. One of the most persistent responses to this work has been in one way or another, a question that goes like this "O.k., o.k, perhaps there is some validity in what you say, and given the enormity of the problems you posit, what then can and should be done?" A very fair question indeed, and my initial response has been and continues to be that the first steps involve the acknowledgment of the massive extent of the crises, particularly of our complicity in their perpetuation and our responsibility in their amelioration. Without in any way conceding on the enormity of our problems or on the necessity for us to come clean on them, I have however, come to see that there needs also to be recognition of those genuine, well-intentioned, concrete efforts by many of our gallant and hard working colleagues. As I walk this line between hope and possibility on one side and despair and futility on the other, I continue to be guided by the example of the Biblical prophets whose message was precisely the importance of balancing moral outrage with the possibility of redemptive action. This consciousness has been eloquently and succinctly described by Reinhold Niebuhr, who in commenting on the prophets said the following: "What they were able to do was to see good in spite of evil and see evil in spite of good and in this way they were able to avoid both sentimentality and despair."

I believe that I have done a far better job of avoiding sentimentality than I have of avoiding despair, and so I, along with many others, feel the necessity of becoming more open to hope and possibility that resides in those who strive to do good.

Service learning for me is a metaphor for such efforts, nurtured in hope and possibility whose future is darkened by the clouds of co-optation and trivialization *and* deserving of our attention, support, and good will. How then are we to nourish such efforts without being seduced by them; and by the same token, how can we be critical of them without crushing them?

Issues of Implementation

Let me first suggest a framework for examining programs in service learning that I came upon as a result of listening to a very brief audio recording of an interview with Willis Harman, President of the Noetic Institute. In this interview, Dr. Harman offers his response to questions regarding what individuals can do in the face of the intimidating task of responding to the enormous magnitude of global problems. He has three suggestions:

1. First, each person should deal with the need for inner transformation by reflecting on one's identity, one's inner struggles and agenda, on what one tends to deny about oneself, and how one messes up with best intentions. I take this to be an acknowledgment that our individual psyches are inevitably involved in our interpersonal and social activities, and moreover, that we need to attend to our own inner disorder if we are to deal with the outside disorder.

2. That individuals should participate in some kind of worthwhile local activity such that they can not only make a discernible impact but also receive reasonably clear and fast feedback on their efforts.

3. We should confront the reality that our whole social system, however destructive and dysfunctional it may be, is, in fact, supported by beliefs that we individually and collectively have accepted. The ability to admit that the beliefs that we have bought into (such as our enthusiasm for a consumer economy) are actually contributing to the world crises is the hardest of the three suggestions to adopt. This is probably because it requires us to face our own complicity in human suffering and the exploitation of nature.

What I especially like about this relatively simple model is the way it provides for an interactive, dialectical process that connects the inner soul, the social persona, and the outside world, thus providing not only for breadth of concern but for personal responsibility on a human scale. It allows us the space within which we can both do and be; reflect and act; be decisive and contemplative; and to deal simultaneously with short and long-term issues. The implications for service learning are clear, as the model suggests the importance of reflecting not only on the particular contexts of the service activities but on personal and ideological matters as well.

Spirituality and Service Learning

I want to add another dimension to this framework, namely that which deals with ultimate meaning, that which integrates the inner being, social being, and the culture. This, of course, assumes the existence of meaning, of some force or energy that provides coherence and wholeness to our existence. Whether the search for such meaning is delusionary and quixotic is surely not clear, at least to me, but what is clear is that we as a species continue to engage ourselves in this search in any number of settings and with incredible energy, imagination, and passion. What we yearn for in this process is to relate and connect what we do on a day-to-day basis to that which has enduring consequence, for in so doing we can avoid drabness, emptiness, and idolatry. In this context, idolatry is to be seen as the worship of phenomena that do not have ultimate meaning or whose connection to ultimate meaning has been blurred or forgotten. My own view is that it is idolatrous to view service learning as a good in and of itself, but is worthy to the extent that it is an important part of a larger good. Indeed, my own enthusiasm for service learning is predicated on the strong belief that it *is* implicated with issues of ultimate meaning and significance. I have been maintaining throughout this paper that we should take seriously the criticisms that service learning reflects self-serving or even sinister motivation. I say that because I believe that we as a people are quite capable of being self-serving and sinister. However, I also believe that as a people we are capable of transcending our self-centeredness and mean-spiritedness and of moving to a consciousness of caring, compassion, and love. Just as we have the responsibility to plumb the wicked impulses that reside within us, we have the parallel responsibility to take seriously those impulses within us that seek the good. What I urge, therefore, is that we examine our attraction to and involvement with service learning as a metaphor of something else, as a symptom of a greater commitment, and as a fragment of a larger whole. In a word, I suggest that we engage ourselves in the important task of naming the phenomena of "service learning" for what it really is for each of us.

It would, of course, be presumptuous of me to attempt to say what service learning really is, but I do want to offer a few possibilities by way of clarifying what I mean by the naming process. I believe in the importance of naming because it provides each one of us the opportunity to exercise our responsibility to participate in the creation of a life of personal and communal meaning. Much of the actual naming process is of course done by a small number of people and groups who have the power to do so, a power which controls and narrows public discourse and personal reflection. Perhaps the best-known example is the familiar observation that Adam first named the animals and then told Eve what they were. In the present instance, we need to question the very concept "service learning," a concept which like all others serves not only to reveal but to conceal. Clearly, there are other names for the phenomena which emerge when we ask ourselves what is it about these ideas that resonates powerfully within us? Why are we drawn intuitively to the programs? What personal impulses are being obscured and silenced by the official rhetoric of the service learning movement?

For example, do we respond positively to the language of service learning because we are drawn to a consciousness of community in which our relationships and connections to each other are more important than our differences and separations? If so, then service learning is not a very apt term. Do we see in the notion of service learning vestiges of a religious commandment to love others, to be as servants, and to attend to the poor, the widowed, and the orphaned? If so, then such a term masks the impulse to do God's work. Is our connection to service learning by way of a deep commitment to the struggle for social justice and democracy? If so, service learning becomes only one aspect of a larger political and social ideological movement. Do we see in service learning the possibility of fostering a sense of spiritual oneness with the universe? If so, service learning becomes a very flat if not misleading term. Perhaps we are truly excited about service learning because it allows us to give thanks for the gift of life; or because it provides us with the joy of creation; or because it allows a space in which we can reflect on the meaning of our lives; or because—you fill in the blanks. The basic assumption I make is that beyond attending to the ordinary dimensions of service learning and its counterproductive possibilities, we need to trust the intuition that there is something of very great worth here, however disguised, masked, and obscured. It is our responsibility to move beyond the conventional professional and psychological discourse and without apology acknowledge our deepest impulse to seek larger meanings than raising test scores, increasing voter registration, and staffing soup kitchens.

Humility, Despair, and Hope

Finally, I want to address the importance of humility, here in reference to the criticism that service learning projects are very unlikely to have lasting impact on our society and culture. Here it is important to draw a line between humility and despair, for it is one thing to be realistic and honest about our capacities and another thing to surrender to a consciousness of determinism and fatalism. The humility I speak to is not about modesty or self-deference but about the acknowledgment of the mystery and awesomeness of the human condition as well as our present social, cultural, and personal crises. I have concluded that there is an inverse relationship between the significance of a problem and its openness to solution. Put more baldly, I do not believe that our most significant problems can be solved. Problems surely can and should be ameliorated, suffering and pain reduced, justice and equity increased, peace furthered, violence lessened, meaning strengthened. To accomplish even such limited gains is exalting and exhilarating for as the Talmud teaches, "It is not for us to finish the task—but neither are we free to take no part in it."

We also know that often we are not able to achieve even modest gains and even more disheartening we sometimes make things worse. How then are we able to sustain our efforts in the face of such obstacles? How do we have the energy to maintain a struggle that promises only modest advances at best and more likely ultimate failure? My response, alas, is a cliché—but an enduring one, and that is we must have faith and trust. But faith and trust in what and on what basis can we sustain that faith? The best I can say is that the persistent search for meaning provides a powerful enough reason to be faithful. My cursory examinations of faith traditions is that they all involve a commitment to human compassion and social justice, although obviously the source of such faith varies enormously across cultural and religious communities. For many, there is a deep faith in the human process of settling conflicts rationally and cooperatively. For others, it is a spiritual faith that speaks to the oneness of all life. In many of us, faith is fleeting at best and its source murky and unreliable. Although, for example, I gain enormous strength from the passion and moral commitments of the prophets, I am still not able to share in their faith in the revealed word.

Cornel West as a believing Christian and a philosopher/theologian/social theorist offers a powerful framework for addressing this dilemma. In his distinction between penultimate and ultimate salvation, he accepts a tragic view of the world in which the struggles for peace, justice and love are destined to fail, but those who nonetheless maintain the struggle receive penultimate salvation as genuine, however tragic, heroes. According to West, such people derive their strength and energy in this extraordinarily frustrating task from their faith in ultimate salvation, that is, through Christian redemption. Those of us who do not share but admire, if not envy, this Christian consciousness can only continue our search for that power that can and does sustain and guide us as we struggle with our moral ambivalences and conflicts. Humanity's greatest achievements would seem to be its persistence in its aspiration for goodness in the face of the incredible pressures for mere survival and self-enhancement.

The arrival of the service learning movement signals that this impulse has been re-energized with fresh urgency and hope. It also provides us with an opportunity to renew our faith in the human capacity to create a life of meaning and wholeness. For that we owe much to those who have had the courage and imagination to challenge the public and the profession to meet its highest aspirations and deepest convictions.

Holistic Education in a Prophetic Voice

Preface

It is important to distinguish between descriptive and normative analyses of education. The former seeks to characterize what actually constitutes educational activity, while the latter seeks to argue which educational activities are more valid, legitimate, and appropriate. When we speak of holistic education in the descriptive sense, we are probably referring to the sensible notion that we must attend to and take seriously the whole realm of human learning. In this sense, holistic education serves as a heuristic and corrective force, reminding us of the dangers of the distortions and dangers that emerge from the extremes of overdeterminism and neglect. Holistic educators tend to perform an extremely valuable function by concentrating on dimensions of education most commonly neglected or abused by mainstream educators as well as by educational reformers. These neglected dimensions include concern for intuition, personal knowledge, spiritual reflections and untapped human potential.

There does not seem to be consensus, however, within the holistic education movement as to whether this concern is primarily a corrective strategy, designed to provide a more balanced dialogue on education by adding important dimensions to it or whether it represents a more normative discourse, in which the argument is that concern for the personal, intuitive, and spiritual is more valuable and appropriate. There are probably elements of both discourses in the work of holistic educators, but the distinction is important because it raises the question of what ultimate criteria and what conceptual framework can help us determine what constitutes valid education. To do so is to immediately and inevitably invoke those moral, political, and social assumptions which inevitably connect with matters of educational policy and practice. There can be no educational policy or practice independent of a social and cultural context, and therefore there is no such thing as "objective" educational theory. The educative process is, for better or worse, inevitably and intimately interrelated with the historic, cultural, normative, political, and economic dimensions of particular communities.

When holistic educators argue that education can be complete only if educators attend not only to the external social and cultural context but also to the inner world of the self and the broader context of the universe, they are both affirming and correcting for socially and culturally, and historically grounded educational analysis. When holistic educators argue instead that "true education" consists of concentrating primarily on the development of personal and spiritual processes that might enable us to transcend our historical, social, and cultural contexts, they are speaking more to a particular affirmation, of a consciousness that might be called metaphysical or mystical. It is one thing to say that humans do not learn by intellect alone or to say that humans are not only social but sentient beings. However, it is quite another thing to say that our pragmatic and material concerns are basically transient, and that they distract us from the ultimate meaning that derives from union with the cosmos. In a word, the difference is linked to how much importance we place on the dialectic between culture and the individual and how much do we place on the individual's connection to the universe.

The holistic education movement's contributions include raising our awareness of the neglect of personal/spiritual/subjective dimensions of education in both mainstream and critical discourses. Conventional educational discourse is of course deeply rooted in the language of technical instrumentalism, positivistic epistemology, competition, and socio-economic advancement. Much of the educational theory of dissent has provided very powerful critiques of mainstream education primarily on grounds that it has perpetuated social and cultural inequality, oppression, and hegemony. As acute and liberating as this critical discourse has been, it has so far been unable to integrate its analysis successfully with serious concern for the spiritual and subjective dimensions of human existence. This paper attempts to address this issue by arguing that the concern for justice and freedom has been informed by a religious sensibility, and furthermore that there is an important place for religious discourse in the project of creating an education that is directed toward promoting peace, justice, freedom, and joy.

In this paper, I argue for the signal importance of an educational process directed at creating a just society and a compassionate culture. My hope is that this analysis responds to the human impulse for a number of powerful, basic, and to some extent, conflicting impulses: autonomy, freedom, equality, justice, community, and fulfillment. Indeed, it is my position that a just and compassionate society is an absolute necessity, even if it may not be an absolutely sufficient condition, for a life of ultimate meaning. I also wish to emphasize that I do not at all intend in this formulation to claim that education is only or primarily about the process of creating a just society. Educational processes involve an incredible range of activities, including acculturation, socialization, training, initiation, as well as the promotion of inquiry and creativity. Important teaching and learning goes on in a great number of sites—within the individual, in families, on the street, on movie and television screens, in schools and universities, in factories, businesses, and so on. My orientation represents both historical and moral dimensions; historical in that my educational concerns emerge from the historical contingencies of the moment. It is moral because I believe that educators in this particular historical moment have a special responsibility to base their policies and programs on a vision of what a good society might be.

The Human Narrative

It seems to be in the nature of human beings to sort out and attempt to make meaning out of our activities, and it is quite clear that this process has produced enormously diverse accounts, narratives, histories, and interpretations. These narratives are more than just interesting and intriguing, for they also help to shape communal and individual consciousness; they provide us with meaning and hence with direction, purpose, and energy.

This paper is written within the tradition of those particular narratives that speak to the human struggle to create more just, compassionate, and peaceful communities. The story of these efforts cuts across time and space and speaks to what is most sublime and most demonic in human possibility. It is not very difficult to see humans as "animals," i.e., being driven by the absolute desire to survive and to satisfy basic needs and gratification. There is ample evidence that humans are capable of doing virtually anything however violent, cruel, and callous in order to satisfy their fundamental needs. What must be remembered, however, is that we live in a culture which accepts and recognizes not only concepts like *cruelty, violence,* and *callousness,* but also as terms like *compassionate, caring,* and *justice.* What is extraordinary, if not miraculous, is not that humans, like other species, are driven to survival and self-gratification but, unlike other species they also struggle to transcend the limitations of such a consciousness. If not all, certainly the great preponderance of cultures and societies create limits on what is considered acceptable and unacceptable conduct and behavior. They develop an ethos or spirit of community which serves as a mechanism to control, inspire, and guide its members. Durkheim has described this process as an integration of the personal and social as grounded in a moral and religious framework. "Morality begins with membership in a group. . . . First, we shall show how society is good and desirable for the individual who cannot exist without it or deny it without denying himself [sic], and how, at the same time, because society suppresses the individual, he cannot desire it without to a certain extent violating his nature as an individual. Secondly, we shall show that society, while being good, constitutes a moral authority. . . . It is impossible to imagine, on the evidence, that morality should serve its unbroken association with religion without ceasing to be itself. . . . Morality would no longer be morality if it had no elements of religion. . . ." (Durkheim, in Nisbet, 194–196, 197).

The history of these efforts to build moral communities reflects the incredible paradox, diversity, contributions, and mysteries of the human condition. It is a history of sharing and emancipation; of oppression and democracy; of the invention of napalm and penicillin; the Ku Klux Klan and the Red Cross; and it has produced villains, heroes, demons and angels. Hitler *and* Gandhi . . . Louis XIV *and* Thomas Paine . . . Mother Teresa *and* Henrich Himmler . . . Joseph Mengele *and* Madame Curie . . . the Peace Corps *and* the Hitler Youth. It is also clear that the notion of civilization making steady and continuous progress toward the achievement of a more just, peaceful, and loving world is a serious distortion of reality. Although there is much evidence that many societies have made gains and positive changes in consciousness—e.g., slavery has been abolished in most of the world— there is the harsh and profound reality that even these gains may be overshadowed by significant regression in other spheres. There is evidence that over 100 million people have been killed in wars since 1700, ninety percent of them in the twentieth century. It is estimated that 2 billion people live in extreme poverty, 450 million suffer from hunger and malnutrition, that 1 in 5 children in America lives in poverty, and that there are upwards of 1 million homeless in America. It is surely easy enough to be disheartened by such findings and to be discouraged by the attendant cynicism, apathy, and sense of powerlessness. A consciousness of impotence and cynicism, of course, compounds and aggravates the enormous pain and suffering that is the consequence of a consciousness of greed, oppression, and callousness. We face catastrophe from the combined forces of evil and apathy, of the dual corruption of power and powerlessness, and from the twin dangers of the affirmation of individual power and the collapse of communal authority.

There are surely new and extremely important dimensions to our present crises, the most paramount of which are the extremely serious risks to the survival of the planet. However, it is certainly not news that the human community faces serious crises from a combination of external threats and the collapse of the moral order. We are, however, not without valuable resources in responding to such calls. Indeed, it is extremely valuable and helpful in such times to reaffirm our most cherished traditions, hopes, dreams, and convictions. A major element in our tradition can be described as a dialectic between affirmation and criticism, or, to use a less linear image, a continuous spiral of criticism and hope: expectations followed by criticism followed by renewed hope and possibility. We have learned not only to dream beyond the narrow limits of human survival and callousness but also to be wary of sentimentality as well as certainty and to be on guard against the violations of our dreams. In the human exploration of our souls, we have discovered a variety of capacities that complicate the struggle for justice—including those of personal deception, denial, evasion, and rationalization. As an antidote to these tendencies, we have come to accept the absolute necessity for maintaining a critical consciousness, a spirit of skepticism, inquisitiveness, and reflectiveness. Indeed, the critical tradition has become so strong and so integral to our culture that it has developed its own set of problematics. Chief among these is to nurture a position of detachment and distance in which a great deal of energy is applied to the analysis and interpretation of ideas, policies, practices but with little if any energy directed at affirmation. Such a posture can and has generated, beyond useful insights and understandings, a high degree of moral relativity, political apathy, and cultural cynicism.

The critical consciousness that I wish to affirm, however, is a part of a wider and deeper vision. This criticism is not an end in itself, but a powerful tool in the service of larger moral, cultural, and spiritual aspirations. In such traditions, criticism is rooted in positive and affirmative commitments which indeed provide the very bases of critique. They are logical consequences of affirmation in that they provide a model and the criteria for making judgments, the heart of the critical enterprise. There can be no criticism without judgment, however implicit and guarded and notwithstanding claims of objectivity and neutrality. Unfortunately, our culture has been able to reify and reduce a critical consciousness through such concepts as "critical thinking" and "objective analysis." This process has the effect of removing (however artificially) technique from judgment and of eliminating the basis and framework within which the critical dimension has been embedded. It is another tragic instance of alienation, in which the meaning-making impulses are actually removed from so-called skills and techniques.

This paper, to be more precise, is grounded in a particular metaphor of affirmation, and a critical tradition, called social prophecy. I wish to emphasize that although this concept has deep and vital roots in the Bible, the clear intention is to employ it metaphorically, recognizing that the consciousness and historic dimension of our time and place are extraordinarily different from those depicted in the Scriptures.

Indeed, strictly speaking, a cornerstone of this orientation, the Socratic tradition, is totally out of the scope of Biblical analysis. Although removed from the historical, cultural, and spiritual particularities of Biblical scriptures, the Socratic traditions, however, have at least one vital parallel: both are critical traditions rooted in a religious vision. When I speak of the Socratic tradition, I have particular reference to the Socrates of the *Apology* in which he attempts to describe the meaning of his life and death. In this account we witness the indictment, trial, conviction, and execution of Socrates as well as the justification of his work and his explanation for accepting his martyrdom. Socrates had been accused of threatening the security of the state by undermining the beliefs of its youth. Indeed, Socrates admits to raising troublesome questions that reveal the shallowness and inadequacies of conventional beliefs. The work is a pivotal part of the narrative of Western civilization since it speaks so eloquently and poignantly to the human passion for freedom and truth, in the face of the forces of conformity and expediency. Socrates is rightfully one of our major heroes, for he not only exemplifies brilliant intellectuality but also enormous wisdom, courage, and dignity. The images of the shrewd, elderly Socrates calmly taking on his tormentors with consummate wisdom and insight energizes us to maintain faith in the power of the mind and the authority of knowledge. The Greek legacy (as embodied in Socrates) includes the enormous power of the inquiring, incisive, skeptical mind to illumine and extend our vision. It is a legacy that has revolutionized the world and one that, despite continuing serious problematics, is surely indispensable.

However, there is an extremely important dimension of Socrates' story as told in the *Apology* that is often neglected if not forgotten. I refer to those passages in which Socrates makes it very clear that he is on a spiritual journey and insists that his intellectual engagement with the citizens of Athens is intimately connected to that journey. Socrates is convinced that his search for greater clarity and understanding is sanctioned and required by the gods and that his queries, examination, and debates represent sacred responsibilities and obligations. In fact, he makes no separation between church and state, religious and secular, spiritual and humanistic, since a life of meaning is one in which all elements are in harmony. Shades of holistic education!

The point is that the so-called Socratic Method is not a method or technique at all. It is not about scoring intellectual triumphs or about making debating points. Socrates was indeed pursuing religious fulfillment intellectually, analytically, and critically not to debunk and deconstruct religious beliefs but to enrich and deepen them. In responding to his indictment Socrates has this to say:

"Gentlemen of the jury, I am grateful and I am your friend, but I will obey the gods rather than you and as long as I draw breath and am able I shall not cease to practice philosophy. Be sure this is what the gods order me to do, and I think there is no greater blessing for the city than my service to the gods. For I go around doing nothing but persuading both young and old among you not to care for your body or your wealth in preference to as strongly as for the best possible state of your soul. . . ." Plato, *The Trial and Death of Socrates* (translated by G. M. Grudge, Hackett Publishing, Indianapolis, 1975).

I confess to not knowing very much about the particular nature of Socrates' spiritual consciousness nor of the specifics of the religious beliefs of his contemporaries. What is vital for purposes of this analysis is the paradigmatic power of an orientation in which keen intellectuality is integrally and symbiotically related to a spiritual and moral vision. This relationship has even more particular relevance for us in the story of the Biblical prophets, a story which contains some of the most central themes of Western morality and spirituality. It is a story with images of slavery and the promise of liberation; of human striving to create communities grounded in a higher law; and of profound commitments to creating a life of piety, justice, compassion, and spiritual salvation.

Again, the point here is not Biblical exegesis but rather to indicate some of the broad but profound influences that the Biblical narratives have had on our consciousness. We can and do interpret great and endearing texts in a variety of ways, and, indeed, it is our human responsibility and destiny to do so. I associate myself with the tradition that sees within the Biblical (as well as other) narratives elements of a profound search for ultimate meaning and a life of justice, peace, and joy. A key part of this narrative is reflected in the accounts described in Exodus in which an enslaved people (the Hebrews) are oppressed by powerful external and brutal forces (Egypt) and by their own sense of powerlessness and despair. The issue of their liberation is linked to the people's capacity to imagine, and hence make possible, transcending their powerfully palpable limits. The prophetic voice (represented here in the figure of Moses) is one which speaks critically and candidly. In this case Moses himself has to struggle to accept the vision and to agree to convince the Hebrews that there is in fact slavery, wholly unnecessary suffering, and totally inhuman misery going on in the midst of luxury and splendor. In addition, the prophetic voice speaks to hope and possibility by invoking higher forces and principles through the development of a higher consciousness. It becomes Moses' task, therefore, to teach the Hebrews that they are not only oppressed but they need not and must not be. Furthermore, it is his task to exhort them to have faith in the power of the mystery to infuse the people with the material, spiritual, and moral energy required to break the physical and psychological bonds of physical oppression and personal despair.

Like subsequent prophets, Moses commits himself to the extraordinarily complex, difficult, and frustrating task of raising the consciousness of the oppressed, confronting the power of the oppression, and dealing with self-doubt, fear, division, and failure. Moses' early reluctance, his own slow awakening, and his inadequacies as a leader reveal the prophet as human, fallible, vulnerable, and believable. The apparent capacity that Moses had to be in touch with the Divine, and to experience and witness the transcendent, marks prophets as people who have dramatically extended the range of human possibility. The image of Moses (presumably the most evolved of the most evolved people) at the peak of Mt. Sinai represents the possibility of humans reaching for the heavens and of an intimate relationship between God and Humanity. What Sinai also represents is the extension of flight from bondage to the quest for a community grounded in a vision of ultimate meaning. The covenant represents a commitment to affirm deeply the vision and to press diligently for its realization.

The basic pattern of critique, outrage, exhortation, hope, possibility, and vision (what has been called the prophetic voice) recurs in other biblical narratives and social texts as well as in history across time and space. In the more literal sense, Biblical prophets are clearly identified within the text (e.g. Hosea, Amos, Isaiah, Jeremiah) and each takes on the role of outraged social critic offering both condemnation of the violation of the Covenant and the possibility of redemption through its reaffirmation. This is very much the configuration of the life of Jesus, who severely castigates the community for not only violating the spirit of the covenant but for profaning it. Beyond his outrage and indignation he provides a message of renewed hope for transcendence through a consciousness of love, humility, and reaffirmation.

Robert Ackerman has argued that the critical function is the very essence of religion, that is, to be alert to the society's reluctance and failure to meet its deepest commitments and to become a voice of protest:

". . . Religion is a perennial source of social critique, but religion . . . always retains the potential of developing a pungent social critique, no matter how accommodating a form they [religions] have assumed. . . . Critique does not exhaust religion, but religion that cannot critique is already dead. . . . What is being suggested here is that the core of religion is potentially critical rather than functional or accommodating" (Ackerman, ix: 24).

It is important to add a note of caution at this point in regard to the problems and limitations of the metaphor of "prophetic voice." For instance, there is the danger of becoming captured by particular interpretations, as it must be recognized that there have been and continue to be serious controversies regarding Biblical interpretation, including those concerning the role and function of the prophets. Furthermore, even if there were a consensus on this, it is also clear that it is dangerous to make direct parallels among the social and cultural milieux involved. That was then and this is now, notwithstanding the reality that the "now" contains important dimensions of the "then." We certainly have the right to be selective about which traditions to reaffirm and which to reject but we also have to accept responsibility for making choices rather than evaluating them, by claiming that we are only repeating universal and/or eternal truths. Furthermore, although I find the tradition of spirituality and morally-grounded social criticism to be extraordinary resonant with our current cultural and political crises, I do not choose to support other phenomena associated with biblical narratives (e.g., animal sacrifices, slavery, conquest, patriarchy).

Within the metaphor of prophet is one very important sub-category, "false prophet," which, of course, raises the basic question of validity. One can be outraged, critical, and indignant and be "wrong," i.e., criticality by itself does not guarantee wisdom or rightness. Ultimately, we search for criteria that validate and generate critical dimensions and whether we do this inductively or deductively is not particularly relevant here. Put another way and more crudely, some prophets are "better" than others and this is not necessarily because their analytical capacities are different but rather because their underlying visions are more or less acceptable. Savonarola, Martin Luther King, Cotton Mather, Ayatollah Khomeni, and Mohandas Gandhi can all be called prophets in that they integrated their political and social movements with deeply felt religious commitments. One person's passion can indeed become another person's zealotry. Therefore, we will want to attend not to *the* prophetic voice but to prophetic voices and to search for those that are most resonant with our vision of a just, peaceful, and joyous world.

The Prophetic traditions have strong and diverse roots in the American experience that are perhaps most clearly seen in America's Puritan origins. Indeed, the impact of Puritan culture and society on our present consciousness helps to illustrate our ambivalence toward a morally and religiously grounded orientation. At best, the Puritans contributed the authority of individual consciousness and of a morally based community; at worst, Puritan society contributed intolerance, rigidity, and self-righteousness. The Puritans apparently were not able to conduct their quest for a more just and equitable society without the certainty that they were God's appointed and chosen agents. Their experience, which is among the great ironies and oddities of American history, helped to foster a quite contrary religious tradition—namely that of tolerance, diversity, pluralism, and the separation of church and state. The collapse of the Puritan dream, however, did not mean the end but only the elaboration of an American moral and religious consciousness. To this day, for better or worse, American culture often reflects an explicit moral and/or religious orientation in a whole array of areas, from popular culture to foreign policy, from family life to the arts. Some of the remnants of Puritan consciousness are clearly vulgar and self-righteous, as in "God Bless America" and the portrayal of the former Soviet Union and Iraq as "evil empires" but much of it is grounded in the impulse to create a world of meaning, justice, freedom, and joy.

The religious impulse is eloquently and powerfully reflected in perhaps our country's most sacred text, the Declaration of Independence. Central to this paradigmatic statement is the notion that "governments are instituted among men [sic], deriving their just powers from the consent of the governed." A political expression of the moral and religious principles that "all men are created equal, that they are endowed by their creator with inalienable rights. . . ." The statement goes on to affirm the vital responsibility of the citizenry to maintain patient but critical vigilance of the government's fidelity to those principles, since, if the government should become despotic, "it is their right, it is their duty to throw off such government." In an echo of Sinai, an emerging people commits itself to a religious and moral vision as the boundaries of a new nation.

As the author of the Declaration of Independence, it is no surprise that Jefferson saw education as a critical dimension in the creation of the new democratic society. The suspicion of government's capacity to oppress, the community's responsibility to be vigilant, and the principle of consent combine to require an informed and critical citizenry. Thus education in America shifted from a focus on the training of ministers and the enlightenment of an elite to an essential instrument of the empowerment of the individual and the preservation of the democratic vision. Later, John Dewey saw formal education as the "laboratory" for democracy, where students and teachers could experience and reflect upon the problems and difficulties inherent in creating a particular world based on a commitment to dignity, justice, rationality, and tolerance. George Counts took this step one step further by claiming for education the responsibility for being part of the power not only to understanding but transform society. In a memorable statement evocative of prophetic rhetoric, Counts once wrote:

"If the schools are to be really effective, they must become centers for the building, and not merely for the contemplation, of our civilization. This does not mean that we should endeavor to promote particular reforms through the educational system. We should, however, give to our children a vision of the possibilities which lie ahead and endeavor to enlist their loyalties and enthusiasms in the realization of the vision. Also, our social institutions and practices, all of them, should be critically examined in the light of such a vision" (Counts, p. 37).

Education, Society, and Culture in the 1990s

What are educators who strive to evoke these prophetic traditions to make of our present historical moment? How well are we as a people doing in the struggle to reduce misery, poverty, suffering, oppression and to increase justice, peace, harmony, equality, and joy? We pose these questions not only because they are obviously of enormous import in and of themselves, but more particularly because they ought to serve as the major point of departure for educators. Organized education is to be seen not precisely in the service of scholarship nor primarily to serve the state or the economy but primarily to serve the task of nurturing, nourishing, and sustaining the quest to meet our highest aspirations most profound commitments. The standards of a society and its culture (and hence of its educational institutions) involve concerns for the degree of freedom, equality, justice, and fulfillment enjoyed by its members.

Recognizing both the importance of affirming our solid and enduring achievements as well as the dangers inherent in profound pessimism does not mitigate the harm and obscene reality of the horrors of our present condition, worldwide as well as nationally and locally. There are no end of indexes, statistics, and observations to demonstrate and evoke the starkness, depth, and extent of profound and unnecessary human suffering. Indeed, this could be demonstrated by a brief exposition of only one of this century's many catastrophes such as World War I, Auschwitz, Hiroshima, World War II, Viet Nam, the sub-Saharan famines, oil spills, the greenhouse effect, Cambodia, and so on. It is extraordinary that such a list can only be suggestive and not definitive because there simply is not the space to list all or even most of the truly horrible events of the century.

There have been a great many attempts to explain and provide meaning for such stupefying phenomena, in the poignant assumption that there are indeed meaningful explanations. Attendant, then, to this terrible material and physical destructiveness has been a corresponding erosion of the spirit. Alienation, fragmentation, anomie, fear, and loneliness are virtually household names and routines. There is deep thirst for meaning and direction as a consequence of an increasing sense of meaninglessness and existential despair. The society and the schools urge us to work hard, strive for personal success, compete with ourselves, our colleagues, and our enemies. Some (too many) people respond with drugs, crime, suicide, and depression. The society and schools extol individual achievement, and indeed equate it with virtue. Some (surely too many) people respond with divorce, loneliness, and anomie. The society and the schools exhort us to be number one and warn that we are risking our loss of economic and political supremacy. Some (far too many) people respond with racism, sexism, jingoism, and homophobia. The society demands more control, discipline, hard work, and competition, and the profession responds with more sophisticated tests and more clever modes of monitoring students and teachers. The people cry out for meaning, wisdom, and deliverance and the society and school respond fearfully with more control, more jargon, more retrenchment, and less meaning and wisdom than ever.

The response of the dominant professional community has been at best evasive and at worst complicitous. Much of the profession has tried to stake out an area of expertise in which the broader cultural, moral, and social issues are left to nonprofessionals. This so-called professional orientation is one in which educators are cast as resource people charged with researching and implementing policy decisions. In a word, to follow but not to shape orders. The great preponderance of educational research is technical, and indeed the term "research" has been reified and reduced to mean experimental, positivistic, quantified investigation. Even the broader cultural, social, and moral issues become objects of study rather than perspectives for affirmation.

A tragic consequence of this narrow, timid, and self-serving professional posture is the appallingly vulgar and ill-informed nature of the public dialogue on educational matters. It is surely true that in the long run basic educational decisions emerge from a social and cultural consensus rather than from professional expertise. All the more reason then for the profession to meet its responsibilities to help the public to frame its dialogue in ways consistent with the complexities, paradoxes, and profundities of the fundamental issues. The moral fabric of our culture is in tatters and the public debates how much homework should be assigned. There are hundreds of thousands of people living in the streets; racial polarization increases; children suffer from neglect and malnutrition, and educators offer up career ladders, standardized tests, more requirements, and more school time. Happily, this is surely not to say that such reactions constitute the entire range of professional response. There is indeed a very lively, imaginative, and provocative body of educational criticism and theory that goes far beyond the toadying and myopic quality of the dominant elements of the profession.

Much of the critical literature speaks directly and cogently to the cultural, social, and political aspects of education and to the necessity for rooting education reform in social and cultural transformation. The term "critical pedagogy" has been loosely applied to this broad school of educational criticism in reference to its major reliance on neo-Marxist critical theory. Critical pedagogy puts a great deal of reliance on raising the consciousness of people's lived experiences particularly as they relate to issues of power, freedom, equality, and justice. This school of thought has made and continues to make very important contributions to educational theory and has energized a great number of educators with its message of criticism, hope, and possibility. Unfortunately, it has also met a great deal of resistance and has largely failed to enter the consciousness of mainstream professionals or the public. There are a number of possible explanations for this failure of these powerful ideas to have more import (e.g., genuine and profound disagreement; the complexities of the analysis and language). Many critical-pedagogy theorists are currently devoting their work to enriching their theoretical underpinnings through moral and psychological inquiries and broadening their political base by adapting a positive inclusive approach, that is, by reaching out to a wide array of marginalized groups.

There are other qualitatively different voices of educational criticism that speak more directly to issues of psychological constriction, spiritual alienation, and ontological sterility. These voices emerge from traditions of progressive and libertarian education, which stress the vital importance of individual freedom, creativity, and unfettered human potentiality. In addition, these voices are often augmented by chords that resonate with New Age themes of spiritual quest, ecological concerns, and cosmological perspectives. This movement has a major advantage over the critical pedagogy orientation in that its psychological and spiritual perspectives are shared by a great many people of the general lay public, although this public has, for the most part, failed to extend these spiritual and psychological perspectives into their interpretation of educational policies and practices. Moreover, what these critical voices add by way of their concern for psychological, emotional, and spiritual matters is diminished by their relatively weak efforts to integrate their ideas with the social, political, cultural, and moral dimensions of the human struggle.

Another critical difference between these two very broad schools of educational criticism is found in the extremely vital issue of assumptions regarding human nature. At the real risk of oversimplification, these differences involve degrees of optimism, pessimism, and cynicism. One side is accused of sentimentality, romanticism, and denial while the other is accused of being overwhelmed, if not energized, by visions of gloom, despair, and futility. This is related in part to theories of change which involve on the one hand the view that change must emerge from fundamental changes in social, cultural, and economic structures or on the other hand can emerge only from significant changes in human consciousness. While both are clearly needed and are surely interrelated, the rhetoric usually stresses one or the other. Those who stress the predominant importance of cultural and social transformation are likely to see such a process as a continuous, quasi-permanent, conflictual, and frustrating struggle with uncertain prospects. Many progressive, or libertarian, or New Age theorists who focus on the psychological and spiritual dimensions are apt to be much more optimistic if not euphoric about the possibilities of quantum leaps in consciousness and are therefore able to envision the possibility of attainable, significant, and dramatic transformation.

To sum up our present section, we see a world at serious risk from a variety of material horrors—famine, disease, oppression, war, pollution—and suffering from a variety of diseases of the spirit-moral numbness, callousness, alienation, and powerlessness. The culture's educational response to these crises tends to promote the forces that contribute to the crises—concern for competition, achievement, hierarchy, and material success. The profession for the most part has renounced its responsibility to provide moral leadership, taking on instead a posture of being detached technical experts. There are important and vital voices of educational dissent and alternatives but they are divided, particularly in their views of the relative significance of psychological and cultural forces and their degree of optimism.

My own view is that educational institutions can only be truly transformed from social and cultural pressures. There is no credible evidence that the schools have ever been a major force in cultural and social transformation. At the same time, it is clear that they are at least both force and resource and it is vital whatever the degree of their influence, that they utilize their valid possibilities optimally. Although it is to the culture that we must ultimately look to for the possibilities of transformation, the profession has an extremely important role in facilitating and guiding public dialogue and social movements. Significant experience as practioners and theorists provides educators with a unique and necessary perspective to interpret the meaning of educational policies and practices in relationship to the culture's most profound aspirations. This responsibility includes not only developing critical and sensitive insights but also the task of making these insights vital and accessible to the general public. This task must seek a balance between the ethical requirements to convey the complexities, paradoxes, contradictions, and sensitivities of the crises with the moral competence to offer genuine and viable possibilities for transformation. I believe that a great deal of the necessary work has already been done by our current educational theorists and visionaries and the hope of this paper is to further the development of a greater degree of consensus among the varying views of these critics.

Education in a Prophetic Voice

In this section, I sketch out an orientation toward education which reflects a selective blending of the voices of educational criticism and vision. This orientation is rooted in sacred and profound traditions that endeavor to speak in a prophetic voice. In addition to being informed by the contributions of these educational critics, I will be relying on the work of Abraham Heschel, Matthew Fox, and Cornel West to enrich and enhance these voices.

These three theologians can all be said to be in the prophetic traditions, although clearly they are from very different perspectives and each offers his own unique contribution. All three passionately affirm the struggle to ground moral, political, and social struggles in spiritual and transcendental visions. I believe strongly that the work exemplified by these three champions of the "wretched of the earth" has

powerful possibilities and implications for educators and those interested in the educative process. Moreover, their work also would seem
to provide a nexus between those educational critics now divided by
their differences on the significance of social/cultural/political forces
as opposed to moral and spiritual ones.

Abraham Joshua Heschel's monumental analysis and interpretation of the biblical prophets rejects the necessity for such dualism. It is
the prophets, according to Heschel, who established the profound
possibility that humans have "the ability to hold God and man in a
single thought." The prophetic consciousness is one in which the
material and the spiritual are not separate categories but vital and
interacting dimensions of human existence. God is seen by Heschel
not as a detached observer eagerly but remotely watching to see how
humans are doing but rather the God of the Prophets is a God of
pathos and compassion whose own being is intimately linked to human destiny. This God is actively involved in the Covenant with humanity and makes it clear that deviations and violations of the Covenant stir divine anger, grief, and dismay. The prophetic sensibility is
one which registers the profundity of the human activities, behaviors,
and policies likely to incur this wrath and grief. In this sense, prophets
are not to be seen as seers, sorcerers, or crystal ball readers but as
shrewd and sensitive social and cultural critics. Their task is to interpret the degree to which the community has been true to its commitments and to speak openly of the serious dangers that will almost
surely result from continuing violations of these commitments. Their
message is, however, more than warning, outrage, and indictment; it
is also one of hope, possibility, and redemption. What is recognized
here is the inevitability of the human propensity to seek advantage
rather than justice as well as the possibility of transcendence over this
propensity. This possibility lies in the dialectic between human imagination and divine energy. Social prophesy exists to re-mind, re-new,
and re-form the human community in the enormously important
struggle to create a humane community worthy of divine approach.

Central to this process is the concept of responsibility, or more
particularly in Heschel's terms, "the ability to respond to divine commitments and imperatives." This ability involves the capacity to be
alert, critical, and active and is absolutely crucial to the struggle for
human freedom and fulfillment. The ability to respond is crucial because humans have the capacity to deny freedom to themselves and to
others because of the reality of the impulse for greed, selfishness, and

personal gain. Indeed, in Heschel's terms, "the opposite of freedom is not determinism but hardness of heart. To be free is to be able to enjoy the fruits of life in a just, caring, and compassionate community" (Heschel, p. 14)

There are other somewhat more subtle barriers to the emergence of such a community besides the propensity toward evil, particularly passivity, despair, and equivocation. Prophets speak with indignity and outrage at both flagrant and insidious violations of the commitment toward the poor, hungry, and oppressed, being well aware of the dangers of both evil and indifference. In words evocative of the passion and eloquence of the prophets, Heschel says:

"Above all, the prophets remind us of the moral state of a people: Few are guilty, all are responsible. If we admit that the individual is in some measure conditional or affected by the spirit of society, an individual's crime discloses society's corruption. In a community not indifferent to suffering, uncompromisingly impatient with cruelty and falsehood, continually concerned for God and every man, crime would be infrequent rather than common" (Heschel, 16).

Matthew Fox, writing from a Catholic perspective, echoes the concept of co-creation in which humans participate in the further creation of a world inspired by a will toward justice, love, peace, and joy. His theology reaffirms a cosmological consciousness, insisting that we situate our being in the universe lest we commit the intellectual shallowness and ontological arrogance of anthropocentrism, an undue concern for human/worldly perspectives. However, his mysticism does not at all take him into a more contemplative position but actually quite the reverse. To Fox, the mystical, the divine, the universal, the human, and the social are to be seen as one, many, and one. The purpose of day-to-day life is to reflect and energize a universe of joy, vibrancy, and love in which we dance with the awe and radiance of the mystery.

Unlike other so-called New Age figures, Fox speaks directly, cogently, and specifically to social, political, and economic concerns. His passionate devotion to the well-being of the planet is deeply informed by an understanding of how our political and economic system contributes to our ecological dangers. Indeed, he speaks out against the spiritual dangers of a religious detachment in which the spiritual agenda of creating a world of justice, and harmony can be ignored. Fox is particularly concerned that we be aware of the distinction between compassion and sentimentality. Human compassion is the process of creating a daily life infused with divine light. Compassion involves genuine sharing of pain and joy and is inherently communal and interdependent while sentimentalism involves detached, shallow, and superficial recognition of others' pain and joy. Compassion provides an opportunity to affirm and manifest human relationship and commitment while sentimentality facilitates separation and irresponsibility.

The struggle for creating a compassionate community is significantly facilitated through art, or more precisely through what Fox calls "art as meditation." In this concept, art is not limited only to the specially talented, but defined as the human process of imagination, creativity, and meaning-working. It is the human genius to play, to dream, to have visions, and to imagine. It is art that gives form to these images, through the creation of rituals, stories, poems, paintings, sculpture, crafts, and so on. In turn, these images guide and help us to interpret our lives and to make meaning of them. Clearly, this process is critical to our responsibility to share in the creation of the world that is part of a vast and mysterious universe, and hence it must be enriched and nourished. It is to the creative process that we must look for our ability to move beyond the horror of our present existence and to imagine and therefore make possible a more loving, compassionate, and joyful world. When we recognize that we have in fact created a world we can accept the responsibility and appreciate the possibility of re-creating it.

Cornel West's academic brilliance and astonishing scholarship is powerfully nourished by his affirmation of the African-American experience and the traditions of the Black Church. He proposes a bold and critical synthesis between Marxist analysis and Christian theology, with particular attention to the plight of the oppressed and marginalized. His work is a superb blending of the prophetic tradition, American pragmatism, and black liberation theology written with eloquence, power, elegance, and authority. He affirms the Christianity that speaks to the poor, the meek, and the oppressed with its promise of ultimate salvation. It is this promise that West believes can provide us with the energy to overcome our fears and dread to struggle for what he calls "penultimate salvation," the redemption that derives from the struggle to create a just and caring community.

He also affirms American traditions of political protest against tyranny and of declaring independence from the domination of European philosophical traditions. In his book *The American Evasion of Philosophy*, West traces the origins of pragmatism to the optimism, individualism, and idealism of Ralph Waldo Emerson and to his efforts to side-step the distraction of metaphysicians. West critically describes and analyzes the contributions of others (such as Dewey, Mills, James, Du Bois, Niebuhr, and Rorty) to this pragmatic tradition and adds his own perspective, which he calls "prophetic pragmatism." West basically approves of the American intellectual tradition of avoiding traditional philosophic inquiry: "[T]he claim is that once one gives up on the search for foundations and the quest for certainty, human inquiry into truth and knowledge shifts to the social and communal circumstances under which persons can communicate and cooperate in the process of acquiring knowledge. What was once epistemological now highlights the values and operations of power requisite for the human production of truth and knowledge. . . . Prophetic pragmatism makes the political motivation and political substance of the American evasion of philosophy explicit. . . . The emancipatory social experimentalism that sits at the center of prophetic politics closely resembles the democratic elements of Marxist theory, yet its flexibility shuns any dogmatic, a priori, or monistic pronouncement" (West, p. 213–214).

West, a deeply committed visionary, is no romantic and has internalized the bitter struggle of his community to make even minimal gains as well as the age-old struggles of the groups across the globe. He addresses the dialectic between tragedy and progress directly:

"Prophetic pragmatism refuses to side-step this issue. The brutalities and atrocities in human history, the genocidal attempts in this century, and the present-day barbarities require that those who accept the progressive and prophetic designations put forth some conception of the tragic . . . yet prophetic pragmatism is a child of Protestant Christianity wedded to left romanticisms. . . . Prophetic pragmatism . . . tempers its utopian impulse with a profound sense of the tragic character of life and history. . . . Prophetic pragmatism . . . confronts candidly individual and collective experiences of evil in individuals and institutions—with little expectation of ridding the world of *all* evil. Yet it is a kind of romanticism in that it holds many experiences of evil to be neither inevitable nor necessary but rather the results of human agony, i.e. choice and actions" (West, p. 228).

This powerful reaffirmation of the human responsibility to avoid the twin perils of "despair and sentimentality" provides us with a language that helps in the struggle against contemporary weariness, anomie, and powerlessness. It is to remind us of both the sublimity of our aspirations and the finitude of our endeavors, although he is not unaware of the lingering sense of futility and meaninglessness that pervades our era. West chides those of us afflicted with this malaise for ignoring the redemptive qualities of a religious consciousness: "The severing of ties to churches, synagogues, temples, and mosque by the left intelligentsia is tantamount to political suicide; it turns the pessimism of many self-depicting and self-pitying secular progressive intellectuals into a self-fulfilling prophecy" (West, p. 234).

The following quotation from West is unsurpassed in its ability to capture the essence of the prophetic tradition in the context of our present moment. It ought to serve as a vital creedal foundation for the development of an educational process that can serve the struggle for a world of love, justice, peace, and joy. It is a statement that immerses us with its soaring hopes and its attainable possibilities:

"Human struggle sits at the center of prophetic pragmatism, a struggle guided by a democratic and libertarian vision, sustained by moral courage and existential integrity, and tempered by the recognition of human finitude and frailty. It calls for utopian energies and tragic actions, energies and actions that yield permanent and perennial revolutionary, and reformist strategies that oppose the status quo of our day. These strategies are never to become ends in themselves, but rather to remain means through which are channeled moral outrage and human desperation in the face of prevailing forms of evil in human societies and in human lives. Such outrage must never cease, and such desperation will never disappear, yet without revolutionary, rebellious and reformist strategies, credible and effective opposition wanes. Prophetic pragmatism attempts to keep alive the sense of alternative ways of life and of struggle based on the best of the past. In this sense, the praxis of prophetic pragmatism is tragic action with revolutionary intent, usually reformist consequences, and always visionary outlook" (West, p. 229).

These powerful and eloquent writers remind us of what our work entails rather than providing us with job descriptions. Our work as educators has little to do with increasing productivity, patriotism, and pride, but much more with meeting our responsibilities to create a compassionate consciousness. Schools should not be objects of detached research and study but subjects of committed search and inquiry. They should be houses of study and affirmation and not sorting and counting houses. An education that speaks in a prophetic voice responds not to the possibility of becoming rich and famous, but to the possibility of becoming loving and just. Its reference point is not the erosion of America's economic and military might but humanity's erosion of its vision of universal harmony, peace, and fulfillment. Such an education is not rooted in strategies, planning, curriculum guides, decision plans, or programs for developing human resources, but rather in the mystery that enables us to dream and hope beyond our present realities.

The educational vision encompasses the awe and majesty of the universe as well as the extraordinary capacities of humans to make meaning and create cultural and social structures. It is an education that commits itself to recreating human consciousness and structures in order to make real our dreams for justice, harmony, peace, and joy. This commitment involves a deep commitment to the democratic process that enables us to celebrate our freedom, interdependence, and individuality. The commitment also requires us to be alert to the inevitable possibilities of cooptation and distortion. It is an education whose starting point is not "excellence" or "achievement" but the grotesque realities of an obscene level of unnecessary human suffering. As members of the human community we need to be reminded that we have created hunger, war, poverty, and oppression, and as citizens of the universe, we must renew our covenant to repair the world. As simultaneous members of the human community and constituents of the universe we can find meaning in the intimate relationship between the pains we have cruelly inflicted and the healing we have lovingly extended.

Such an education links heaven and earth, moral and spiritual consciousness, and society and the individual. It also vitally requires all human energies—the mind, the intellect, the body, the soul, and their unity. It must take into account our history and our traditions of knowing and must seek to benefit from accumulated knowledge and wisdom. Such an education requires the development of skills, experience and expectations, writing, reading, knowledge of various symbolic systems, deep understanding of several cultures, languages, and histories, significant understanding of several modes of research, the capacity to create and imagine. It is an education in which knowledge, criticality, and skills are necessary but not sufficient since such capacities need to be informed by moral energy and enriched by social and practical skills required of those who would make a world.

What is also required is the courage and determination to maintain the struggle, particularly as our education will likely reveal the depth and persistence of injustice, greed, callousness, and cruelty. We can take solace and comfort from the reality that the task of creating a just the world is a relatively new one in the context even of human, never mind geologic history. Moreover, we must celebrate the majesty of a struggle that binds us to the highest ideals of those who came before us and that will inspire even greater aspirations by those who come after us. As it is written, "The task is not for you to finish, but neither are you free not to take part in it."

References

Ackerman, Robert, 1985. *Religion as Critique*. Amherst, MA: University of Massachusetts Press.

Fox, Matthew, 1979. *A Spirituality Named Compassion*. Minneapolis: Winston
Press.

Heschel, Abraham. 1962. *The Prophets*. New York: Harper and Row.

Nisbet, Robert. 1974. *The Sociology of Emile Durkeim*. New York: Oxford University Press.

West, Cornel. 1989. *The American Evasion of Philosophy*. Madison: University of
Wisconsin Press.

Social Transformation and Holistic Education: Limitations and Possibilities

Background and Assumptions

I believe that the term *educator* has had a misleading and problematic effect, for it has enabled us to participate in the fiction that educational issues have a reality of their own apart from the social and cultural context. At its most distorted, the term can mean a person who is an expert on what and how students learn, i.e., a skilled technician or craftsperson who specializes in what happens in the classroom. This distortion has at least two important troubling dimensions; first, there is the myth that the educational process can be separated from the historical and social context, and second, there is the absurdity that educators are primarily, if not only, educators. Educators like everyone else are responsible for the creation, preservation, and/or the re-creation of a social system, or, if you prefer, a community. Whatever else people are called upon to do, they have the inevitable, agonizing, and exhilarating task of constructing ways in which we are to live with each other. Each of us participates willy-nilly in this extraordinarily vital process, however unaware we might be, however tiny or major our impact, however beneficial or destructive the contribution.

Some people (e.g., educators) are lucky enough to be in positions where they are explicitly called upon to articulate and act upon a vision of the good life. I often tell my students that there are no such things as educational issues; there are instead a number of moral, spiritual, philosophical, psychological, social, and cultural issues that get expressed and acted out in educational settings. In that same spirit, let me add that there are no educators per se, but more profoundly, there are moral and spiritual leaders who exercise their responsibilities in the context of educational settings. These moral and spiritual educators presumably have some strong ideas on what is involved in imagining and developing a life of individual and communal meaning, and their particular work has two aspects: (1) the creation of an educational community that in critical ways reflects that broader vision; and (2) in creating teaching and learning activities that can nurture and nourish that vision. The real issue is clearly not what specific term we use to call ourselves but more importantly, how we name our work and I would suggest that the naming must reflect our awareness of our deep and intense involvement in the inevitable, awesome, and continuous process of creating community. Indeed, John Dewey has defined education as "the making of a world."

Certain processes and institutions are inevitable in developing community, most notably a moral framework which informs a political and economic system that creates and distributes the rights, responsibilities, and rewards of citizenship, i.e., a system of justice. However, what holistic educators know only too well, these political and economic policies and institutions interact with other important dimensions of our lives and moreover, we must insist on an education that seeks to integrate *all* facets of human life, being sure to avoid a one-sided or distorted vision of human being.

There is, of course, some intended ironic criticism here since it has been my view that, by and large, holistic educators have tended to focus much more on the personal and spiritual than on the social and moral dimensions of education. This is ironic to me, because I believe that in their zeal to rightfully point out how conventional educators have a truncated vision of learning, holistic educators tend to substitute an equally truncated, albeit more aesthetically satisfying, vision of learning. It is quite true that holistic educators are making an enormously important contribution to our society and culture by emphasizing such neglected areas as the intuitive, the artistic, the creative, and the mythopoetic, and for that they deserve our thanks and approbation. What is spectacularly exciting is that the conceptual framework of the current holistic-education movement provides for the possibility of a *truly* holistic education, one that seeks to integrate the inner self with the outer self and thereby connect the personal with our social, cultural, moral, political, and economic contexts.

Not only must we be wary of a narrow professionalism that renders our work as being in "the field of education." We must also be suspicious of formulas that proclaim the importance of "keeping politics out of education," as if that were even possible. We must also guard against the preciousness that seeks to keep us all shielded from the harsh realities of social injustice and political oppression. Perhaps most importantly of all, we must have the courage to confess and witness to the ways that we and the educational system are part of, and have created, sustained, and legitimated this injustice and oppression. Not only must we be fully aware of our political, economic, and social contexts, but we must reaffirm and renew our commitments to our social vision of the just, loving, and joyous community.

To be an educator without a social vision is like being an artist without an aesthetic, and to be a holistic educator without a social vision is to be like an artist without a soul. It's not that easy to be a visionary educator, however, since what we want is not any old social vision but one that enables us to transcend to a consciousness of beauty, love, and compassion. Indeed, it is vital to be reminded that conventional education does in fact reflect a social and cultural vision, and in so doing it serves a particular political and economic ideology. Let us then take a look at the relationship between the dominant educational discourse and how it is related to social, political, and economic considerations.

The dominant ideology puts an incredible amount of emphasis on the difficulty that the United States has had in maintaining its military and economic primacy in the face of foreign competition and that our prosperity depends on our reestablishing that supremacy. It is this ideology that drives the current reform movement in stressing so-called higher standards, greater mastery of knowledge, greater reliance on test scores, and more demanding instructional techniques. This orientation is neatly captured in President Clinton's 1994 State of the Union speech in which he said, in the context of voicing support for alternative forms of schooling, maintaining that such efforts are worthwhile ". . . as long as we measure every school by one high standard: Are our children learning what they need to know to compete and win in the global economy?" This is hardly ambiguous and its bluntness and vulgarity should hardly be surprising since it represents, I believe, mainstream public opinion and the primary focus of professional energies.

In an increasingly global economy marked by extraordinarily intense competition, corporations are engaged in a frenzy of efforts at gaining, if not an edge, at least survival. Mergers, buyouts, downsizing, layoffs, and union-busting are obvious manifestations of this hysteria, spurred on by the fantasy of enormous wealth and power as well as the nightmare of being wiped out. This kind of vicious competition has contributed to a very significant reduction in the number of satisfying job opportunities and to incessant and cold-blooded efforts to reduce personnel costs. The result is a sense of unease and anxiety among us all, as we become increasingly vulnerable to economic misfortune, threatening not only such material things as savings, medical care, and educational opportunities but our hopes and dreams for peace and justice.

What *must* be understood is that these trends are reflected *in* and facilitated *by* current educational policies and practices, or, at the very least, that is what most of our political and educational leaders are advocating. Schools, community colleges, and universities are all being asked to teach more technical and vocational skills, to be more selective and demanding with students, to test more, and to create closer partnerships with business. This is *not* about nourishing souls, it is not about individuation or *even* about encouraging learning. It *is* about harnessing educational institutions to the President's vision of "competing and winning" in the race to be the richest and most powerful nation of all.

It is well to remember that so-called public schools are state agencies under the direction of civil servants answerable to elected officials who are, in turn, answerable to particular individuals and interest groups. The thrust behind the establishment of state financed and controlled compulsory education in the nineteenth century (which was strongly resisted by a number of different groups for a variety of compelling reasons) was to require a common school experience for all children in an effort to create a common American culture. They would be required to pray and read the Christian Bible and learn the traits expected of the WASP middle class: piety, respect for authority, cleanliness, obedience, perseverance, hard work, civility, and delay of gratification. Such traits not only constituted the ethos of the dominant cultural vision, but not surprisingly, meshed with the requirements of the new industrial order with its insatiable demand for compliant and reliable workers. I would submit that this agenda still operates, even though it is clear that the rhetoric has been somewhat altered in response to changes in the form in which these issues are currently framed. There is at least one major exception to this generalization and that, ironically enough, has to do with the emphasis on democracy, which had a very clear, strong, and urgent place on the agenda of nineteenth century advocates for compulsory common schooling. How different it would be if President Clinton had suggested that the one standard for schools be not "winning in the global economy" but instead nourishing and deepening the spirit of democracy.

Response

If we have anything in common as professionals, citizens, and humans, we have responsibilities and we all have the ability to respond. If educational institutions do, in fact, have an effect on society, then presumably they can be a force for positive transformation as well as for the maintenance of the status quo. How then are we as educators to respond to the social, cultural, and economic crises of our time particularly if we are to accept the premise that we are inevitably involved in them whether we like it or not? To borrow from a familiar slogan, can we move from being part of the problem to being part of the solution?

I must necessarily begin with a confession that I take the tragic view of life, that is, I see our lives as fated to involve heroic and virtuous struggles that ultimately end in failure. I resonate with the Sisyphean experience of meaning and dignity deriving from continuous and never-ending engagement in the task of creating a better world in the face of an awareness of its futility. This is based not only on my own perhaps impoverished inner spirit but on an analysis of the effects of various social movements for reform and political struggles for genuine revolution and transformation. The story of such efforts certainly contains many truly inspiring sagas of courage and determination as well as solid and enduring successes. Yet many of the gains are short-lived and even if some problems are resolved, new even more difficult ones appear. The story of public education in America is surely a case in point, for in spite of the imagination and perseverance of thousands of dedicated and talented educators and the availability of any number of wonderful ideas and programs, the sad reality of the matter is that in general the schools are less creative, less playful, less joyful, and less stimulating than they were ten or fifteen years ago. We have made very little if any progress in reducing hostility, violence, racism, sexism, homophobia, and warfare. Poverty and homelessness persists while the standard of living and sense of security continues to erode even for the middle class. Our economists seem, in spite of their brilliance, unable to either understand or manage an economy that is cruel and relentless. Welfare programs seem to be counterproductive, pesticides turn out to be deadly to humans, and antibiotics produce ever stronger, more dangerous viruses.

I do not see this view as necessarily cynical or despairing because for me it is very strongly tempered by the majesty of human persistence in the teeth of this storm of resistance to our earnest efforts. I joyfully join with those who would damn the torpedoes, light candles, fight the good fight, or who use any other cliché that celebrates the human impulse to participate in the covenant of creation. Indeed, I have to admit that I scorn the view that pessimism is an excuse for passivity and inaction. However, having said that, I need also to confess my parallel antipathy to sentimentality, that is, a consciousness of mindless optimism that is a product of blindness, denial, wishful thinking, and fear. My position is that we must not be daunted by the magnitude of the task of creating a just and joyful community, but we must not add to its difficulty by underestimating what is involved. I am continuously energized by the Talmudic admonition that even though the task is not ours to finish we are not free from the responsibility of engaging in the task.

The task of creating cultural and social transformation is greatly magnified by two powerful, if not embarrassing, realities: (1) in spite of all our crises and fears, the dominant ideology of growth, achievement, success, privilege, individualism, and conquest is extremely alive and well and thrives in most if not all of us; and (2) there are no broad alternative ideologies that are accessible to the public that could compete with the dominant ideology. The spirit of free enterprise and the sanctity of the concept of market are triumphant, virtually uncontested (especially with the collapse of the Soviet system and the weakening of the social democratic movements in the West), and venerated not only as ultimate truth but as a thing of beauty. There can be no greater indictment of our entire culture and particularly our entire educational program than this shocking state of affairs- that with all our knowledge and with all our creativity, imagination, and sensibilities, we find ourselves without a serious competitor to a system that is killing us with its popularity. If nothing else, this speaks to an immense failure in imagination but at a deeper level, it represents the triumph of one set of spirits over another. The spirits of individual gain, self-gratification, hedonism, competition, and possessiveness are beating the pants off the spirits of interdependence, peace, joy, and love. Our culture demands ever more products, thrills, innovations, titillations, scandals, sensations, daring-do, outrageousness; it is ever more mean-spirited and vengeful, increasingly paranoid, violent, and destructive. The dissenting elements of the culture surely provide a great deal of criticism but precious little in the way of affirmation. Ironically enough, one of the few groups offering some alternative is the Christian Right, which however, insists on wrapping the banner of capitalism around the Cross. It, therefore, becomes an imperative that educators accept their responsibility to participate in the process of not only providing and using the tools of cultural and social criticism but in nurturing and expressing the impulses of affirmation. Criticism without affirmation is not only a contradiction in terms but carries with it the destructive elements of sterility and paralysis. At the same time, let it be said that affirmation without criticism is not only intellectually suspect, but also fraught with the possibility of dogmatism and self-righteousness.

At this point, it is essential to temper my pessimism about the absence of alternative social-political-economic paradigms by celebrating the enormous amount of energy and talent that is being expended in the effort to make for a more just and peaceful society, as expressed in innumerable projects and movements. I have in mind comprehensive and ambitious programs in the ecology movement, for example, with its myriad projects in recycling, consciousness raising, educational activities, legislative efforts, political lobbying, and activist campaigns. There are many parallel efforts in other realms—concern for child abuse, civil rights, the handicapped, world peace, women's rights, liberation movements for any number of oppressed groups, the labor movement, gun control, concern for the homeless, for refugees, for the starving, and so on.

The spirit of the sixties was not born in that era, it was and *is*, a reenergized and renewed expression of the American and human tradition of giving a damn, of responding to ancient and deeply felt impulses to transcend existing limitations to a consciousness of love, joy, and peace for all, and celebrating the mystery and beauty of life. That spirit is very much alive in the 1990s as reflected not only in major programs like the ones I have just mentioned, but also in the innumerable and unpublicized daily acts of social responsibility, communal involvement, and personal engagement, such as doing volunteer work, political campaigning, comforting the sick, the afflicted, and the wounded; speaking up at PTA meetings and in legislative bodies for reform; writing letters to the editor, and just as important, actively witnessing the pain and suffering in the land. Such efforts must be strongly recognized, joyfully celebrated, and widely disseminated for a number of very important reasons, beginning with the necessity to provide support and encouragement for those involved. In addition, it is vital to resist the rising tide of understandable and somewhat justifiable despair that is being fanned into a consciousness of futility by a campaign of disinformation claiming that the 1960s was really about drugs, sex, and rock and roll and that the flower children of that era are now all stockbrokers. Those who want to hold on to the present paradigm want very much for us to believe that we have lost our sense of idealism, hope, and commitment, and it is vital that we give the lie to that self-serving slander.

We must also be in touch with these positive movements and activities in order to join with them, to form coalitions, to learn from them, and to contribute to them. In a broader sense what I am strongly suggesting is that educators need to align their work with other groups and movements as an important part of its involvement in and responsibility for the continuing development and creation of community, culture, and society. In this context, I want to reiterate my notion that we must work to broaden the concept of educator as someone skilled in classroom and school activities to include one who connects classroom and school to a social and cultural vision. Educators are social leaders, cultural advocates, moral visionaries, spiritual directors who choose to do their leading, advocating, visioning, and directing in institutions labeled schools and universities. We must always be mindful that the public and most private schools were not and are not set up for deep social and cultural transformation; actually it's the opposite for they function primarily as preservers and conservers, as forces of stability, continuity, and predictability. In this sense we as educators are already aligned with particular social and political forces and if we want to teach "against the grain of history," it would make a great deal of sense to do so explicitly, consciously, and deliberately. It also makes sense for those of us interested in working for social transformation to team up with like minded people who happen to operate in different but complementary realms. In this way educators can participate in the dialogue, help shape the strategy, and develop the policies that provide for a far greater degree of articulation between educational and political, social, economic, and cultural matters. This makes sense for two other reasons. First, it would be more honest and forthright to acknowledge the inherent interconnections, and second, this process is going on anyway but without the significant proactive involvement of the profession. It is no accident, for example, that many, if not most schools are now replete with computers for they are there because particular businesses and industries planned for them to be there. In other words, educators are usually called upon to figure out how to use their expertise to further the goals of certain others—politicians, economists, business leaders, and cultural leaders. I say that it is time that educators be involved in the process of which social, economic, political, and cultural goals need and ought to be furthered.

One very important implication of such an analysis for educators has to do with the significance and limitations of particular curriculum and instructional practices, especially those that are appealing, humane, imaginative, wise, and constructive, that is, the good kind. Alas, I have concluded with many others that such wonderful ideas and programs as cooperative learning, peer teaching, whole language expressive writing, and nature walks will by themselves have little impact on social and cultural transformation unless they are integrated into a holistic concept in which the boundaries between education and society become very blurred. We must end the delusions of single variable research, namely that we can isolate and separate educational elements and that a limited amount of significant change on a small scope will ultimately lead to significant change on a grand scale. No, my friends, the answer is not more imaginative curriculum and more sensitive instruction when the question is how can education contribute to the creation of a more just and loving world. The answer lies more in seeing such work as absolutely necessary but clearly insufficient; in connecting our classroom to our spiritual and cultural visions; and in accepting the reality that our social, cultural, economic, and political structures are integral and inevitable elements of the school curriculum. If we insist, however, on using a discourse that posits a sharp distinction between society and education then I would have to say that changes in the culture and society will come long before changes in the schools and not vice versa.

There is yet another response to the question of the place of education in society, and that is to be far more humble and modest about the significance of our work as educators. This attitude seems always appropriate, if not potentially liberating, but nonetheless has the danger of being implicitly irresponsible and collusive. It is however, possible to hold on to both the requirements of humility and responsibility by seeing ourselves as part of a larger struggle in collaboration not only with others but in connection with those who precede and follow us.

Having said all that, let me hasten to add that working to improve and enrich the lives of students within the school boundaries is a vital and necessary part of our work, and when we do so we are striving to respond to our highest moral and spiritual aspirations. In fact, it must be said that life in the classroom *is* the real world in those moments; not only a preparation *for* life but part of *life* itself. We must therefore affirm, support, and honor those who have worked and continue to work courageously and creatively from day to day, week to week to week, year to year for an education that is loving, nourishing, and stimulating. Such work sustains and warms us all and undoubtedly contributes not only to short-range gains but to longer-lasting ones as well. We can here again take a cue from holistic education by being mindful of the differences and connections between microcosm and macrocosm. In a very profound sense, every moment in the classroom is a sacred one and has within it the possibility of transcendence and connection. In that sense, the classroom itself becomes an arena for the struggle or, if you will, a place that invites the possibility of transforming the banal to the profound, the vulgar to the beautiful, and the profane to the sacred. Alas, it also provides the possibility within the power of the alchemy of education of turning gold into dross and innocence into savagery. Indeed I believe the stakes are that high, and if they are not we needn't bother and fuss so much over our work, but the fact that they are endows our frustrations with the mark of tragedy and our perseverance with the glow of majesty.

What More Can Be Done?

I want now to speak more directly to issues regarding what we as educators might do to respond to our social, political, and economic crises (notice I did not say educational crisis) in addition to striving to connect enriching and life-giving classroom experiences with other complementary cultural and social movements. I especially want to address the matter of the particular contribution that those in holistic education could make to this effort. Before I get to that, however, I want to mention what I believe is perhaps the most important contribution all educators can make to the well-being of our society and culture, and that is the matter of informing the public. As I have stressed, education in a democracy is ultimately a matter of public policy, and as such its shape and content must be determined through public dialogue, debate, and decision. Our democratic principles require that this dialogue and debate be guided by reasoned, informed, and open-minded processes. Unfortunately, I find the quality of public discourse on education to be appalling in its simplistic and reductionist analysis as well as the dreariness and conventionality of its visions of change. This level of discourse sharply contrasts with what appears to have been a very sophisticated and impassioned public debate in the mid-nineteenth century over the issue of mandating publicly financed compulsory schooling. The current sad state of public discourse on education, however, is by no means limited to cabs, bar rooms, and to talk shows but can be heard in legislative halls, in the offices of government officials, the board rooms of corporate America, and the towers of academe. The quote from the President's State of the Union speech that I cited is noteworthy not only for its crudeness and vulgarity but for its resonance with mainstream, middle-class public opinion. Indeed, when President Bush announced his mindlessly shallow Education 2000 program, the Democrats complained bitterly that the Republicans had stolen their ideas! I regret to say that this deplorable state of public discourse on education has been aided and abetted by our profession in acts of both commission and omission. Although it is not for the profession by itself to make public policy on education, it has a vital role in informing, shaping, and clarifying the dialogue and debate. It can do this by virtue of its expertise and experience by providing thoughtful, thorough, and critical reflections on the issues and by insisting that the public take these reflections seriously. In this way the profession can act as the intellectual and professional conscience of the public. However, it is my experience that the profession withholds a great deal of its insights and understandings from the public and is more likely to provide material that is more technical than substantive, more sentimental than critical, and more distracting than candid. I see nothing to be gained and a great deal to be lost when the profession plays the role of enabler in the public's fatal addiction to avoidance and denial.

The Role of Holistic Education in Social Transformation

I wish now to discuss the particular and critical ways in which the holistic-education movement could significantly contribute to redemptive social and cultural transformation. The most important contribution lies at the very heart of the movement, and that is its root metaphor of wholeness and interdependence and its rejection of dualism and alienation.

Affirmation of connection and integrity, passion for harmony, peace, and wholeness can only deepen the connections between our inner and outer selves, between individuals and the community, between the material and the spiritual, between humanity and nature, between Planet Earth and the universe and all the other possible betweens and amongs. Peace, justice, love, harmony, and meaning are each and all indivisible—they are neither to be rationed nor circumscribed; none of them individually sufficient, all of them are necessary, each of them is identifiable and all of them blurrable with each other.

I am convinced that a key educational element to the possibility of social and cultural transformation is the nourishment of imagination. One way of regarding our current crises is to see them as failures of imagination, as an inability to envision, for example, an economy without poverty and where there can be meaningful work for everyone, or an international order that can be maintained without recourse to violence, or a social system based on sufficiency for all rather than luxury for a few. Holistic educators need not be convinced about the importance of imagination for have they not only continuously and passionately argued for the necessity of encouraging the creative process but also demonstrated their faith in the extraordinary and untapped genius that resides in human imagination. It is time to direct the incredible power of fantastic, fanciful, and daring flights of imagination not only to the arts and letters but to fresh new social and economic visions, to developing more aesthetically pleasing ways of living together, and to designing more creative and life-giving social institutions.

However, when we consider the connection between the elements of holism and imagination, it becomes time to exercise extreme caution and to be in touch with our requirement of humility. What I mean here is that the impulse to image and create a coherent and whole vision of meaning, purpose, and destiny is as irresistible as it is dangerous, inevitable as it is futile, and redemptive as it is idolatrous. Indeed, in our current intellectual climate we have come to see, for better or worse, all cosmological, social, even scientific formulations and visions as acts of human imagination and construal. In this perspective, we see narratives, paradigms, contexts, contingencies, and particularities rather than dogmas, truths, eternal verities, certainties, and grand theories. This orientation has been both liberating and harrowing in that it has helped us to renew the importance of human agency in its constructivist sense. However, it has also made it virtually impossible to fully and totally affirm a firm and sustaining framework and rationale for our cherished beliefs. The death of certainty cuts two ways: it undercuts both dogmatism and conviction, both rigidity and steadfastness, and in so doing it sponsors both diversity and relativism. The incredibly powerful research on issues of race, class, culture, and gender has revealed not only that an immense variety and diversity have been lost, hidden and/or suppressed but that our lives have been largely guided by a particular vision of particular and privileged groups. The good news is that this vision, as a human construction, and as an act of human imagination, is not inevitable and hence can be replaced. The bad news is that we don't seem to have a replacement of commensurable appeal and power. We are between a rock and a hard place, for on one hand we see the necessity and feel the reality of a coherent worldview, but our intellect and history remind us of the dangers and foolishness of grand narratives. We value and revere the power of the human imagination but realize that it is able to produce evil and destructive designs. We see the necessity for boldness and transformation but recognize our limitations; we want to discover meaning and truth but recognize that there is extraordinary diversity in how they are named. We want to act but we are unsure and unclear what to do since everybody and everything seem to be right and/or wrong. We want to be sensitive to diverse views and perspectives but are fearful that we can be paralyzed by fairness. Is it possible to have strong convictions without being self-righteous, to be audacious without being grandiose, and to be imaginative without being idolatrous?

The theologian Walter Brueggemann has directly addressed such questions as they relate to Christianity in his book, *Texts Under Negotiation*. Brueggemann insists that it is the church's role to preach rejection of our current materialist and present-oriented vision and to replace it with a worldview that accepts divine creation and ultimate redemption. However, he clearly recognizes the obstacles and offers a far more modest and humble process of change based on the metaphor of *funding*.

"It is not," Brueggemann writes, "in my judgment, the work of the church. . . to construct a full alternative world, for that would be to act as all preemptively and imperialistically as all those old construals and impositions. Rather, the task is a more modest one, namely, to *fund*— to provide the pieces, materials, and resources, out of which a new world can be imagined. Our responsibility, then, is not a grand scheme or a coherent system, but the voicing of a lot of little pieces out of which people can put life together in fresh configurations."

He goes on to say that this new world is not to be given whole in one moment but, ". . . is given only a little at a time, one miracle at a time, one poem at a time, one healing, one promise, one commandment. Over time, these pieces are stitched together, all of us in concert, but each of us idiosyncratically, stitched together in a new whole— all things new" (Brueggemann, 1994).

I believe that such a formulation can be applied to education and that we can be bold and visionary in our endeavors, yet humble and modest in our expectations. As educators we certainly have pieces, poems, miracles, promises, and commandments to offer as part of the new collage and stand ready to stitch them together with offerings of other groups and individuals. Holistic educators have their own ways of contributing to this funding, feeding, nurturing, nourishing, and legitimating project, and it is vital to affirm them even as we are aware of their piecemeal quality. It is surely no small thing to be part of a quilt especially if we are talking of a new quilt of harmony, justice, and meaning.

How then might holistic educators contribute to the fund of pieces, materials, and patches that will constitute significant portions of that quilt in process? Let me count the ways. There is the matter of spirit— the concern for the soul, the divine, the mysterious, the inner self, the tacit, and the unconscious. There is the openness and insistence on legitimating diverse ways of knowing—aesthetic, intuitive, kinesthetic. Holistic educators put special reliance on developing close and warm human relationships not as instruments of manipulation but as essential to human meaning and existence. Children, and for that matter people, become the center of concern, not as in self-centered but as foci of connection to each other, the community, the planet, and the universe. Holistic educators are among the very first to affirm the ecological consciousness that stresses the vulnerable but vital interconnections among all forms of life, and teachers have much more to contribute to the struggle to sustain and nourish Mother Earth. Holistic educators are also unique in their insistent and heartfelt invitation to joyously celebrate the wonders of creation and the continuous miracle of life. This optimism, hope, determination, and energy are literally refreshing and renewing, a much-needed antidote for the nay sayers and grumps of the likes of me.

I also urge holistic educators to extend another one of their unique capacities, that is, the genius of being able to reach out and touch others. In this case to help to break down the barriers among other educators committed to transformation albeit with differing orientations, such as those in critical pedagogy, feminist groups, and those working in the area of curriculum criticism. Perhaps their concern for wholeness and their openness and optimism could enable them to be a principal catalyst for more harmony, complementarity, synergy, and integration among like-minded educators. The burden for this responsibility clearly does not rest only on the shoulders of holistic educators since other groups must move away from their positions of smugness and preciousness and have the sense to broaden and deepen their understandings in dialogue with those they have not really encountered.

Having said all that, please indulge me as I return to my previous condition of fear and foreboding. Even as I celebrate the optimism of holistic educators I can't help but worry about the future. Do we have the time to rely on the emergence of a new collage, a transformed quilt, and a new whole? It is true that there have been dire predictions of calamity in all ages, and it is true that we have survived any number of catastrophes. But it is also plausible that we may be running out of lives and that we ought to be extremely careful that we not be taken in by our resistance to wolf crying. Many ecologists indeed have said that it is already too late to save the planet, and many social critics see the inevitability of permanent violence and war created by the increasing gulf between haves and have-nots as exacerbated by the population explosion and the depletion of the earth's resources. Our educational task surely includes providing a critical awareness of our condition, but perhaps our most pressing immediate task as educators is the development of a pedagogy of hope and possibility. All of us need to wrestle with this task and to probe within ourselves to find a source of renewing and reenergizing our own faith and hope without denying the magnitude of the dangers we face. As for me I find such energy in the prophetic traditions of the Bible and in its modern manifestations such as liberation theology. This tradition combines criticism and affirmation, anguish and hope, humanity and the spirit, this world and eternity. Reinhold Niebuhr has characterized the Biblical prophets as being able to "be confident that life is good in spite of its evil and that it is evil in spite of the good and in this way both sentimentality and despair are avoided." The prophetic tradition emphasizes a continuous collaboration between humanity and God in which both humans and God are free but interdependent and in which people are responsible to fulfill a divine destiny. I have to admit to some nervousness in using the G word, especially in an academic setting and given my own wavering agnosticism. Harvey Cox has helped me in this regard by suggesting this formulation:

"God [is]" whatever it is within the vast spectacle of cosmic evolution which inspires and supports the endless struggle for liberation, not just from tyranny but from all bondages. 'God' is that power which despite all setbacks never admits to final defeat" (Cox, 1973).

With that concept of God in mind, let me close with yet another quote from a theologian, this time the eminent Jewish scholar, Jacob Neusner. Neusner has translated and written a commentary on a book from the Talmud usually titled *Sayings of Our Fathers* but which Neusner translates as *Torah from Our Sages*. In a section discussing the insights of Rabbi Hillel, Neusner points to issues of hope as he examines Hillel's insistence that over time "God corrects the imbalances of life—pays back the evil and rewards the good." Although Neusner readily admits that this is hardly a description of reality, he goes on to say:

"We, for our part, must preserve that same hope for justice, even in the face of despair. We have to believe, despite the world, that God cares. . . . But part of the meaning of having faith in God is believing there is justice when we see injustice, believing there is meaning when we face what seems an empty accident. Ours is not a time for complex explanation. We cannot appeal to how things come out right in the end. We have been through too much. Ours is an age that demands simple faith—or no faith at all. All the standard explanations have—proved empty. But Hillel's also was an age that gave no more evidence than it does now that God rules with justice. Yet Hillel said it, and so must we: against it all, despite it all. There is no alternative" (Neusner, 1994).

References

Brueggemann, Walter, 1994. Texts Under Negotiation: *The Bible and Postmodern Imagination*. Minneapolis: Fortress Press.

Cox, Harvey, 1973. *The Seduction of the Spirit*. New York: Simon and Schuster.

Harman, Willis. Interview on audio tape, Noetic Institute, 1991.

Part Three

EDUCATION IN A SPIRITUAL VOICE

Social Justice, Curriculum, and Spirituality

Preface

There are times moments when I find the culture's extraordinary reluctance to respond honestly to the realities of social injustice to be ironic and troubling but most of the time, I am horrified and outraged. As I write, we have just finished a Presidential campaign that the press criticized as dull; in which the incumbent glowed about his tough stand on crime and his pride in "ending welfare as we know it"; while one of his opponents delighted in attacking affirmative action and immigration and the other candidate seemed to be overcome with anguish over the public deficit. There was virtually no mention of poverty or racism; no reference to hunger and homelessness; no sense of outrage at unnecessary human suffering. Instead of debate on the plight of the homeless there were ploys to attract soccer moms; the war on poverty had been replaced by a crusade for middle-class tax relief.

Meanwhile, mainstream educators seem to be focused on devising more sophisticated testing and tighter control mechanisms and many educational critics are engaged in fierce battles over the fate of the universe and the nature of deconstructionism. Some educational visionaries would have us believe that what we really need in education is an end to dualistic thinking and a consciousness of spiritual oneness with nature and the universe. While politicians spin, educators test, critics reflect, and theorists parse, there are people eating dog food, teenagers turning tricks, children dealing in drugs, and families living in boxes. I say all this because I believe that it is intolerable that there be any educational discourse without continuous reference to the presence of the pain and suffering that is rooted in human greed, irresponsibility, and callousness.

The Rise and Fall of Curriculum

Although the field of curriculum theory has been declared moribund, it is perhaps fairer to say that it appears that many theorists have given up on the notion that reforming the formal school curriculum is the key to social, if not educational reform. In response to this disenchantment with curriculum development, much of what goes on in the name of curriculum discourse today tends to be mostly highly theoretical and ideological in nature. The vacuum of dialogue on what should we teach has been largely filled with discussion of instructional and assessment issues. Indeed, it would appear that even the politicians have discovered the language of the hidden curriculum as they call for an education that responds to the concerns of competing in the global economy and for "a return to values." The once powerful demands for more demanding science, history, and math courses as well as for a more academic curriculum now seem like part of ancient history.

Herbert Kliebard has helped to clarify how the various curriculum controversies have been played out in the schools historically. It is his position that the story of twentieth century American school curriculum can be seen as the struggle among four broad competing educational groups:

"First there were the humanists, the guardians of an ancient tradition tied to the powers of reason and the finest elements of Western cultural heritage. . . . [The second group] "led the drive for a curriculum reformed along the lines of a natural order of development of the child" . . . based on scientific data. [Third, there are] "the social efficiency educators . . . also imbued with the power of science but, their priorities lay with creating a coolly efficient, smoothly running society. . . ."

Finally, there were the social meliorists who felt that "new social conditions did not demand an obsessional fixation on the child and on child psychology; nor did the solution lie in simply ironing out the inefficiencies in the existing social order, The answer lay in the power of the schools to create a new social order"(Kliebard 1986, 23–25).

Kliebard's conclusion is that none of these orientations ever became dominant as the schools tried to accommodate to pressures from each of these groups: "In the end, what became the American curriculum was not the result of any decisive victory by any of the contending parties, but a loose, largely unarticulated, and not very tidy compromise" (Kliebard, p. 25).

This typology helps us to see that the continuity of our educational concerns as important aspects of these orientations can be easily detected in contemporary dialogue on educational policy. Surely, for example, the debate on multicultural education reflects the agenda of what Kliebard calls "the humanists," and certainly critical pedagogy is very much in the tradition of the "social meliorists." However, there are other forces in American culture that influence the curriculum which are not as apparent in this formulation. For example, the persistence of the arts and athletics in the standard curriculum over time cannot be explained entirely or even largely by these four orientations. There is also the recurring phenomenon of using the curriculum as a vehicle for promoting nationalism (patriotism) and/or ideology (democracy), and the term "social efficiency" only begins to suggest the current obsession with competing in the global economy.

Underneath and cutting across these four approaches and their variations are what I would term fundamental educational imperatives, in which we are called upon, nay commanded, to earnestly and conscientiously pursue certain ideals. The most familiar and enduring cultural formulation of such imperatives urges us to seek "the True, the Good, and the Beautiful." Others would want to add to these commandments the injunction to pursue Meaning. These commandments are so profoundly revered and have become so powerfully internalized that they have come to constitute the spiritual foundations of education. Put another way, no matter what the specific educational goals may be, there is the underlying demand that we reach these goals without violating the canons of these fundamental imperatives.

Today, perhaps the single most powerful and pervasive of these educational commandments is "Thou Shalt Seek the Truth." In modern times, truth has come to be typically defined as accurate and precise knowledge; information that can be verified through empirical and/or logical processes. The triumph of Enlightenment thought is testimony to the primacy of this imperative, with its basically unchallenged demands for precision, proof, reason, analysis, detachment, and skepticism. We are enjoined to seek this kind of Truth, however difficult and unsettling it may be and regardless of the consequences, presumably in the faith that the Truth will make us free. Not only is this pursuit presented as a moral and aesthetic imperative but as a pragmatically essential dimension of creating a progressive civilization. If nothing else, American education is about preserving and enhancing the intellectual and aesthetic processes of pursuing this kind of Truth. Critics and defenders of the educational status quo unite in their dedication to the values of critical rationality insofar as they give us valid information and knowledge that at least approaches the Truth. Our schools and universities constantly test for accuracy and precision, for right answers, and for the presence of compelling evidence. Indeed, the mottoes of two of our oldest and most prestigious universities—Harvard and Yale—are simply and boldly translated as *"Truth."*

This is surely not to say that the school curriculum centers on the acquisition of knowledge for its own sake, or that universities are singularly committed to the search for Truth. What I am saying is that whatever the social and cultural goals may be (job training, national solidarity, human development, social change, personal fulfillment, etc.), we are deeply committed to pursuing them within a context of intellectual integrity. i.e., we all want to be sure to be accurate, precise, rational, and knowledgeable. Indeed, at the cost of appearing to be gratuitous, I want to reaffirm my own strong commitment to an education strongly rooted in reason and rationality.

Having said all that, it is also clear that such an education is not without criticism. There are those who insist on the validity and significance of other ultimate goals such as wisdom or goodness. It is also clear that although knowledge and intellectual acuity may be necessary, they are surely not sufficient conditions for wisdom and goodness. Our history has made it painfully clear that smart people can do hateful things and that the impulse to be cruel and callous is not significantly mitigated by acquiring knowledge or analytic skills. Even more troubling is the phenomenon of people deliberately utilizing knowledge (truth) for destructive purposes. The design and production of Zyklon B, napalm, and land mines require the same degree of intellectual mastery as the design and production of antibiotics and computers. Manipulation requires as much insight as does enlightenment; knowledge of the how people learn is as useful to the wizards of Madison Avenue as it is to the gurus of Sesame Street.

There is, of course, another strong educational tradition that seeks to go beyond the pursuit of information and knowledge, namely that of the pursuit of Meaning. In this tradition, knowledge is an important dimension of this pursuit and Truth is thought to be metaphysical in nature. Abraham Joshua Heschel expresses this orientation eloquently:

"Socrates taught us that a life without thinking is not worth living. . . . Thinking is a noble effort, but the finest thinking may end in futility. . . . The Bible taught us that life without commitment is not worth living; that thinking without roots will bear flowers but no fruit. . . . Our systems of education stress the importance of enabling the student to exploit the power aspect of reality. . . . We teach the children how to measure, how to weigh! We fail to teach to revere, how to sense wonder and awe . . ., the sense of the sublime, [and] the sign of the inward greatness of the human soul" (Heschel 1955, 36, 216).

Postmodernism: The Worm in the Apple

It is surely not for me to enter into the seemingly interminable and torturous scholarly debate about the meaning and significance of this concept except to be clear on what I make of all this hullabaloo. Beyond all the smoke of battle and prolixity is the harsh reality of a very serious crisis of authority. We have come to see more and more clearly how much of our understanding of the world is contingent on such matters as history, culture, gender, class, and above all, language, and how much we have been confusing universal truth with particularist interpretation. The very tools of Enlightenment thinking itself have, ironically enough, undermined its most basic and profound project—that of affording human liberation through reason, objectivity, science, technology, and detachment, a project now described by many postmodernists as delusional.

This critique goes beyond eroding our epistemological grounding (as fundamental as that is) and extends to questioning the nature of and commitment to our core moral aspirations. It would appear that not only have we committed the sin of being wrong about the nature of Truth, but we have compounded that sin by utilizing these errors in such a way as to provide privilege and advantage to some. What is involved is not only the sin of intellectual arrogance but the evil of political oppression. Walter Brueggemann puts it this way:

"The practice of modernity . . . has given us a world imagined through the privilege of white, male, Western, colonial hegemony with all its pluses and minuses. It is a world that we have come to trust and take for granted. It is a world that has wrought great good, but also has accomplished enormous mischief against some for the sake of others. The simple truth is that this constructed world can no longer be sustained, is no longer persuasive or viable, and we are able to discern no larger image to put in its place. . . . The imagined world of privilege and disparity is treasured by all who live in the advantaged West. It is treasured more by men than women, more by whites than blacks, but all of us in the West have enormous advantage" (Brueggemann, 1994, 18–20).

The notions of the social construction of knowledge, the close relationships between power arrangements and constructions of reality, and the problematics of essentialist formulations, although surely not new, have had a profound effect on all cultural institutions, including education. What we face amounts to an intellectual and moral crisis that comes in a most importune time of enormous peril from the forces of greed, divisiveness, and hatred. What we urgently need is a common understanding of our plight and a common vision that can save us from ourselves. In a time when we seek community, we are confronted with the realities of its ambiguities and problematics; at a time when we long for authentic identity, we are required to face the indictment of essentialism; in a time when we feel impelled to speak out at the injustices inflicted on marginal groups, we must deal with the ways in which the definition of these groups has been deconstructed; and in a time when we search for the moral vision to sustain us through despair and cynicism, we must confront new insights on how ideology impinges on our moral quests.

The implications for education are deeply troubling, for as we have indicated, underlying the various curricular approaches has been the profound commitment to the pursuit of Truth in the more restricted sense of critical rationality and/or the metaphysical sense of ultimate meaning. Much of postmodern thought would seem to undermine both of these quests. If truth is an illusion and meaning a delusion, then what are we to teach other than basic literacy, numeracy, and the conversation-ending assertions of postmodernism? How do we make a rational and coherent plan for education when many brilliant theorists make a compelling case that rationality and moral coherence are no more than charming fictions?

Enter Spirituality

It is hardly surprising that in an atmosphere of political, moral, and intellectual crisis we as a culture would look to the spiritual as a path toward sanity and hope. The extraordinary surge of interest in matters religious and spiritual is as deep as it is broad, expressing itself not only in religious fundamentalism and New Age spiritualism but in such movements as liberation theology, feminist theology, and Jewish renewal as well as in such phenomena as alternative approaches to healing and to organizational management.

This interest has also manifested itself in education, as reflected in the recent publication and popularity of a growing number of articles and books on spirituality and education. There are a growing number of authors like Dwayne Huebner, Jeffrey Kane, Kathleen Kesson, James Moffett, Ron Miller, Parker Palmer, and Douglas Sloan who are writing directly on issues at the intersection of education and spirituality. There are also other major curriculum theorists whose works surely are spiritual in nature even though they do not necessarily use religious or spiritual language as their primary form of discourse. For example, Nel Noddings' daring and challenging work on caring and compassion speaks to matters of the spirit and to the centrality of human connectiveness while Jane Roland Martin's focus on nurturance, relationship, and responsibility is a powerful affirmation of the deep inner impulses for love and intimacy.

However, proclaiming the bond between education and spirituality does not begin to resolve our problems, since that only begs further questions. Whose spirituality? Which spirituality? How are we to accept the authority of particular spiritual orientations? In other words, the same critiques that have rendered other educational formulations problematic require us to examine critically the claims for a spiritually grounded education. Indeed, the history of religious and spiritual expression requires us to be specially alert to its particular problematics, e.g., the possibilities of dogmatism, zealotry, authoritarianism, and irrelevance. The whole notion of an education based on spiritual beliefs goes totally counter to what we have learned about the danger and implausibility of visions that emerge from "grand narratives."

And yet, the power of the spirit is the very energy we need lest we fall into the paralysis and cynicism that are the consequences of moral despair and intellectual confusion. Even as intellectuals scoff at facts as fictions, reform efforts as self-serving, and moral visions as pretentious, there is vast and needless human suffering in our midst. Millions of human beings are malnourished and maltreated; millions of people do not have adequate housing, medical care, and education; and the gap between rich and poor has grown to obscene proportions. Even more disheartening is the way that we as a people, nation, and profession have failed to begin to fully accept the depth and gravity of this human suffering, never mind taking responsibility for it. The problem is surely not rooted in a lack of understanding, knowledge, and information. There can be no doubt whatsoever that we know about the suffering and that we have the material and intellectual resources to significantly relieve if not eliminate it. However, the great irony and shame is that we cannot utilize the extraordinary knowledge and expertise that we have accumulated to meet our most profound moral commitments. This is largely but not entirely because the spirits of greed, suspicion, hate, and division are so pervasive and dominant in our culture.

The reality of immense human suffering is made even more unspeakable by its origins in human stupidity and cupidity, as our failure to redress these sins provides proof enough of our capacity to do evil. Surely, we have enough understanding of the intellectual underpinnings of our efforts at creating a just and loving society to make some judgments about them. As far as modernism is concerned, my view is that now is the time to proclaim that the long run has finally arrived and that it is terrible. And as far as postmodernism is concerned, all I have to say is that the misery and suffering of millions of people is not a socially constructed metaphor but is as real and certain as misery and suffering.

How then do we go on with our commitments in a time when we have clear responsibilities and fuzzy authority, and how do we generate hope and vision in an era of uncertainty, despair, and disenchantment? This is not merely a challenge that educators must address but one that requires creative and thoughtful responses from all aspects of our society and culture. One very helpful response has been presented by Walter Brueggemann in his book *Texts Under Negotiation*, in which he struggles with the implications of postmodernism for another influential cultural institution, the Christian church. After acknowledging the power and influence of postmodern thinking, he goes on to offer some suggestions on how the Church can sustain its efforts in the light of this disquieting critique without in any way loosening its commitment to its worldview based on divine creation and ultimate redemption:

". . . It is not, in my judgement, the work of the church . . . to construct a full alternative world, for that would be to act as preemptively and imperialistically as all those old construals and impositions. Rather, the task is a more modest one, [namely] . . . to *fund*—to provide the pieces, materials, and resources, out of which a new world can be imagined. Our responsibility, then, is not a grand scheme or a coherent system, but the voicing of a lot of little pieces out of which people can put life together in fresh configurations" (Brueggemann, 1994, 22).

He goes on to urge his colleagues to create places of meeting where people can come together to share their "funds" but not to make "claims that are so large and comprehensive that they ring hollow in a context of our general failure, demise, and disease. It is rather a place where people come to receive new materials, or old materials freshly voiced, that will fund, feed, nurture, legitimate, and authorize a *counterimagination of the world* . . . an imagination that is not at all congenial to dominant intellectual or political modes" [emphasis in original] (Brueggemann, 23).

V. A Modest Funding Proposal
I want to move past all the postmodern handwringing about the nature of reality and truth as a troubling, interesting, and useful critique but one that is marginally relevant and fundamentally distracting to our moral responsibilities. Surely, the suffering and the pain are real enough and there is no great mystery about what is required to ease that suffering. In spite of this, one of the horrible ironies of the past few decades is a serious erosion in concern for social justice, e.g., concern for the poor and the homeless. Much of the responsibility for this lies with those who have chosen to see the poor as irresponsible, unskilled, and/or an impediment to the demands of a highly competitive global economy. However, the erosion has been heightened by the neglect of many of those who have traditionally been active in drawing attention to the plight of the poor, a neglect that is not so much the result of a change in moral conviction as it is a consequence of being distracted by other important concerns. Among such concerns are postmodern thought, cybernetics, and the ecological crisis, all matters of enormous import and significance. There are undoubtedly important connections among issues of social justice, computers, ecology, and postmodernism but my view is that priority for social justice has been significantly eroded, if not superseded. I reject the notion that we cannot pursue social justice till we get our epistemology right as well as the notion that issues of social justice must be seen only in the perspective of the fate of the universe. My point is not to discount the importance of such powerfully significant issues as the nature of truth, the impact of technology, or the preservation of the planet but only to argue that we not be held hostage to them or not allow ourselves to be distracted from our nonnegotiable, permanent, and solemn responsibility to work for the elimination of unnecessary human suffering.

At the same time, and in spite of the devastating postmodern critique, the commitment in the academy and among educators (conservatives as well as radicals) to the pursuit of knowledge and critical rationality seems as passionate and relentless as ever. The dedication to being rational, precise, accurate, perceptive; the solemn vows to conduct careful research and thoughtful inquiry; and the devotion to creating new knowledge and discovering the laws of nature constitute the ultimate raison d'être of contemporary formal education. One way or another, educators pay homage to this Holiest of Grails, for whether it's vocational education or critical pedagogy, whether it's a book report or a dissertation, a manifesto or a monograph, we want it to be grounded in the name of the Spirits of rationality, knowledge, and inquiry and meet their demands for accuracy, precision, and reliability.

My intention is by no means to reject these Spirits as false gods, only to put them in perspective and in their proper place. Let us begin with an examination of the aesthetic values of pursuing knowledge and understanding for their own sake. My sense is that even as educators and scholars embrace pragmatism and functionalism and as they make eloquent and poetic claims for the benefits of increased knowledge and understanding (e.g., as necessary for citizenship or for personal meaning) there remains an abiding love and passion for the search and accumulation of knowledge and understanding per se. This seems reasonable enough as an educational goal for the relatively limited number of people with that highly specialized sensibility, but hardly plausible as the Ground Zero of all curriculum being.

There is also the problematic nature of the pragmatic claims for knowledge since it has become eminently clear that even though highly knowledgeable and understanding people tend to be richer, more powerful, and more famous, they are also among the most dangerous and evil. This is certainly and emphatically not to say that smart equals bad, but only to say that it is often the case that people use their smarts to do bad things. Power in the United States is not in the hands of the illiterate and intellectually dense; I dare say that we would find a disproportionate number of highly educated (or at minimum, highly schooled) among the movers and shakers of Wall Street, Madison Avenue, Capitol Hill, Hollywood, and all the other power centers of our society and culture. It must also be said that many of the people who genuinely do serious good are also very knowledgeable and understanding. And that, my friends is the whole point.

At the very least, the persistence of such claims suggests that increasing knowledge and understanding is supposed to have some consequence over and above the fun and profit of simply finding and having it. The very simple and obvious "truth of the matter" is that education for increased knowledge and understanding should be

grounded in a deeper commitment to pursue a larger good than studying for its own sake. My own explanation as to why heightened understanding and knowledge continues to be used for bad things is that we
have not demanded that, if and when it is to be used, it be used *only*
for good things. I believe that there are three basic reasons why we
haven't made such demands:

1. Some of us genuinely like finding truth for its own sake.
2. Some of us really want to do bad things.
3. Some of us don't know the difference between good and bad.

To those in Group One, I offer respectful tolerance; to those in
Group Two I have only contempt, but to those in Group Three, I offer
some suggestions.

My most basic recommendation is that we ground our education
not in the pursuit and adoration of truth, knowledge, understanding,
insight, critical rationality, interpretive schema, or analytic tools, but
rather in a relentless and whole-hearted quest for the attitude formerly
known as *agape*. I say this because I have come to see the wisdom in
that all-time, oldest, and corniest of all clichés that it is only unconditional and dispassionate love that can truly overcome unnecessary
human suffering. It is a wisdom that persists across time and space in
spite of vulgarization and oversimplification and in the face of scorn,
ridicule, and cynicism, including more than my fair share. I am convinced that a people grounded in a consciousness of *agape* would end
most human misery even as I realize that such a statement is somewhat tautological as it can also be said that human misery is rooted in
lack of human caring and compassion. I am also very much aware that
a project for an education based on nourishing a human consciousness of agape is incredibly ambitious if not outrageously pretentious
or just plain impossible. However, I do not see such a project as any
less ambitious, impractical, pretentious, or possible than the Enlightenment project of human freedom through increased knowledge, understanding, and insight. Indeed, I believe that developing the capacity for understanding and insight alongside a commitment to nourishing
the capacity for love is a whole lot more practical than teaching people
only to be critical and thoughtful.

Mary Daly's definition is helpful:

"In the fullest sense, *agape* is God's love. It is generous love, not
appetitive in the sense that there is need to satisfy that in oneself
which is incomplete, not stimulated by or dependent upon that which

is loved. It is indifferent to value, seeking to confer good, rather than to obtain it. It is therefore, spontaneous and creative, and it is rooted in abundance rather than in poverty" (Daly, 1973, 210).

The idea that we as a people could attain such a consciousness seems remote, if not the stuff of delusion and fantasy. However, the idea that all people have the capacity for the development of an equally intense critical consciousness seems no less daunting and improbable. A major difference is that most educators as a matter of faith readily accept the call to work as if people have both the need and the potential to develop a critical consciousness, continually pressing students to stretch and expand their critical skills. Indeed, the educational project for the development of a critical consciousness is deeply embedded in the whole array of our curricular and instructional repertoire. It has been well organized and its elements subdivided into any number of categories, e.g., literacy and numeracy; the sciences and the humanities; writing skills, analytic and interpretive skills; research skills; reliance on theories of cognitive development; and the use of laboratories for experiments. The point here is that schools and universities approach the task of developing intellectual acumen not as a special program but as a Spirit that is to energize and permeate all aspects of its academic program with at least the implicit understanding that the effect of all the particular intellectual skills adds up to something more than the sum of its parts, i.e., a critical consciousness.

What I am suggesting here is parallel to that approach, i.e., not a special program or course in moral education or caring (although these are not unreasonable possibilities) but a larger, deeper, and more endemic commitment to the project of nourishing and demanding the enhancement of the human capacity to love. In doing so we also encounter problematics parallel to that of the commitment to develop critical consciousness, e.g., issues of definition, resistance, and complexity. As educators and citizens, we have the responsibility to continue to engage these issues and problems as difficult and perplexing as they are. It surely is not that we are without resources in such an endeavor for one of the marvels of human life is that people over time and across space have seriously and profoundly involved themselves with the question of how we are to live with each other with justice and love. As a result we have an extraordinary heritage of powerfully enduring ideas, images, and visions of love and social justice as well as the legacy of remarkable children, men, women, and groups who have endeavored to embody them.

It is easy enough to realize that many of these visions have been betrayed, that many of these formulations conflict with each other, and that much misery has been inflicted in their names. This is a reality that we must not ever deny or rationalize and one that represents a human potential for stupidity and cruelty that we dare not discount nor minimize. At the same time, and without blinking from the horrors of some of our best intentions, it must also be acknowledged that in spite of all the turmoil and divisiveness, there really does exist an important space of common moral affirmation in which there is a very large degree of consensus, even if some of this is limited to rhetoric. It is a space worthy of passionate embrace and zealous protection that is no less real but perhaps more vulnerable than the privilege, domination, and greed occupied by the space of human conflict. These items of consensus are admittedly general, perhaps ambiguous and even vague; yet their very persistence in spite of the intellectual and empirical battering they have taken is nothing short of miraculous.

Perhaps the most basic and most profound is our belief in the preciousness of life itself and in that context, our affirmation of the right of every person to a life of dignity and respect. I really do believe that we believe this even though there are reservations to this commitment. For example, there are those that say that certain people, like serial killers, child molesters, and rapists, should be excluded from this affirmation by virtue of the unforgivable nature of their crimes. I admit to my own deep ambivalence about forgiving and affirming such people, but I am clear that we should not let the worst of the world shape our moral visions and am equally clear that the vast majority of us are not vicious and hateful criminals. As educators, we can surely affirm the dignity of children, even if we are perplexed and grieved when some of them act out in anger and violence. At the very least, we can reaffirm our commitment to enhancing the dignity of those students who are not hateful and continue to struggle with how to respond to those who are.

These reservations notwithstanding, the roots for the affirmation of life with dignity run very deep and wide in our history and in our religious, spiritual, and moral traditions. They are embraced, surely in a variety of discourses, by people of all faiths, colors, denominations, classes, genders, ethnicities, creeds, and epistemological preferences. Such affirmation is reflected in the Bible, in the Koran, in the Declaration of Independence, the U.S. Constitution, the Gettysburg Address, the Pledge of Allegiance, although regretfully, they are not exactly prominent in Goals 2000. Indeed, the United Nations Universal Declaration of Human Rights (which all member nations are required to uphold) begins with this assertion:

"*Whereas* recognition of the inherent dignity and of the equal and inalienable rights of all members of the human family is the foundation of freedom, justice, and peace in the world, . . ." Later on in the preamble,the statement goes on to require that "every individual and every organ of society, keeping this declaration constantly in mind,shall strive by teaching and education to promote respect for these rights and freedoms and by progressive measures, national and international, to secure their universal and effective recognition and observance."

However, educators bent on connecting curriculum-making with such stirring discourse need to be reminded of the dangers of grand narratives and magisterial programs. As Walter Brueggemann points out in support of his notion of "funding the pieces, materials, and resources out of which a new world can be imagined. . . . What is yearned for among us is not new doctrine or new morality, but new world, new self, new future. The new world is not given whole, any more than the new self is given abruptly in psychotherapy. It is given only a little at a time, one miracle at a time, one poem at a time, one healing, one promise, one commandment. Over time these pieces are stitched together into a sensible collage, stitched together, all of us in concert, but each of us idiosyncratically, stitched together in a new whole—all things new" (Brueggemann, 1994, 24–25).

I would like to suggest a few such pieces of the collage that certainly can give us direction and an agenda. Firstly, the concepts of agape or unconditional love are at once daunting and controversial, laden with so much baggage that it can be a non-starter. We might begin more modestly and perhaps more realistically by taking Charity James suggestion of substituting the concept of "respect" for the notion of agape as a goal of education. She has this to say:

"Swami Muktananda teaches that the true *dharma* (way, path, religion in the non-dogmatic sense) is to 'welcome one another with great respect and love.' I find this helpful because respect is more difficult for the ego to fool around with than is love or compassion. It seems to be a truly manageable proposition to build an institution and a process on an ethic of uncompromised mutual respect. And of course if we make (and encourage) the steady practice of respecting others, the privilege, the great attainment, of loving will increasingly flow toward us" (James, 1980, 8).

This adds up to respect for life itself and for the affirmation of human dignity for all. In order to move such an affirmation beyond mere rhetoric, I suggest that we can agree on some minimum standards of what it means concretely to affirm human dignity. These standards not only help to define basic human dignity but they also serve as part of the conditions under which individuals can find meaning and fulfillment. I want to suggest standards that are not only consistent and resonant with our consensual moral commitments but are also eminently and immediately technologically, logistically, and materially doable. They are simultaneously simple and profound, traditional and radical, spiritual, and material:

Every person should have enough to eat. Every person should have adequate shelter. Every person should have proper health care. Every person should be afforded dignity and respect. Every person has the responsibility to participate in efforts to ensure that these requirements are met.

Notice that I have *not* said every person should have the opportunity to *pursue* adequate diet, shelter, and health—these are not areas that are to be left to chance or the market, nor are they to be rationed as scarce commodities or awarded as prizes, but instead are the inherent and inviolable rights afforded by membership in our community. There are important questions, of course, as to what constitutes adequate diet, shelter, and medical care, and there are legitimate questions concerning the conditions under which individuals can be said to forfeit these rights. Important as these questions are, they are still marginal ones and are no excuse to put everything else on hold. The uncontested dignity of the vast majority of human beings should not be held hostage to the very few who try our patience. In summary then, we can, at least partially, fund what Brueggemann calls "that which can help us to imagine a new world" by grounding our educational program in the commitment to respect human life by ensuring adequate food, shelter, and health care for all, with the understanding that there are unsettled questions, problems, and policies that need to be debated within that commitment.

For educators, generally speaking, this would mean that the Spirit of this commitment would pervade the rhetoric, consciousness, and energy of the schools to the point that it would be taken for granted and assimilated as much as the Spirits of critical rationality and the accumulation of knowledge are. Indeed, the decisions on content selection and instructional emphases would be largely driven by the con-

cern for which bodies of knowledge, which research skills, which resources, and which attitudes are most likely to further the commitment to human dignity.

More particularly, schools would be required to examine their policies, rules, and regulations on the basis of their consonance with this
commitment. To make them consonant would surely mean drastic
changes in these policies and rules, which by itself tells us a great
deal. For example, what does it mean to have a grading system at all
in a situation where we are endeavoring to promote deep and profound respect and dignity for all? Imagine the impact on the schools if
all students, faculty, and staff were required to treat each other with
utmost respect. Imagine what the effect would be if that policy was
considered as vital and enforced as firmly as the policies forbidding
violence and drugs in the school. How affirming this would be for
those educators who have devoted their lives to honoring their students as precious and unique beings.

This is surely not to say that such a process is without controversy
and difficulty since it would certainly and very quickly generate any
number of torturous and anguishing dilemmas since we would have to
constantly consider what most deeply and truly constitutes and en-
hances human dignity. However, this is not essentially different from
the complex and contradictory problems that educators face currently,
the difference being one of focus and priority. Moreover, it cannot be
but enormously beneficial that educational discourse be driven by the
heuristic of vigorous dispute and argument over which educational
policies are most likely to enhance human dignity!

Further, we would need an educational psychology less concerned
with instruction, measurement, and evaluation and more with the conditions under which people can learn to love and respect themselves
and each other. We would need to have more research that delves into
the human impulses for community, compassion, and social justice,
and there would need to be more analysis and understanding of the
forces that disrupt those impulses. Our history needs to be enriched
with more of the language, stories, and images of the costly and courageous struggles for social justice that sanctifies our past, gives energy to the present, and provides hope for the future. Our art can be
the vehicle not only for self-expression and the evocation of form but
also as the creative and imaginative processes that can give voice,
shape, and image to the community of justice, love, and joy for which
we so ache. Indeed, our failure to create communities of justice and
love is not so much a reflection of the failure of the intellect but of the

failure of the imagination to envision a life where both freedom and equality can flourish.

The commandments to seek Truth and the processes that facilitate it would be replaced by the commandments to seek Justice and the arts and sciences that yield it. To pursue the pleasures of the mind while there are bodies in pain is to be seen as aberrational rather than quaint, more as an indication of self-indulgence than as a sign of grace. We must be mindful, however, that both minds and bodies are terrible things to waste. The capacity for love can only mature when it is nurtured and enhanced by the enormous powers of human rationality, imagination, and creativity. In this way, education becomes the integration of body, mind, and spirit.

A Last Word

I accept as a matter of course that life is extremely complicated, contradictory, and messy and I have spent a great deal of my career learning, teaching, and writing about the incredible tangle of ambivalence, uncertainty, and perplexity that is involved in dealing with educational issues. I have, inevitably, also come to learn about the problematics of problematics, particularly in their capacity to obscure and paralyze and so I come not to praise complexity but to give it a rest. Some very important issues are quite clear and eminently simple:

No person should have to go hungry, homeless, or without health care. We have the material and logistical capacity to make this possible. In spite of this, millions endure the pain and humiliation of hunger, homelessness, and poor health.

I would submit that these facts be the dominant and underlying elements of *all* discussions and debates on educational policies and practices. The realities of widespread unnecessary human suffering should replace issues of competing in the global economy, of accountability, of computer instruction, of school-based management, of multicultural education, even of critical pedagogy, eco-feminism, and spirituality as the starting and ending points of any and all educational dialogue. It is inconceivable to me that we could do otherwise than be constantly aware of and attentive to the shameful way we have reneged on our most profound commitments and responsibilities to our brothers and sisters.

Let us not ask how the problems of human misery illumine and demonstrate the importance of our favorite specialized projects like success in the global economy, accountability, computer instruction, school-based management, multi-cultural education, critical pedagogy, eco-feminism, or spirituality. Let us, instead, reaffirm our commitment to human dignity for all and insist that before anything else, all people should have enough to eat, adequate shelter, and proper health care. I believe very strongly that there are educational processes that can significantly contribute to these goals and that we should concentrate our energies on them as our number one priority. There is no number two.

It may be useful to see this task and responsibility as "spiritual" rather than "educational" since it does raise and reflect the most profound questions of existence. What is the origin of this intense impulse for social justice that is so pervasive across time and space? Why do we have this urge to seek meaning and to link the details of our everyday world with visions of the sacred? Asking and responding to such questions are spiritual acts in themselves. When we sense the pain of suffering, the ache of responsibility, and the joy of justice we are surely in the presence of Mystery.

Heschel helps us to clarify this phenomenon:

"To the speculative mind, the world is an enigma; to the religious mind, the world is a challenge. The speculative problem is impersonal; the religious problem is a problem addressed to the person. The first is concerned with finding an answer to the question: what is the cause of being? The second, with giving an answer to the question: What is asked of us? . . . In spite of our pride, in spite of our acquisitiveness, we are driven by an awareness that something is asked of us; that we are asked to wonder, to revere, think, and to live in a way that is compatible with the grandeur and mystery of living. What gives birth to religion is not intellectual curiosity but the fact and experience of our being asked" (Heschel, pp. 111–112).

Within this Mystery is an astonishing Truth: We are asked to regard each other as sisters and brothers, to be their keepers, to strive to respect, if not love them, at minimum not to hurt them, and surely to provide for them. An education grounded in that Mystery and Truth is light years away from the mean-spirited and vulgar spirit of our operating educational model. Nor, it must be said, does this educational vision guarantee a cosmic consciousness. Yet it provides a perspective that is both practical in its application and idealistic in its hopes; doable in its possibilities and daring in its aspirations; traditional in its roots and radical in its critique.

The opportunity to develop a pedagogy of human dignity is an awesome one for it goes beyond our *professional* obligations to our *human* responsibilities as co-creators of our world. What makes it so exhilarating is its very awesomeness, i.e., the opportunity to match human capacities with a sacred vision, to engage in a task that is grand *and* realizable, and to make the educational process truly redemptive, not merely profitable.

References

Brueggemann, Walter. 1994. *Texts under negotiation: the Bible and postmodern imagination*. Minneapolis: Fortress Press.

Daly, Mary. *"Love"* in *Dictionary of history of ideas*. vol. 2, 1973. New York: Charles Scribner.

Heschel, Abraham Joshua. 1955. *God in search of man*. New York: Farrar, Straus, and Giroux.

James, Charity. *Spirituality and education*. Unpublished manuscript, 1980.

Kliebard, Herbert. 1986. *The struggle for the American curriculum*. Boston: Routledge and Kegan Paul.

Education as Sacrament

This essay represents a talk I gave at a meeting of a group of lay and religious people involved in a process of integrating the ideals of the Order of the Sacred Heart into their schools. This process was a very serious and determined effort to make profound and lasting changes in Sacred Heart schools on five continents, an effort that eventually produced a report with detailed (and controversial) recommendations. I was deeply moved by the dedication and commitment of those involved with this project, which was not merely directed at amelioration and reform but at radical transformation rooted in a vision of justice and love.

It is a genuine privilege and blessing to have the opportunity to participate in this truly extraordinary endeavor by the Society of the Sacred Heart and the Network of Sacred Heart Schools to deepen and make real their deepest and most cherished religious and moral commitments. This endeavor not only provides educators interested in grounding their work in a transcendent moral and spiritual vision with a powerful and compelling model, but even more importantly, offers vital energy and hope to those struggling for a better world. Make no mistake, education is indeed about making or not making a better world and one of the most important contributions made by Sacred Heart educators is that they, unlike almost all other educational leaders, make this goal explicit, clear, and central. Indeed, one of the great scandals of the present public and professional dialogue on education is the way we have successfully disguised our most fundamental crises by trivializing them, by converting the profound struggle for meaning into the vulgar pursuit of competitive advantage.

John Dewey said that education was about "creating a world" an echo of the tradition which impels humans to fulfill the promise of creation through the struggle for a life of love, justice, peace, and joy. Without for a minute denying or minimizing the complexity of educational policies and practices, it would seem that there ought to be no doubt that the purpose of *all* institutions and endeavors, including education, should therefore be to meet that very commitment, i.e., to create a world embedded with our deepest and most cherished hopes. This broad and universal human responsibility is, in the American experience, further enriched by the ultimate connection between education and democracy. Let us also be reminded here that democracy—a political theory—is rooted in the moral and spiritual notion that every person is inherently worthy and that all persons are equally deserving of dignity.

While all this may sound obvious if not cloyingly familiar, let me quote André Gide: "It *is* true that everything has already been said. But it is also true that nobody was listening, so it must be said again." What must be said again is that the educational process in all institutions, especially schools and universities, needs to be rooted in the commitment to build a democratic society that makes possible lives of meaning in the context of a caring, just, and joyful community. This must not only be repeated but also be said with strong reaffirmation, and not only because people haven't been listening but because, tragically and scandalously, our society and culture seem bent on creating quite a different world, one of hierarchy, privilege, inequity, injustice, moral callousness, personal gain, and international competition. So while we might all accept Dewey's notion that education is about creating a world, we must extend the analysis beyond definition and description to the more basic and important moral question, namely, what *kind* of world do we wish to create?

Alas, the dominant streams of education policy and practice run not in the currents of love, justice, and joy but in the straits of inequity and competition. This situation is all the more tragic because it corrodes the true spirit of the impulse to teach. My view is that educators find themselves, for the most part, to be unwitting and naïve accomplices to those who are bent on perpetuating a society and culture that is in sharp conflict with our deeply felt moral and spiritual vision. Even worse, many educators and many in the public sphere are not even aware of the chasm between the dominant educational ideas and our highest aspirations as a people. Indeed, many educators in their haste and pride to be professional and knowledgeable, i.e., to be experts, actually deny the social, cultural, moral, and religious implications of educational policy and practice. What we have is a powerful and awesome coalition between those committed to the political, social, and economic status quo and those who insist on sticking their collective heads into the blinding muck of neutrality and objectivity.

This situation is perhaps best illustrated by a highly influential document, a report that gave fuel to what is called our current educational reform movement. I have in mind the report *A Nation at Risk,* commissioned and endorsed by the Department of Education during the Reagan Administration. This document, ostensibly directed at making basic educational changes, offers an extremely revealing picture of the essentially unchallenged assumptions about the purpose and nature of American education. First of all there is the title—*A Nation at Risk*—not a culture or society at risk; not a people at risk, not democracy at risk, not justice, equality, or even a way of life, but the Nation. Clearly the highest priority is given to the nation state, and the report is all about how the educational system has failed to respond to the needs of the state. Never mind the irony that this comes from an Administration elected on a platform that identified the government not as the solution but as the problem.

Not only does the report arrogantly and blithely posit the role of education as servant to the state, but, incredibly enough, it blames the schools for the nation's crises. The report in effect says: The nation is at risk! Fix the schools!! This position is outrageous and supercilious because it assumes not only that the educational system is the root of the problem, but even more disingenuously, that this system is autonomous and independent. What is crucial here is to remind ourselves are educators not only, for the most part, under the political control of powerful public groups, but also that the values, attitudes, and consciousness of educational institutions necessarily and inevitably reflect the values, attitudes, and consciousness of the larger dominant society and culture. How could it be otherwise? How could an institution with millions of Americans drawn from every class, constituency, area, and group be so isolated and autonomous from public consciousness? The imperative—fix the schools—seems to say that we wish to make significant changes in our society by not changing anything *except* what goes on in schools. It would be easy to write off such thinking as shoddy and shallow (which it certainly is), but more importantly it does reflect a very deep reality about dominant views on education. The nation is akin to that of the lord of a vast estate who takes his servants to task for problems that interfere with the smooth running of the estate, problems like broken fences, missing livestock, and dirty rugs. The Lord is irate at these lapses and admonishes the servants for being lax, if not slothful. Educators are expected similarly to solve problems posed by their overseers, to afford technical solutions to issues defined by the wise and powerful.

The heart of the report, however, is how the authors define the nature of the risk that the nation is at. What are the crises that make our leaders tremble? What is it that should lead educators to contriteness and shame? What threatens the very core of our life? What threatens the republic and the American way of life?

The crises according to the report are twofold and both crises are united by a concern for national domination. The first threat is perceived as the challenge to our preeminence as a world power in the deadly arena of geopolitics. Here the major competition was the Soviet Union, although this particular threat to our hegemony seems to have evaporated. The other major threat is economic and pertains to America's standing in the race for profits, and here our enemy/competitors have been Japan and Germany, but now include the European Union and the Asian Tiger nations. In a word, our nation was considered to be at risk because we might not be number one in the international political and economic realm, and hence our nation's highest priority was to widen our lead and in some cases catch up with the threats of the time.

The report also maintains that at the root of the crisis is an educational system mired in mediocrity and permissiveness populated by dazed and under qualified teachers working hard but ineffectively with stupefied students bent on a life of drugs, sex, and rock and roll. The solution is obvious—educators and students need to get their act together, and the honest, God-fearing, hardworking public needs to exercise its indignation at the mess and support the painful but necessary task of serious reform. The basic message for educators was quite simple and direct: Students need to know more, work harder, be more obedient, and above all else, be tougher competitors. The code word for this was "excellence," an interesting and effective use of a concept that produces a warm glow in most people. There are, of course, many shades of meaning in the concept including the Greek concept of *arete* which refers to the importance of striving to fulfil the sacred within each person. Alas, excellence in *A Nation at Risk* is not about being godlike but about inter-personal and international competition, that is, about encouraging people to excel at the expense of others.

The response of Tweedle-Dum—i.e., the dominant voice of the established profession was inevitably, Yes indeed! Me too! You bet! In less time that it takes to switch band wagons, the profession was ready with its expert counsel for programmatic change based, of course, on careful research. The basic elements of the professional response included: more sophisticated tests to be given more often; stricter modes of accountability; longer school days and years; more requirements; emphasis on mastery, competencies, and the acquisition of particular bits of knowledge; increased requirements for teacher certification; testing of teachers, and refined techniques, tied to merit pay, for evaluating teachers. In short, a program of tighter control, intensified competition, hard work, and a severely narrowed and truncated conception of education.

There were other responses, albeit muted, scattered, and discounted. Some were outraged to see our crises framed in the context of developing a competitive international edge. For these people, there were far more compelling crises, indeed, crises that are to a large measure the consequences of the very competition that we were being asked to intensify. I share the belief that our most serious crises involve the staggering degree of worldwide poverty, hunger, and homelessness; that our very existence is threatened by economic greed and moral callousness; and that our security is made dangerously vulnerable by the arms race, the proliferation of chemical and nuclear weapons, the intensification of nationalism and chauvinism and the ecological ravaging of the planet.

As a citizen I am appalled by the arrogance reflected in *A Nation at Risk*, a report that reeks with an obsession with power, control, domination, and certainty. As an educator, I am dismayed by the timidity and disingenuousness of the professional establishment in its zeal to do its master's bidding. As a profession, we ought to, and I believe do, know better, in every sense of that phrase.

The public response was even more disheartening although it should not have been a surprise, because the authors of *A Nation at Risk* report were astute enough to gauge the political winds and cynical enough to fan them. The report, at least in its broad assumptions and conclusions, seems to have resonated with public frustration with the schools and fears for their families' future. It is surely understandable that people would have these concerns and worries. The dominant culture, however, seems to have swallowed the whole package—that our priorities should be to increase our competitive stance with other nations and that the schools need to be tougher and more rigorous. The public opinion seems, by and large, to favor programs of increased testing, tighter controls, and stiffer requirements.

I have discussed what I believe to be the dominant thrust of what is called the educational reform movement for two reasons: first, because this movement is extremely important and influential, and secondly, because it offers a powerful point of contrast with the extraordinary efforts of the Society of the Sacred Heart and the Network. This contrast not only reveals a difference in educational strategy and beliefs, but, more importantly, it sharply illumines contrasting notions of what kind of world we ought to create. One perspective speaks to the perpetuation of a world grounded in hierarchy, competition, and material success, while the other is informed by a spirit that seeks justice, love, and community.

Perhaps the single most famous sentence in *A Nation at Risk* is the following: "Our once unchallenged preeminence in commerce, industry, science, and technological innovations is being overtaken by competitors throughout the world." The authors of this report look out at the world and see hostile competitors threatening our superiority. Their counterparts in the Sacred Heart Order look out at the world and see a far different scene:

"In every corner of the world, we see the same images. They are world images of crises, broken promises and broken people, cultural domination, oppression of women, disintegrating social fabric, militarism. Images of despair across all age lines, unemployment, racism, economic exploitation, violence, images of drugs, broken families, meaninglessness, the rich get richer, the poor get poorer."

The dominant professional establishment responds to the political and public demands for reform with a newly formed enthusiasm for tighter controls over teachers, learners, and what is to be learned in the name of what is euphemistically called "effective schools." In contrast the Society of Sacred Heart chooses to see its educational task as involving a deep and profound risk, and here I quote:

"We risk creating options *within* essentially unjust systems and educating only agents of change rather than agents of transformation in a truly evangelical sense."

This is not a dispute over techniques, not a matter of conflicting research findings, and not a debate about issues that can be settled by expertise. Clearly, such issues are involved and entangled but the essential difference is between very different ways of being in the world. From this perspective, both orientations can be considered to be radical in the sense that radical refers to "root" issues, to the very basis of the world we endeavor to create. One radical position is rooted in assumptions about the inevitability and validity of competition, hierarchy, and materialism, which demands an education directed toward maintaining the status quo as either unchangeable or preferred, or both. The other radical position is rooted in a commitment to the human opening to love, community, and justice, in which education is seen as nurturing these impulses. In this light, the issues, of course, become, as they ought, much more serious and fundamental and afford the possibility of seeing education as either a sacred or profane activity.

What is truly remarkable and inspiring about the efforts of the Society of the Sacred Heart and the Network is that they represent one of the very, very few approaches and, maybe the only one that constitutes a serious alternative to existing educational models. To be more precise, I have not seen any statement that integrates an education policy with a spiritual vision as well as the present documents do; nor have I seen any group as serious as the Sacred Heart Order and the Network in their determination to implement ideas of such profound significance.

The predominant notions of education, of course, reflect a predominant sense of what kind of society and culture we want. It is true that our educational system has some variety, diversity, and choice, but within a very limited framework. Operationally, this means that what the dominant public and profession has produced in the way of accessible educational options amounts to a selection comparable to the difficulties involved in choosing between a Zenith and a Sony television set. The work of the Sacred Heart Society in contrast, provides us with an opportunity to make choices akin to choosing between television and poetry.

It seems to me that the Sacred Heart Order is meeting its most fundamental responsibilities as a religious institution, which to me are to provide standards of criticism to the existing order and to offer ways to improve any shortcomings that derive from this process. It is surely the prophetic function of a religion to insist on an adherence to a society's deepest commitments and highest aspirations. With that prophetic impulse comes the further responsibility to offer energy, hope, and new possibilities—in the realization that as humans we are open to both powerlessness and transformation. Our religious traditions demand that we confront our failures but also provide us with the energy to overcome them. What gives us the possibility of a life of meaning necessarily involves enormous, sometimes painful, struggle as we confront the inevitable tensions between the impulse to settle for a life of conformity, achievement, and personal satisfaction and the impulse to create a more abundant and joyful life for all. By providing such a radical vision, one in which we are asked to take the Gospel seriously, the Society and its Network remind us of the true significance of educational choices. It also provides testimony to Elie Wiesel's assertion that "we live in biblical times." Perhaps we ought to conduct our lives as if our history were to be read by our great-grandchildren as they seek to find wisdom and inspiration in the past.

Surely, what the documents call for requires immense political, moral, and psychological struggle, and, even more risky, they will require us to let go of some of our most cherished and deeply ingrained values and beliefs. It is chilling and threatening to face the possibility that some of our taken-for-granted ways of being in the world may seriously clash with our basic spiritual and moral values. We profess belief in the brotherhood and sisterhood of all peoples, yet we maintain armies, harbor distrust, punish enemies, and take overwhelming pride in our national and cultural identities. We believe passionately in social justice and equality, yet we seek ways to gain an edge, to obtain the very real and unequally distributed privileges of our society. We affirm the dignity of work but provide a minimum wage that is below our official standard of poverty and continue to complain about how hard it is to get a good house-cleaner. We affirm the diversity of cultures but are indignant when the notion of teaching an exclusively European tradition of literature is challenged. We want equality for all, but we want our own children to do well on the SATs. We want quality education for all, but we want to find out how we can get our own children into an Ivy League college. We want everyone to have high self-esteem, but we insist on grades. We want our children to be autonomous *and* obedient; to be generous *and* competitive; to be concerned with the group *and* to look out for Number One. We want racial equality, but not in our neighborhood. We want to provide political refuge to the victims of oppression, but not if they are Haitians. We want to put an end to sexism, but are very reluctant to allow women to be ordained.

These conflicts are not between God and Satan, not between the Good Guys and the Bad Guys, but rather reflect the paradoxes, dilemmas, and conflicts that emerge out of our own personal connection to a highly complex and bewildering society. These issues are of course magnified for us as we live in a particularly perilous and chaotic or historical moment.

The goals of the Sacred Heart report provide us with the exhilarating opportunity to define ourselves not as pedagogues, bureaucrats, and experts but as participants in the sacred covenant to create a world of justice, love, and meaning. Exhilarating, yes; easy and fun, sometimes; difficult and frustrating, yes. Why teachers are always so tired and why so many in teaching and other helping professions burn out can indeed be explained by the frustration and despair that emerges from the realization of how wide the gap is between what we ought to do and what we are in fact doing. Ironically enough, it is this very tension and struggle that also attracts us to the vocation of teaching and service in the first place. Teaching is the noblest profession, and when its nobility is vulgarized and trashed, it is a time for despair and tragedy. An urgent educational and public need is to find ways to counter the dramatic increase in despair, pessimism, and cynicism. Part of this need is being met by a barely recognized broad movement that seeks to energize and ground progressive social and cultural policies in religious images and imperatives. This movement (more accurately, a number of different but related movements), to me, represents a serious effort to revitalize the prophetic mission of religion. It is seen dramatically in among other places in various theologies of liberation being developed by any number of oppressed peoples and groups.

Michael Lerner, the editor of the Jewish journal *Tikkun*, speaking of how Judaism provides both understanding of and relief from the pull of pessimism and realism, says:

"Early Judaism proclaimed that the world could be turned on its head, that the powerful could be defeated by the powerless, that a whole new world could be constructed . . . This conception of possibility stood in opposition to the various religious systems that provided the metaphysical foundations for existing systems of oppression. . . . The Egyptians saw history as a repetition of patterns that were built into the structure of necessity. [This] led to a political quietism, an acceptance of systems of oppression as ontologically given and unchangeable. . . ." (p. 10, *Tikkun*, V. 5, N. 5).

Lerner also reminds us, that the Bible reflects Lerner sees different understandings of the divine consciousness. In the Torah ". . . a struggle between the moments in which we can truly hear the voice of God as the force that will allow us to break the patterns of the past and believe in the possibility of creating a world governed by mutual caring, love, peace, and justice; and the moments in which that voice is drowned out and all we hear is the legacy of inherited pain and oppression which presents itself as the voice of common sense and reality (just as everyone else is cruel and ruthless toward 'the other,' the stranger, so must we be, because that's the way of the world" (p. 92).

He goes on to discuss a theology of pessimism which he condemns as idolatrous. "In practice, idolatry is the belief that the way things are in the world is all that can be, the reduction of the ought to the is, the abandonment of the belief that the world is governed by a force that makes possible the triumph of good over evil . . ." (p. 93).

In this context, education can be thought of as the energy that helps us to hear the divine voice that urges us to create a world of peace and justice and helps us to drown out the din of the voices urging us to buy, consume, compete, and achieve. To the extent that education is part of that process, education becomes a sacrament, the process by which the ordinary invites the possibilities of becoming holy. Indeed, our vocations are to be seen as devoted to the struggle to accept, confess, and forgive our weakness as we affirm our determination to fulfil our commitments. This constant tug between the best and worst within and among us and the redemptive nature of that struggle is eloquently described by Cornel West in his brilliant account of the African-American experience of Christianity in his book *Prophesy Deliverance*. Let me quote a small sample:

"Contradiction and transformation are the heart of the Christian gospel. The former always presupposes what presently is; the latter, the prevailing realities . . . this dialectic of imperfect products and transformative practice, of prevailing realities and negation, of human depravity and human dignity, of what is and the not-yet constitutes the Christian dialectic of human nature and human history . . . For Christians, the realm of history is the realm of the pitiful and the tragic. . . . The pitiful are those who remain objects of history, victims manipulated by evil forces; whereas the tragic are those person who become subjects of history, aggressive antagonists of evil forces. Victims are pitiful because they have no possibility of achieving either penultimate liberation or ultimate salvation; aggressive antagonists are tragic because they fight for penultimate liberation, and in virtue of their gallant struggle against the limits of history, they become prime candidates for ultimate salvation. In this sense to play a tragic role in history is positive . . ." (West, 1989, 17–18).

West goes on to describe prophetic Christianity as concerned with both existential and social freedom. Once again I quote:

"Existential freedom is an effect of the divine gift of grace which promises to sustain persons through and finally deliver them from the bondage to death, disease, and despair. Social freedom is the aim of Christian political practice, a praxis that flows from the divine gift of grace; social freedom results from the promotion and actualization of the norms of individuality and democracy. Existential freedom empowers people to fight for social freedom, to realize its political dimension" (p. 18).

As I understand this formulation, Christians are empowered to engage in the difficult and never-ending struggle against evil and sin by their faith in redemption. West, in his characterization of this struggle as tragic and redemptive, avoids the twin traps of sentimentality and despair. He speaks to a Christian praxis, the process by which Christians endeavor to seek this salvation through careful and continual examination of how the Gospels become palpable and vital.

Clearly, the educational work that you do is a part of that Christian praxis, uniting the educational, social, and the religious. Your task is to create a seamless web among your educational practices, social beliefs, and religious faith. This praxis is cyclical, continuous, and ever-changing. More particularly, you are now faced with yet another challenge by the Society. This challenge is surely as vital as the preceding ones so courageously and creatively initiated by the Society. If this new work is not successful, the thrust of the prior work will be seriously blunted. What I want to emphasize in the strongest possible terms is that this so-called "implementation" stage should be conducted with the same reverence, humility, and passion that the prior process has reflected. The process of making a clearer and deeper bonding of Christian faith and educational practice is itself a sacrament, an important dimension of Christian praxis. The fundamental requirement for this process to be fruitful is the willingness of people deeply committed to Christian praxis to struggle with the opportunity and challenges. This will require that you confront your doubts, fears, and confusions and see them as potentially valuable to the further development of the vision. Praxis is not putting theory into practice, it is examining theory and practice from both perspectives. The responsibility of practioners is not only to inform their practice with theory; but also to develop theory as informed by practice. It is of course difficult to know the difference between contribution and sabotage, between being critical and being defensive, between being open-minded and empty minded. What is clear is that this process is extremely important, sensitive, complex, and difficult, and that the participants must have both initial commitment and faith as well as strong and compassionate support from each other and the larger community.

I believe that if you conceptualize this next stage as sacramental that you could very well decrease your reliance on the language and metaphors of industry and productivity. Indeed, I urge you to consider the full significance of such terms as "implementation," "accountability," "training," "evaluation," "middle-manager," "assessment," "action plan," and so on, in light of your tradition and your vision. I suggest that as you ponder complex and concrete issues and problems that you worry not what Lee Iacocca would say about this or that but rather what Jesus would say. Accountants are important, but balance sheets are not to be confused with confessions; evaluation forms can be useful but they are not to be equated with the process of witnessing. As important as form, order, and system are, their danger is in their potential to be reified or, as I prefer to name it, to promote idolatry. They can become substitutes for the truly sacred, and furthermore they can be easily subverted by those who are reluctant or resistant to the fundamental premises of your vision. Filling out forms sometimes helps us to escape the anguish of freedom and the awesomeness of fully meeting our responsibilities. There is a danger here that you may blur the differences between accountability and responsibility, since responsibility is not about counting and blaming but about our ability and willingness to respond to our covenants.

The task is awesome, exhilarating, terrifying, and glorious. The risks are high, but the risk of not seriously engaging in the processes are even higher. The sacred errand that you pursue has consequences beyond you and your communities, because the larger culture also yearns to ground its efforts in an enduring vision of meaning. I believe that for the most part public and private schools in America are intellectually and morally bankrupt, devoid of energy and direction. I hope that your ministry can be extended to include sharing your insights and wisdom with other educators, be they public, private, religious, or secular. The work that you do offers hope and possibility for them and for the public, and I urge you to accept this responsibility as well.

What I have tried to do in this paper is to underscore both the importance and significance of the efforts of the Society to transform its educational ministry. Many of us are apt to refer to this process as involving "the bottom line," but you have chosen another image, that of the divine spark and how this spark is to warm and light our way. I have tried to indicate the significance of this effort by contrasting your vision with the dominant, semiofficial vision of education. One vision suggests that the wolf should lie down with the lamb, another urges us to train lambs to be wolf-like. One vision urges us to beat swords into plowshares while the other version urges us to do the reverse. One vision urges us to love our neighbor, while another urges us to compete with them. Some would have us see the poor and the meek as blessed, while others would have us see them as burdens. One vision implores us to be more cunning, more productive, and to seek meaning in consuming and hedonism. The other vision prays that we search for wisdom and find meaning and redemption in the struggle to create a world of love, justice, peace, and joy.

All of us should be immensely thankful for the work that you have already done and for the commitment that you have made to continue. I offer you my most heartfelt wishes and prayers that your work continues to reveal that which inspires and redeems it.

References

Lerner, Michael, "Editorial," in *Tikkun*, vol. 5, no. 5.

West, Cornel, 1982, *Prophesy Deliverance*. Philadelphia: Westminister Press.

Moral Outrage and Education

Cultural Transformation and Education

We are asked in this volume to consider relationships among education, transformation, and information which implies that there is good reason to believe that they are in fact closely connected and that we are in an era that requires social and cultural transformation. Therefore, it would seem appropriate as we approach the end of a millennium to consider very broadly the notion that a sophisticated education is a critical dimension of a peaceful, prosperous, and joyful society. One of the major goals of this century has been to enlarge and expand opportunities for formal education at all levels, a project that has shown impressive accomplishments in both scope and magnitude. It has also been a century of incredible scientific and material achievement and of enormous spiritual devastation—a century when small pox was eliminated and genocides were perfected, when we have come to believe in the big bang theory for both the beginning and end of life; when God died a most untimely death.

In the United States of the last moments of this millennium, we still have far too many poor, far too many rich; we have far more hatred, bigotry, racism, sexism, classism than we say we want; we have a culture that emphasizes achievement, competition, conquest, and domination at the expense of compassion, caring community, and dignity. The abomination of homelessness persists but it has vanished from the media and political platforms except from those who promise to shield us from the unpleasant presence of those who have no shelter. Poverty persists and increases but instead of a discourse of poverty we have a discourse of welfare; instead of a war on poverty we have a campaign for middle-class tax relief. There is a growing gap in incomes, a widening gap of trust among racial and ethnic groups, increasing homophobia, xenophobia, and whatever phobia it is that covers fear and loathing of the other. A dismal record indeed for a talented and enterprising people and a shameful state of affairs for a powerful and wealthy nation that claims sacred status, one explicitly founded on the principles of liberty and justice for all.

The added shame of this situation is that our educational system has contributed to and colluded with much, if not all, of this. Our most powerful and influential leaders call upon education to meet the demands of a cruel economy and a meritocratic culture. The great bulk of formal educational policies and practices reflect and facilitate structured inequality, rationed dignity, rationalized privilege, and self-righteous hierarchy. Moreover, much of the rhetorical justification for this violation of our commitment to a vision of liberty and justice for all comes from the ranks of the school and academy. Perhaps most disturbing of all is the realization that the movers and shakers in government, business, communications, advertising, banking, et. al., that is to say those institutions that shape our lives in critical ways, are people who almost surely have had what we have come to accept as a "good education." It is the very people who have brought us to our present plight who are among the brightest, most articulate, most creative, most imaginative, and most reflective people in the land. It would seem that at the very least, we need to re-consider what we mean by a "good education."

Moreover, the professional educational community has largely responded to our crises with characteristic opportunism, timidity, and accommodation, exercising their skills to meet the demands of the dominant political forces. What would seem to be required is a pedagogy of moral and spiritual transformation but instead our profession has fashioned a pedagogy of control and standardization focused on technology, competitiveness, and materialism. There is, however, in spite of the overwhelming dreariness and blandness of the present professional educational discourse, some extremely encouraging work that is being done that has great power, hope, imagination, and daring. I have in mind the work being done in what I would call a pedagogy of transformation and meaning. Educational ideas directed at the search for social justice and personal meaning. Among the prominent writers in this mode are Henry Giroux, Michael Apple, Svi Shapiro, Nel Noddings, Wlliam Pinar, Ron Miller, C.A. Bowers, Jane Roland Martin, and James Moffett, all of whom address basic issues of cultural and existential meaning as the necessary framework for developing educational policies and practices. It is work which at least holds out the possibility of challenging the dominant educational discourse of achievement, competition, and standardization and of stimulating the public and profession to reexamine the relationship between our highest aspirations and prevailing notions of schooling.

I want very much to affirm and celebrate this work even as I speak to how its very insights and analyses testifies to the limitations of some of our most valued educational traditions and public schooling. What this work does in its affirmation of serious reflection on fundamental issues of justice meaning in a context of their complexity, ambiguity, and perplexity is, among other critically important things, to highlight the problematics of detachment, independent thinking, and critical rationality. It must be pointed out that I am lumping together educational orientations that have important differences among them, e.g., the difference in the emphasis put on social, political, and economic concerns as opposed to writers who emphasize personal development and human growth. However, among the very important connections are their commitment to social and cultural transformation *and* their reliance on critical rationality, personal reflection, openness and respect for varying perspectives, and good faith dialogue.

I certainly would not want to quarrel with this educational approach, and indeed I am proud to be part of an intellectual and professional community and tradition that is deeply committed to them. However, I increasingly find that such an orientation, necessary as it is, is not anywhere near being sufficient to respond to our present set of existential, social, political, economic, moral and spiritual crises. The twin roots of this doubt are in the sense of moral outrage that I share with many people at the depth of unnecessary pain and suffering in the world and simultaneously in the absence of moral outrage of so many people. Not only do I affirm the validity of this outrage, I consider it an absolute requisite to serious efforts at cultural and educational transformation. I am also very much aware of the problemmatics of a pedagogy of moral outrage, not least of which is the psychological reality of the resistance and hostility to it when it is perceived to be guilt inductive. People simply do not want to hear constant messages of disaster, gloom, and suffering and are wont to tune out jeremiads as hysterical if not counterproductive—the perfect defense mechanism. In addition, there is the frustration that comes with the awareness of the depth, enormity, and scope of the problems that engenders helplessness if not despair. Yet it is difficult for me to see in the absence of a passionate commitment to the plight of the suffering how we can seriously address the really vital issues that threaten our existence as a caring people.

In addressing the matter of moral outrage I have had to confront three basic questions: what are the criteria for morally outrageous phenomena? how do we come to internalize them? and third, what is the authority and source of these criteria? I have some sense of the first issue as I affirm what I believe to be our basic human moral framework of liberation, dignity fulfillment, and peace for all. Having said that let me quickly acknowledge that this is in no way suffices as a satisfactory response. The question regarding how we come to learn to have moral commitments is obviously a very complicated and controversial one and with it comes a very strong and rich tradition of reflection and theorizing. Moreover, there is some very interesting and intriguing work going on in educational theory today in this realm as reflected in the work of such people as Nel Noddings, James Moffett, and Jane Roland Martin. However, the harsh reality is that the public schools are very far away from paying serious attention to such questions and issues largely because they do not have the political will or intellectual tradition to accept this responsibility.

Moreover, I believe it is time to question the broader notion that we can significantly effect social and cultural transformation primarily or even largely through serious study and dialogue. It is more than a little disquieting when we consider the poignant effects of critical rationality on our struggle to find meaning and create a morally sound and spiritually satisfying path to personal fulfillment, cultural richness, and social justice. This process has inevitably confronted us with enormously diverse perspectives, incredibly perplexing dilemmas, extraordinarily complex ideas, and a fathomless set of paradoxes. Because of these realities we have learned to be cautious of generalizations, suspicious of certainty, reverential toward difference, and wary of affirmation. We have learned about the historical, political, and subjective nature of knowledge and have had to respond with critical and skeptical detachment lest we be seduced by self-serving rhetoric masked as universal truths. We have become so smart that we find it extremely difficult to believe in anything except the contingency of knowledge and the inevitability of conflict. Our critical studies have taken us to spiritual and moral inarticulateness if not silence; our detachment has led us to the emptiness of the marginality of interested but paralyzed bystanders; and our tolerance has forced us into an unwilling consciousness of moral relativity.

Part of my skepticism is directed at the whole notion of there being such a thing as an educational enterprise, i.e., the difficulty of the reification of education, of separating out certain processes and phenomena from a larger framework of meaning and labelling them to be "educational." I have come to believe that such a reductionism serves to blur the intimate relationships among critical cultural, political, and social phenomena and education and to nourish a myth of an objectivity based on technical expertise. Perhaps it is time to tell ourselves that Education is an emperor without clothes and that we need to return to the realms of the fully clothed. It seems rather ludicrous to me to have this vast array of sophisticated, well-trained, and creative people called "educators," sitting around in their offices and classrooms with nothing to do except to define and solve "educational problems." Where do these educational problems come from? Do they exist as such, in a conceptual vacuum, outside of any larger context? Educational problems, per se, would seem to be of a secondary (no pun intended) nature; they necessarily arise as a consequence of other issues and concerns, e.g., the efforts to teach literacy emerges from a variety of motivations: to facilitate productivity, to strengthen democracy, for personal empowerment, to name a few. Indeed one of the prime activities of educators is to determine objectives and goals in an Alice in Wonderland effort to figure out the reasons we're doing what we're doing! To me it is quite extraordinary that we are constantly being asked to state our goals (a process which, incidentally, rarely, if ever, results in changing what we do). If there is uncertainty about our educational goals, then how could we possibly continue to teach what we do? How could such uncertainty arise in the first place? Presumably, if we do not know our goals, then we should stop whatever it is we are doing and restart only when we know what the goals are. Of course, much of the goal-stating effort is largely disingenuous, since politically it usually adds up to a post-hoc justification of what we already are doing. However, beyond the cynicism and ritualism, I believe that the impulse to ask the question of educational purpose reveals an unsettling lack of confidence in the validity of what we do and masks a deep and genuine uncertainty of our moral direction and a suspicion that we are morally and spiritually lost. This brings me back to the third question regarding moral outrage: what is its authority and source?

My position is that above and beyond studying educational processes we as educators are required to wrestle with issues regarding the nature of our culture's highest aspirations and most cherished visions. In addition, we as educators need to ground our work in a vision that in some significant way resonates with what matters most and is of the most profound nature, to matters of cosmology, religion, and spirituality. One needs to proceed from this point cautiously and carefully because I believe that figuring out what it is that matters most and what constitutes profundity can be an extremely difficult, elusive, and anguishing process since we are dealing here with issues of extraordinary importance, ambiguity, and complexity. A particularly complex and elusive dimension of this process is sorting out the role of spirituality in this quest. I would like to share part of my own sorting out process in the next section of this essay. I do so not to be particularly autobiographic or to claim that my quest has produced radically new answers to profound questions but because I believe that the questions, processes, and insights that I came to accept are shared by many if not most of those interested in personal and cultural meaning and transformation. Obviously, individuals will address these issues on the basis of their own unique background, history, and orientation and indeed I believe that the process of sharing individual quests can greatly contribute to the task of reflecting on both our differences and commonalities.

Education and Spirituality

The context of trying to connect education to spirituality, passionate commitments and to matters of ultimate concern has been and continues to be a difficult and confounding struggle which has certainly not led me to a resolution but clearly has led me to a source of authority. I came to a place where I realized that I would not be able to respond in depth to the question "to what should we be committed?" unless I was willing at some basic level to accept a starting place, a point of departure, a fundamental frame of reference, or to put in more contemporary terms, I would need to be part of an interpretive community. It was at this point that I truly encountered capital M Mystery for I came to this conclusion in part because I realized that what I was looking for involved a process which gives life to existence, which animates, energizes, and gives direction, or as it is written, that which represents the spirits that reside within our midst. Perhaps this is in part what is meant by the term, spiritual—literally, that which inspires and gives breath to. The first Mystery then has to do with the source of this energizing spirit; although I am prepared to accept, albeit gingerly and hesitantly, the importance and reality of these spirits, I remain among the baffled about what they are, where they come from, how does one find them and what does one do with them when one does.

The second Mystery for me has to do with the reality that I find myself generally drawn to religious issues and particularly and increasingly so, to the study of Jewish religious traditions. At first, I saw my interest as part of the way to provide further justification and validation for my work on an educational orientation that focused on equality and social justice and found powerful support for this in such traditions as the writings of the Biblical prophets. However, I quickly realized that what was going on was more than the usual kind of academic scrambling for post-hoc rationalization that passes for carefully considered inquiry. I was astonished to find, generally speaking, this material to be simultaneously familiar and fresh, old and new, accessible and remote. It was as if I was revisiting an important and suspended part of my consciousness even though I do not remember ever being in that state, at least in any systematic, thorough, or direct way. My formal religious training had been minimal, perfunctory, superficial and banal if not counter-productive and misleading and yet it would seem that my work had been significantly influenced by traditions I had largely ignored and misunderstood. I still cannot fully explain why this would be so. Nor do I entirely comprehend why I am still so strongly drawn to examining Jewish sources but I am and I find myself relying increasingly on them for that which animates and informs my work. My reactions to these materials is varied, if not contradictory—I find much that is affirming and energizing; there is a great deal that I do not accept, much I do not even understand; some seems directly relevant to my work and much of it seems quite removed from it; some of it troubles me and all of it intrigues me.

Will Herberg points out in his book *Faith in Biblical Theology*, that it is what we remember and what we expect that shapes our quest for faith. According to Herberg, ". . . the act of faith is double: the existential affirmation of *a* history as one's redemptive history and the existential appropriation of this redemptive history as one's personal background history, and therefore in a real sense the foundation of one's existence." (pp. 40–41). Accordingly, I seek to ground my work in my hopes as they are informed by what I choose to remember and by what I want to expect. I expect and accept meaningful existence and that as educators we must do our work within a larger framework of meaning, that which is of utmost importance to us and constitutes the substance of our very deepest commitments, those which Paul Tillich calls matters of "faith and ultimate concern." Tillich describes faith as:

". . . the state of being ultimately concerned: the dynamics of faith are the dynamics of man's ultimate concerns. Man . . . is concerned about many things, above all about those which condition his existence, such as food and shelter. Man in contrast to other living beings, has spiritual concerns—cognitive, aesthetic, social, political. Some of them are urgent, often extremely urgent, and each of them as well as the vital concerns can claim ultimacy for a human life or the life of a social group. If it claims ultimacy it demands the total surrender of him who accepts the claim, and it promises total fulfillment even if all other claims have to be subjected to it or rejected in its name"(p. 1).

It certainly makes sense that we determine our goals, purposes, and strategies within a framework of faith and ultimate concern and it also makes sense that within this frame we are wise to study, reflect, and dialogue. While we need not insist on linearity we, however, are still beset with the greatest of all difficulties, that of determining our faith and what constitutes matters of ultimate concern. The processes of critical rationality can operate with enormous power both within and without such frames of faith and ultimate concern but by themselves they cannot bring us to affirm a faith or celebrate an ultimate concern. Study, reflection, and analysis cannot be at the center of an education for meaning, although they surely can and ought to be among the inevitable and valued partners in the task of naming and acting on our faith. I believe that we are living in a time when there is widespread earnest and heart-felt searching for the other critical partners.

Indeed, it may be that it is the very human desire and impulse to seek faith and ultimate meaning that is itself another critical partner. The modern condition is one in which we seem to seek rather than express faith and one that requires that we do so in order to pursue hope, and sustain our struggle to create a just and loving community. Franz Rozensweig in describing the rationale for a center of adult Jewish education said that at one time people went from the Torah into life but now is a time when we must go "the other way round from life . . . back to the Torah" (p. 152). The modern age is one in which we encounter the world not with faith and a sense of ultimate meaning but with skepticism, wariness, and suspicion and convinced that we are better served by being armed with knowledge and critical rationality. This approach has certainly served many purposes well but it has also exacerbated our alienation and anxiety leading us to be even skeptical about our skeptical armament. Many of us indeed seek the faith and framework of meaning that can enable us to understand the evil that has befallen us and that can help to sustain the impulse to resist if not overcome it and return to traditional and sacred sources like the Torah. However, it is one thing to study sacred traditions and sources of wisdom and quite another thing to be nourished and energized by them. This generates yet another search—the search and struggle for the disposition, accessibility, and openness to faith and the desire and willingness to be nourished by the sacred.

Abraham Heschel teaches us that we can learn to faith only when we wonder, for only when we truly wonder we will be able to confront the awesomeness and sublimity of creation. He says in *God in Search of Man*, "Mankind will not perish from want of information; but only for want of appreciation. The beginning of our happiness lies in the understanding that life without wonder is not worth living. What we lack is not a will to believe but a will to wonder" (Heschel, 1955, p. 46). It is this wonder that inevitably brings us to confronting the awesomeness of the most fundamental questions of origins, purpose, and destiny—the overwhelming and disturbing mystery of existence. Heschel says that this mystery ". . . is not a symptom for the unknown but rather a name for *meaning* which stands in relationship to God. . . . Ultimate meaning and ultimate wisdom are not found in the world but in God, and the only way to wisdom is through our relationship to God. That relationship is *awe. . . . The beginning of awe is wonder, and the beginning of wisdom is awe. . . .* Awe enables us to perceive in the world intimations of the divine, to sense in small things the beginning of infinite significance, to sense the ultimate in the common and the simple; to feel in the rush of the passing the stillness of the eternal" (Heschel, 1955, p. 74, 75).

Faith then is not a function of study, not the result of research and analysis, not the culmination of reasoned reflection but rather emerges from wonder, awe, and engagement with the infinite. Heschel is not unaware of the educational implications of such a formulation for education. ". . . Our systems of education stress the importance of enabling the student to exploit the power aspect of reality. To some degree, they try to develop his ability to appreciate beauty. But there is no education for the sublime. We teach the children how to measure, how to weigh! We fail to teach to revere, how to sense wonder and awe . . . the sense of the sublime, [and] the sign of the inward greatness of the human soul" (Heschel, 1955 p. 36).

It seems that an alternative response to issues of ultimate meaning is to dismiss essentialist questions about the meaning of life, human nature, and the course of human destiny as naive, irrelevant, or sentimental if not stupid and dangerous. I have chosen to speak from the perspective of traditions that assume quite the opposite, namely that these questions are the *only* ones worth asking and moreover, from the grounding of a tradition that takes commitments very seriously. As Rabbi Heschel has said, "Socrates taught us that a life without thinking is not worth living. Now, thinking is a noble effort, but the finest thinking may end in futility. . . . The Bible taught us that life without commitment is not worth living; that thinking without roots will bear flowers but no fruit . . ." (1955, p. 216).

I affirm traditions that not only recognize that as humans we are fated to create our world but believes that above all we are called upon to create a world resonant with divine intention—a world of peace, justice, love, community, and joy for all. These are traditions that accept as givens the potentials of human abilities as well as the limits of human fallibilities; they posit our capacity to be generous as well as to be selfish; to be angelic as well as demonic; compassionate as well as cruel; wise as well as foolish. Such traditions revere knowledge but only as it is tempered with the wisdom that advances justice and mercy; a perspective that acknowledges the enormity of the task but dismisses human despair as sinful; and one that represents a consciousness of unmitigated outrage in the wake of cruelty and injustice but always in the faith that witness, confession, and healing offer the possibilities of transcendence and redemption. What is absolutely crucial to redemption is human responsibility and human agency since these traditions require that we act as God's agents, dedicated and committed to constructing and sustaining intentional communities based on joy, love, peace, and justice.

As educators we should not be merely committed to education, we should instead be more deeply committed to human dignity; we should not dedicate ourselves to higher learning but to a high standard of living for all; our responsibilities are not to select the best students but to eradicate privilege; our commitment must not be to the market economy but to the Golden Rule. It is idolatrous to commit oneself primarily to the preservation of History, Biology, or any other discipline or field when there is injustice, inequality, and hatred in the land.

We need not be concerned with a decline in test scores; we need to be outraged and obsessed with an increase in unnecessary human suffering. As educators we must not offer justice, joy, and love as rewards or luxuries but affirm them as requirements for a life of meaning. Personal dignity is not something to be rationed and manipulated but cherished as something inherent and inviolable.

Yet in spite of our prior commitments and vows, it is certainly true as well as tragically unnecessary that we have created a world in which justice, love, peace, and joy are unequally distributed and that is why it is truly a blessing when we try to reduce this inequity situation by situation, one person at a time. However, our commitment must extend beyond the enrichment and support of particular individuals as worthy and commendable as that goal surely is. We must recognize that the sources of the inequality, inequity, and injustice lie not only within the souls of individuals but also within the structures of our economic, political, and cultural institutions. Our present economy requires poverty, our current culture demands elitism, our existing political system necessitates hierarchy. Our commitments, therefore, extend to the creation of a just world beyond merely making accommodations to an unjust system; we are called upon to both heal the wounded *and* to create healthy environments, to respond to both the effects *and* the sources of injustice. As educators we need to be concerned not so much with minimum scores as with minimum wages, not with classroom deportment as much as with business ethics, less with the distribution of grades than with the distribution of wealth. More accurately, we need to be mindful of the links between classroom pedagogy and social policy as there are, in fact, close relationships between minimum scores, classroom deportment, the distribution of grades and minimum wages, business ethics, and the distribution of wealth.

Educational Implications

The Public Schools and Transformation

Is this an oxymoron or a cherished vision? A delusional fantasy or the stuff of dreams? Is it a useful way of distracting us from the necessity of deeper structural change or the conviction of the inevitable triumph of good sense? Much has been written and much has been expected of the possibilities of public education and of course, much has been written on how the public schools act not as agents of liberation and enlightenment but as engines of the dominant classes.

Perhaps it would be useful to pause on the term "transformation" and examine it as a neutral rather than a polemical term, i.e., there are all kinds of possible transformations some of which we may like and some we may not. The common schools of the 19th century endeavored with a great deal of success to transform a group of largely rural, multicultural, multilingual regions into a unified, industrial, and WASP nation. The schools of today are striving to transform us in such a way that we can accommodate to a cybernetic culture and multinational economy. It must be remembered that public schools are bureaucratic agencies of the state which are required by law to follow the policies of publically elected officials who have total fiscal control of the schools. If there are to be transformative functions assigned to the schools, the assignments will be made by those in power, i.e., by the established dominant interests. In addition, we must also confront the reality of an entrenched professional bureaucracy which largely works for self-serving inertia and stasis. Although there is an honorable and modest history of the profession calling for genuine social and cultural transformation it is a story of very little impact. At the same time it must be said that the profession has been able to make a great many technical changes (e.g., in instruction, curriculum, and assessment), but even these are usually absorbed into the basic schooling frameworks set by the dominant power structures.

However, what I believe is meant by transformation in the context of this book has to do with a fundamental change in moral and spiritual consciousness in which we reject the excesses of individualism, materialism, competitiveness, and acquisitiveness. The kind of transformation that is required is one that energizes us to pursue personal meaning, social justice, world peace, and ecological harmony. The difficulty is that those who favor this kind of transformation do not have the political clout to direct the energies of our social and cultural institutions and hence it is quite naïve to expect that the public schools can be a primary source of such a transformation. After all, public school educators are under quite strong political, professional, and community controls which work to put enormous pressure certainly not for moral and spiritual transformation but on the intensification of our present consciousness. Most teachers are over-worked and underpaid; and most come out of a tradition that stresses professionalism rather than social reform. What we will have to do is to work harder to create the cultural and social conditions that will enable the public schools to do their part in changing consciousness. Schools are not there to thwart the will of those in power so if we want to change society it is simply neither fair or wise to ask the schools to be in the vanguard. This means that educators who want to work for transformation cannot limit themselves to schools, community colleges, universities and the like but need to be involved with other and larger cultural movements.

Obviously, there are many forces and movements working for the kind of transformation being described, some of them political, others economic, and others ecological. I want to speak directly to the enormous force of the current interest and involvement in spiritual matters that up to fairly recently has been misrepresented as a rise in religious fundamentalism. There is surely a dramatic increase in religious fundamentalism but there is a broader and more widespread phenomenon of spiritual seeking and struggling that cuts across class, religions, and ideology. As I have already indicated, some of this energy has been expressed in the professional educational literature, a literature not noted for its daring. My own view is that we as educators, citizens, and humans ought to involve ourselves more directly and openly in this larger realm since it is my belief that the transformation that radical educators seek is fundamentally spiritual in nature. More particularly, I believe that we as educators need to engage in the struggle to affirm spiritual beliefs and to integrate this struggle into our professional responsibilities.

There are ancient spiritual truths that must be asserted—truths that do not constitute information but wisdom, that do not emerge from research but from the soul, and are not matters of consensus but of affirmation. For me it is abundantly clear that we *are* our sisters' and brothers' keepers and we are inevitably and intimately connected to each other and to nature. It is clear to me that we suffer enormously from the loss of this truth and the resultant profound alienation. It is because of this that we seek to reclaim our holiness and in doing so we will end the isolation, suicide, murder, pillage, and pain we inflict on ourselves, each others, and the planet. Scientists, theorists, and philosophers now tell us of our intimate and inevitable interconnectedness with society, culture, history, and nature and have made it possible even for skeptics like me to approach the essence of spiritual consciousness, the belief in the oneness of being. Indeed the question of being our brothers' and sisters' keeper becomes moot when we begin to realize that we are very likely not apart from but a part of our brothers and sisters.

This consciousness impels us to renew our struggle for direction, meaning, and guidance with determined intensity—Heschel says, "Man is not the same at all times. It is only at certain moments that he becomes aware of the heart-breaking inconceivability of the world in which he lives and which he ignores. At such moments, he wonders: what is my place in the midst of the terrifying immensity of time and space? what is my task? what is my situation?" (1955, p. 130). His own response is powerfully unequivocal: "He who seeks an answer to the most pressing question, what is living? will find an answer in the Bible; man's destiny is to be partner rather than a master, there is a task, a law, and a way, the task is redemption, the law is to do justice, to love mercy, and the way is the secret of being *human and holy*" (1955, p. 238).

How are the rest of us to respond to Heschel's challenging questions? Walter Brueggemann urges us to respond to such questions in a consciousness of confession and grief. Confession refers to a process in which we affirm our basic aspirations, hopes, visions, beliefs and commitments as well as to admit to our failures to act on them. This is very likely to be a matter of both celebration and grief for as we remember our communal and personal spirits we will undoubtedly be renewed by the energy and joy of this wisdom and as we remember our history we will surely be horrified and mortified by our refusal to live by them. Brueggemann makes it very clear that we cannot omit the grief process for that is a necessary part of the process of confronting the chasms between our hopes and realities, our human responsibilities for the pain and injustice in the world, and recommitting ourselves to our cherished destinies. In his book *Hopeful Imagination*, he invokes the work of the Biblical prophets as a metaphor for how we might address our present cultural and religious state which he characterizes as a parallel exile for serious believers. In his concluding chapter, he offers three themes: "1. *Grief* is offered against establishment *denial and cover-up* Jeremiah regards as a lie. 2. *Holiness* is proclaimed against conventional theology that never quite faces the otherness and always hopes for and forms a *utilitarianism* that links God's holiness to some historical purpose. 3. *Memory* is asserted against *amnesia* in which nothing is noticed or critiqued and everything is absolutized in its present form. . . . *Grief* should permit newness. *Holiness* should give hope. *Memory* should allow possibility" (pp. 131–132).

It is poignantly if not tragically clear that much of our culture is a long way from acknowledging its responsibility for such hideous phenomena as slavery, poverty, war, racism, sexism, inequality, and hunger. This refusal to take responsibility and hence to grieve and mourn for the pain we as a community have inflicted represents to me the limitations of an education grounded primarily in critical rationality, study, and the exchange and analysis of information. Indeed, many of our most learned and reflective commentators have used their vast store of knowledge, insight, and information to celebrate a smug and intoxicated triumphalism of capitalism, consumerism, and meritocracy, American-style. It is obviously impossible to grieve if there is no sense of significant loss, or even more strikingly, if there is a sense of significant gain! Instead of compassion for the suffering, we have learned to blame the victims or to make them invisible; many curse rather than bless the poor; and rather than seeing others as God's children, many of us see human beings through the lens of potential customer or expendable worker. The dominant culture does not celebrate justice but competition, does not value unconditional love but grooves on conditional rewards; its rituals are not of communal solidarity but of partisan triumphs, and its energies are not rooted in a divine impulse to seek oneness but in a frantic spirit of greed and acquisitiveness.

What I think is required for genuine transformation is an education that emphasizes the processes that I have been discussing in this piece, awe, faith, the struggle for ultimate meaning, commitment, confession, moral outrage, and grief. In the present political and cultural realities, these cannot be a significant part of the public school experience, largely because they go counter to both public and professional expectations of the role of these schools. For the most part, parents want their children to succeed and look to the schools to provide them with the wherewithal to gain an edge in the struggle for privilege and advantage. Academics, for the most part, want to preserve their disciplines and areas of study while school administrators are preoccupied with maintaining good will and stability. Moreover, the public schools are politically positioned to be as accommodating and acutely sensitive to community pressures as possible, effectively making them hostage to the demands of zealous and determined groups. The possibility of introducing on a widespread basis, serious spiritual and moral consciousness or even dialogue to educational policy and practice is extremely remote, if for no other reason than the political clout of the Christian Right. The cliché that the public schools try to be all things to all people and consequently fail to fully satisfy anyone is basically true and must be accepted as a consequence of our political and social structures.

The daring, intriguing, and imaginative ideas of James Moffett and Nel Noddings are instructive to this issue. Moffett basically attacks our culture as bankrupt and our schools as perpetuating a ruinous consciousness and argues forcefully and courageously that only an education that is primarily and radically directed at personal development through various spiritual disciplines can save us from ourselves. He makes a very compelling argument for this approach and I believe with many others it merits serious public and professional dialogue. However, as attractive and creative as these ideas are, I would have to say sadly and ruefully that there is virtually no possibility that they will see very much of the light of day in the foreseeable future of public school practice. They are far too threatening to the dominant thrust of those who dominate public spaces.

The ideas of Nel Noddings on teaching children to wrestle with the enduring and complex issues of fundamental belief are also quite daring for public school although much less radical than those of James Moffett. Noddings urges schools to provide safe and supportive opportunities to study and discuss such ideas as theodicy, immortality, the existence of God, and the nature of evil, surely a sensible and valid idea. Her plan is not, however, to make such study the focus of the curriculum but to introduce them as relevant spin-offs and dimensions of the traditional discipline-based curriculum (e.g., math, science, history, English, foreign language). She advocates that teachers commit themselves to teaching for understanding of varying beliefs; to an attitude of "pedagogical neutrality"; and to an approach that allows them to take a position but insists that they acknowledge and recognize differing views. All in all, I see this as a very prudent and pragmatic way for the schools to deal with such vital issues but the relative cautiousness and lines of demarcation of her proposals only emphasizes the limited range of public school possibilities. It is not an approach that is designed to transform the culture or galvanize spiritual struggle, moral outrage, awe, and passionate commitment but one that hopes to stimulate students to study and reflect on the fundamental questions of existence within the traditional framework of the schools as they are. And yet even such sensible and modest proposals are within our present context relatively controversial and radical with little likelihood of gaining broad support in the mainstream of educational practice. If schools are, at best, reluctant to provide for serious discussion of the most important questions of human existence, then how can we expect them to be a prime mover in the struggle for cultural and social transformation? We mustn't and shouldn't.

What Can Be Done?

Accepting the educational limitations of critical rationality for changing consciousness and the political liabilities of the public schools does not in any way mean that educators are irrelevant and marginal to the struggle for a just and loving world. It does mean that we have to re-examine the claims that we have made for enlightenment education and the public schools in the context of a commitment to social and cultural transformation. It does not mean that we should accept the anti-intellectualism that denies the undeniable and absolutely essential liberation and inspiration that can and does emerge from study, research, dialogue, understanding, and analysis. It does mean that we need to seek other sources for the energy, wisdom, and courage to sustain the struggle for meaning. It does not mean that we should cede and surrender the public schools to the forces of either bland-ness or zealotry; nor does it mean that we should not continue to engage in the public and professional struggle for a humane and liberating education. It does mean that we must give up the falsely reassuring and naive way in which we equate democratic education with public schooling.

It does mean that we as educators may have to give up some of our precious programs and pet solutions, or at least be more modest about their possibilities. There is nothing particularly sacred about whole language learning or experiential learning, nothing specially ultimate involved per se in the teaching of poetry or going on field trips or even in journaling. Indeed, it is possible to turn the teaching of imagination and critical thinking into a sacrilegious act when people use their newly augmented imagination and criticality to make a buck at the expense of others, to exploit the environment, to find tax loopholes, or to encourage teen-agers to smoke. The use of portfolios may stimulate imagination, it is surely more sophisticated than conventional, reductionist assessment, and it no doubt will afford more opportunities for advancement to more people. At the same time, portfolios have, can, and will be used to facilitate and enhance elitism, privilege, and hierarchy. On the other hand, however dubious we may be of the value of particular educational technologies, there is something clearly sacred and very special involved in promoting human dignity and social justice and to do so as educators.

Indeed, our deepest commitments should be the same as all other people: they cannot, should not, must not be anything less than those contained in our culture's highest aspirations and most cherished dreams. Our differences with other groups lie not in the substance and nature of our commitments but only in where and how we act on them. The struggle for creating a community of peace, love, joy, and justice must go on in every sphere, including, of course and perhaps especially in educational institutions. We are not primarily educators, we are first of all God's agents, active partners in the covenant to create a community of peace, justice, love, and joy who, parenthetically, have decided to exercise our responsibilities to this project in places called schools and universities. Educators are called upon to pursue justice, to choose life, to cherish freedom for all, and to love their neighbors as themselves, maybe more but certainly not less than anyone else. Our profession will not be ennobled by feeding the engines of material growth, personal success, intellectual mastery, or national supremacy; it is ennobled by its devotion to spiritual development, individual dignity, moral sensitivity, and universal peace.

My view is that if and when public school educators commit themselves to the task of participating in the continuing responsibility to create a just and loving world, the nature of their work would change dramatically and profoundly even within the context of severe restriction. It is possible to do at least some of what Nel Noddings suggest, that is to engage students in serious dialogue on profound issues within the existing curriculum. It is possible to do what Jane Roland Martin suggests and that is to create a more nourishing and loving classroom environment where students are affirmed as they thoughtfully probe their world. It is also possible to add some of the opportunities for spiritual growth that James Moffett suggests into existing classrooms. The suggestions that William Pinar makes about the importance of aesthetic opportunities for students to reflect on their inner lives and those of Henry Giroux that students and teachers critically examine the contradictions of their lived experiences are extremely important and doable possibilities. None of these orientations may become central to the schools but that doesn't mean that they can't have some impact in some however modest way.

This is an era of increasing cynicism, despair, and helplessness and a time when many suggest that the best we can do is either to ride out the storm or reduce the damage as much as possible. Still others say that the apocalypse is now and that we should abandon ship and/or learn to tread water. I take a different view, namely, that we should renew our commitment to creating a world of peace, love, justice, and joy with greater determination, passion, and vigor precisely *because* these are such desperate times. It is surely proper to count our blessings and to affirm our vision at times of genuine cultural and social advancement but we have an even greater responsibility to remind the community of its covenant in times of danger. This is a time when we must vigorously and passionately counteract the cynicism and despair which only deepens and extends the danger. The times call not for capitulation or curtailment of our commitments but in affirming, as Herberg suggests, what we remember and what we expect. We ought to remember the enormous amount of unnecessary human suffering and we ought to remember our vows to redeem that suffering with the creation of a better world. We must expect that this requires a great deal of human agency, determination, and will, and we must have faith that these efforts will ultimately succeed. We must remember the magnificent acts of courage and sacrifice that millions have offered in the struggle for a just and loving world.

Let us as educators, citizens, and human beings have faith in our ultimate commitment to the creation of a just and loving community. Easy to say, hard to do. Unless we take into account our amazing human capacities and that mysterious spirit that is the source of that faith that energizes and inspires them. Each of us must search for the community of meaning that provides, protects, and enriches that source. It is in these communities that we can find the authority for our moral outrage and the energy to sustain the struggle to preserve the hope that is required to meet our responsibilities. Responsibility without a moral and spiritual framework becomes psychological guilt, the kind of meaningless and unrooted dis-ease that cripples people into deafness if not hostility to human suffering. The difficulty in recognizing, enduring, and responding to morally outrageousness is, I believe, related to spiritual alienation, i.e., a failure to affirm. The reality is that we need more help than good intentions, critical rationality, and tolerance can provide in our vocation to create a just and loving community for all. We and our students need to have the faith that there are such additional resources available in that realm called the spirit.

I find great consolation in what Michael Lerner said in 1994, "The ultimate Force governing the world, the Force that has created the entirety of Being, is the energy that presses for transcendence toward a world in which all Being manifests its fullest ethical and spiritual potential, a world in which human beings recognize one another both in our particularity and in our ability to manifest ethical and spiritual possibility. That Force exercises a spiritual pull within all Being to move beyond what is to what it ought to be. . . . [T]he God of Moses is a Force that transcends all limits and makes it possible for us to do the same. This God is the Force that makes for the possibility of possibility" (p. 65).

I am further moved by what Michael Lerner's teacher, Rabbi Abraham Heschel, wrote in 1951: "Only one question . . . is worthy of supreme anxiety: How to live in a world pestered with lies and remain unpolluted, how not to be stricken with despair, not to flee but to fight and succeed in keeping the soul unsoiled and even aid in purifying the world." (Heschel, 1951 p. 179).

I am deeply comforted to know that Lerner, Heschel, and I as well as countless others across time and space have been and will continue to be stirred by what was written in the Talmud 1800 years ago: "The task is not ours to finish, but neither are we free to take no part in it."

Summary

The focus of this essay has not been on information nor even on education but rather on the part that education plays in the infinitely more important issue of our moral condition. It is my view that this must be the starting point of all serious discussions of all issues of public policy, including of course those involving education. I share the position that we as a society have fallen tragically short of our commitment to create a just and loving community for all and furthermore, that our educational institutions and orientations are complicit in the violation of this commitment. This failure can be seen as the triumph of a consciousness of materialism, individualism, competitiveness, and hierarchy as well as a function of increasing cynicism, loss of energy, and rising despair.

I believe that the most powerful element that is lacking in the necessity for the kind of transformation that is necessary to renew our commitments is a sense of profound moral outrage. The road to moral outrage would seem not to be paved neither in good intentions nor in more critical rationality, sophisticated knowledge, and clever analysis. The more direct path would seem to be the one marked "spiritual," since the nature of the commitments that generate moral outrage will emerge from our most profound sense of what constitutes ultimacy. This would suggest that educators need to seriously address their own views on what is of ultimate concern in order to explore the moral and spiritual commitments that ground their educational orientations.

It is clear to me that the public schools are sharply limited in their capacity to be a major force in such a transformational process but whatever possibilities exist should be energetically pursued. It is also clear to me that educators need to have the courage to accept the limitations of deeply cherished notions of the traditions of liberal education without in any way denying their necessity. Educators need therefore to be at once more modest and more bold; modest in their expectations of what public schools and critical rationality can do and bolder in their hopes in the possibilities of awe, faith, grief, confession, and spirit.

References

Brueggemann, Walter. 1986. *Hopeful Imagination*. Philadelphia: Fortress Press.

Giroux, Henry. 1988. *Teachers as Intellectuals*. Granby: Bergin and Garvey.

Herberg, Will. 1976. *Faith in Biblical Theology*. Philadelphia: Westminster Press.

Heschel, Abraham. 1951. *Man Is Not Alone*. New York: Farrar, Straus, and Giroux.

Heschel, Abraham. 1955. *God in Search of Man*. New York: Farrar, Straus, and Giroux.

Lerner, Michael. 1994. *Jewish Renewal*. New York: Putnam.

Martin, Jane Roland. 1992. *The Schoolhome*. Cambridge: Harvard University Press.

Moffett, James. 1994. *The Universal Schoolhouse*. San Francisco: Jossey-Bass.

Noddings, Nel. 1993. *Educating for Intelligent Belief or Unbelief*. New York: Teachers College Press.

Pinar, William. 1976. *Toward a Poor Curriculum*. Dubuque, IA: Kendall-Hunt Publishing.

Rosenzweig, Franz. 1955. *On Jewish Learning*. New York: Schocken Press.

Tillich, Paul. 1957. *Dynamics of Faith*. New York: Harper and Row.

A Pedagogy of Faith
in an Era of Triumphalism

Happy Days Are Here Again

These are times that future historians might refer to as another "era of good feeling," a time of relative consensus and harmony on basic structural issues when the center is the place of political choice. We are led to believe that there is a low rate of unemployment; that investors are in ecstasy; that the welfare rolls are shrinking; that the Evil Empire has been reduced to a pitiful and impotent shambles; and that the crime rate is falling. There are even moments when many Republicans and Democrats embrace each other in the redemptive quest for centrist consensus and harmony. There is, to be sure, the continuation of partisan bickering and rancorous battling for political advantage, much of it simultaneously trivial and uncivil. Moreover, there are some disquieting grumbles that often find some expression: some still worry about the effects of another inevitable downward swing in the economy; some do not believe that there is a safety net for those no longer in welfare programs; and, of course, there continues to be those who bring up the longer range, seemingly intractable problems, such as racism; sexism; environmental dangers; world wide poverty; continuing geo-political tensions; and the profusion of weapons of mass destruction.

However, the bridge to the twenty-first century seems to be constructed by a consciousness built on consolidation and consensus on the broad configuration of social and cultural policies. We seemed to have ardently and desperately, if not lovingly and longingly, adopted a consciousness rooted in the values of the market—aggressive, if not ruthless, competition; the frantic acquisition of material goods; the avid, if not mindless pursuit of pleasure; the glorification of the individual; and the avoidance of long-range commitments to grand ideals. This consensus also indicates that a number of other traditional values have either been downgraded or totally rejected: a deep concern for social justice; a serious commitment to community and economic equity; the quest for meaning; and devotion to nourishing mercy, compassion, and love.

Accompanying these consensual acts have come some disturbingly subversive outlooks—a sharp increase in cynicism, suspicion, distrust, passivity, and despair. Voter turnout and interest are down as are confidence and reliance on government, while no institution is spared public ridicule and contempt, from law to medicine, from the media to the Church. It has taken less than a generation for such terms as *paranoia* and *conspiracy theory* to move from the realm of arcane jargon to household usage. We have come to view the plight of the disadvantaged less as an opportunity to ease their plight and more as an opportunity to put an end to malingering, less a chance to be just and more to be punitive. Affirmative action is attacked because it does not sufficiently reward individual merit and education, and health services for "aliens" is to be denied because aliens, per se, are not deserving.

We have come to a point in our meritocratic myth that we can openly justify highly discriminating policies in responding to human necessities, where human rights come to be seen not as inherent but as privileges to be earned. Medical care, education, meaningful work, and a living wage are to be rationed, not so much because they have to be but because they should be. Racism, sexism, and homophobia grow not only because of their long intractable history but also because of the general increase of distrust and fear of others as the plague of the doctrine of the survival of the fittest returns in a more sophisticated and perhaps more deadly mutation.

However, we may be crazy but we're not stupid, since we as a culture seem to know that, even in our complacency, we are at serious risk. In spite of all the hype, all the proclamation of the end of history and the arrival of New Era economics, this happy time seems to be a rather joyless one with deep undercurrents of fear and loathing. People are working harder and with more anxiety; class, race, and gender conflicts seem harsher and more intractable, personal relationships, if anything, seem more problematic than ever, and much of the middle class seems to be deeply worried about the future. One is not sure if this is less an era of good feeling than an era of grudging fatalism, more a time of shrugging and struggling and less a time of celebrating and exalting.

The sense of helplessness, passivity, and grudging acceptance is significantly heightened by the lack of any serious attractive and plausible alternative ways of being and doing. There is an extraordinary ideological vacuum that seems to have been totally filled by the agenda of the global, free market economy.

Speaking very broadly, the sterility of alternative socio-economic political paradigms is probably due to at least four major historical forces, notwithstanding the obvious popularity of global capitalism. One is the belief, rightly or wrongly, that the communitarian vision of social democracy, as reflected modestly in American liberalism and more robustly in European socialism, has not only been betrayed by bureaucratic bungling and authoritarianism but is inherently conducive to them. Second is the perception that the history of utopian and idealistic movements is one of inevitable disillusionment and failure, a perception made more compelling by the diminishing effects of the various liberation movements of the sixties. This more recent wave of disillusionment only serves to magnify the deep pessimism that emerged as a result of the unspeakable horrors of twentieth century genocide, global warfare, famine, and political terror. Last has been the intellectual traditions of postwar existentialists and postmodern theorists which have provided renewed reasons and theoretical justification for pessimism and despair. The notion that justice and humanity are the products of rationality and science died at Auschwitz and Hiroshima. Moreover, recent insights from deconstructionist and feminist theory have shown us how us how presumably liberating values such as individuality, detachment, and objectivity have been turned into instruments of hegemony. Disenchantment and cynicism are a deadly team.

On one hand there is a sense that the vacuum fillers, i.e., the global economy and consumerism, have perhaps brought an end to the great ideological debates; yet, on the other hand there is the sense that what has really ended is our will and ability to engage in further fundamental debate. There is a paradox that in the wake of the triumph of individual freedom there is so little public disputation of fundamental social and cultural structures that the very freedom exemplifying the entrepreneurial consciousness seems to have stifled basic social inquiry and silenced serious public debate.

The End of Education

We may also be witnessing the demise of the concept of an education rooted in criticality and imagination, one directed at creating a more just and loving community. Education is increasingly seen as an applied technology, as providing the up-to-date information instrumental to maintaining a competitive edge, personally as well as culturally. There is, in addition to this economic focus, some emphasis on systematic education for acculturation, as reflected in the concern for multiculturalism and character education, although the direction in these areas is clearly a conservative one. Moreover, the notion of education as a force for critical analysis and social reconstruction grows increasingly weak as it moves into the marginal realms of fantasy and nostalgia.

The reasons for this decline are connected to the social and cultural issues described above—the sense of complacency, the lack of alternative social frameworks, the loss of optimism and hope, and the erosion of moral commitments. One of the great hopes of Enlightenment thinking has been that rational discourse and scientific research would free us from the tyranny of determinism and the restraints of conventionality. The idea being that we need not be controlled by destiny which, in reality, turns out to be only a mask for human institutions and practices that could be examined and improved through careful, critical, and imaginative thought. The Biblical dictum that "the truth shall make thee free" was transformed from a statement of spiritual liberation to a motto of humanism's project for individual autonomy through knowledge and rationality.

However, the centrality of knowledge has become increasingly problematic as knowledge in the marketplace becomes bits of fragile information, while in the Academy, it tends to take on the character of fragments of contingent and tentative presumptions. This would seem to squeeze the value of knowledge and rationality for personal and social transformation and transcendence between the rock of knowledge as useful and the hard place of knowledge as socially constructed. Many committed to the vision of the free market share the notion with many postmodernists of the fragility and perishability of knowledge and concurrently, a deep distrust of theories and visions. Call it cynicism or call it insight, it still gets down to a situation in which the culture relies less and less on a critical and imaginative education for social and personal redemption. The earnest hope that serious, heavy-duty scholarship is inextricably linked to progressive ideology has been dealt a serious, if not fatal, blow.

This, then, is the constellation of factors that threaten the vitality of a critical pedagogy of liberation and transformation: a consciousness of Arrival in which we believe we have finally reached consensus and solution on an ideal (or as close to ideal as we're going to get) social structure, one framed in the discourse of the market; an acceptance of the inevitability of division and inequity as a necessary, if not desirable aspect of the human condition; the erosion of confidence in what academics call "grand narratives" and what conservatives call "pipe dreams"; and the virtually total co-optation of education as instrument of preserving and enhancing the dominant culture.

It is much more difficult to make the case for a pedagogy of liberation and criticality when there is even less enthusiasm for an ideology of liberation and ever more skepticism about the intellectual validity of criticism and theory. However, it is also likely that this time of complacency and inertia coupled with despair and danger is not historically unique. Indeed, it is in just such times that responsible educators are of utmost importance, as they must be prepared to reenergize their faith in human imagination, intelligence, and agency and develop educational resources that can countervail the debilitating currents of smugness, drift, and neglect. Apart from the extremely formidable theoretical and professional barriers to such a project, there is, however, the rather embarrassing intellectual problem of finding valid alternative sociocultural paradigms that are accessible, plausible, and compelling. Where do we look for such ideas? To whom should we go for visions that are fresh and vibrant, free of rejected discourse and discredited baggage? More, to the point, are there any such formulations out there?

I want to suggest that there probably are, but they surely are not readily available and even if they were, there does not seem to be the requisite cultural readiness to render them credible or even discussable. In place of the notion that educators should offer alternative ideas and visions, I would suggest we work on an interim project, namely, educating for a consciousness in which transformation is necessary and possible; one in which we know that we are capable and required to have achievable dreams. Such a pedagogy is directed at subverting the triumphalism and complacency that blind us to intentional and unnecessary human conflict, suffering, and injustice. This pedagogy aims at undermining faith in a status quo that works to the

advantage of some at the expense of a great many. It is not a pedagogy of a particular vision but one that rejects a vision that accepts
anything less than a community of justice, love, and joy for all and a
pedagogy of faith in the human capacity to hope and work to create it.
It is about teaching people the possibility of a liberating and transformative education, i.e., a pedagogy of hope, or as we used to call it,
faith.

A Pedagogy of Faith

In this instance, I speak of a particular faith, one rooted in the conviction that we as humans will continue our commitment to work for a
just and loving society and that we have the moral, creative, and intellectual capacity to create one. I believe we are at risk in maintaining
this conviction and that one of our more urgent tasks is to shore up
this faltering faith.

It has become abundantly clear that the restoration of this faith will
not emerge from rational and critical discourse alone.

I believe we would be wise to take seriously the idea that much
pertinent and relevant wisdom and insight is to be found in what has
been called the mythopoetic; the realm of myth, music, dance, drama,
literature, folk wisdom, spirituality, and religion. I refer, in particular,
to that wisdom that is miraculously and simultaneously metahistorical
and contemporary, that which not only gives us insight into the human condition, but helps to nourish and deepen the impulse to create
a better world.

I want to examine, in this essay, the possibilities of religious discourse for contributing to a pedagogy of faith. My view is that certain
religious traditions can be especially relevant and helpful in these times
of despair, cynicism triumphalism, and powerlessness. Indeed, religious sensibilities may very likely emerge from the necessity to respond to situations like our own when meaning and hope are both
seriously lacking and needed. Religious thought, therefore, can be seen
as a demonstratively safe and effective antidote to despair as well as a
bracing tonic for rejuvenation. Moreover, religious traditions, situated
at the intersection of cosmology and history, explicitly deal with the
conflict of the ideal and the actual, demanding that we probe our deeds
in relation to notions of ultimate meaning.

There is nothing new about suggesting a pedagogy of faith, since
these issues have been the topic of much of our literature, art, phi-

losophy, and other sources of wisdom. Moreover, the inculcation of faith has surely always been a central concern for religious and spiritual education. However, the notion of purposely and systematically promoting faith in the capacity for social transformation in today's public schools seems, to put it mildly, highly problematic, if not the stuff of fantasy.

Not least of the problems is the powerful Constitutional injunction to maintain the separation of Church and State as well as the widespread apprehension of matters spiritual entering the curriculum. (This on top of the much more problematic issue of vigorous resistance to *any* pedagogy directed at cultural transformation.)

I strongly believe that from a political point of view, this constitutional restriction is a very wise and sensible one, in that it gives us safety from the threat of a particular kind of arbitrariness and dogmatism. In a pluralistic and democratic society we must always be on guard against institutions rooted in exclusiveness and privilege. I read the First Amendment as a proscription against the impulse of religious institutions to impose themselves on the society through positional power. In other words, there is to be no reserved place at the official political negotiating tables for organized religion. Given the continuing history of some religious institutions, it seems a prudent safeguard for the preservation of personal freedom, and given the history of some nations, it seems like a sensible way to safeguard religious expression and diversity.

However politically wise this separation may be, it does not mean that we have not been or should not be influenced, individually and communally, by religious aspirations and ideas. Indeed, it is quite possible that in our zeal to maintain the separation we may have thrown out the tyrannical baby of the institution with the healing bath water of spiritual renewal. Although the historical excesses of religious authoritarianism clearly justify our wariness and suspicions, we must also be careful not to overlook the extraordinary contributions that religious institutions have made to the quest for freedom and justice. Indeed, I tend to see reactionary and repressive religious policies and practices, at least generally, not as constitutive but as betrayals of their visions; not as essential and primary elements but as historically determined deviations. My point is simply to urge that in our understandable zeal to guard against the worst aspects of religious history that we not forgo the opportunity to benefit from its more majestic moments.

More particularly, I want to focus on the role that religion has had and continues to play in fundamental social criticism. Indeed, Robert Ackerman, in his book *Religion as Criticism*, believes that it is social criticism that gives religion its passion and legitimacy: "Religions have risen as legitimate protests against societies and ways of life, providing in the process the overpowering foundations for laying down one's life to improve the lot of humanity. . . . Critique does not exhaust religion. But religion that cannot critique is already dead. The main thread of religion may be one of potential opposition or criticism of a surrounding society by the development of a picture of life as how it should be lived. . . . What is being suggested is that the core of religion is potentially critical rather than functional or accommodating." (Ackerman, 1958, ix, 24).

Notice that the distinction Ackerman makes is between a critical and accommodating religion rather than between a repressive and a liberating religion. Religions, unlike the Academy, combine critique with transformative visions so that our difficulties with religion, ironically enough, have to do with both their tendency to accommodate *and* their refusal to accommodate. Some are impatient when religion serves to preserve and validate the status quo, while others are critical of religious leaders who suggest "fundamental" changes in the society and culture. I would also note how this distinction plays out for formal education, which is also expected to serve as a force for accommodation and preservation, a view that is sharply contested by those who urge that education serve as a force for fundamental change.

It is, therefore, vital to be able to distinguish among religious policies, practices, and traditions as to their relative orientations toward the existing social and cultural order. To summarily dismiss religious ideas and formulations as reactionary because some, if not many, of them serve repressive and cooptive functions is as absurd as giving up on art because there are some reactionary artists. Indeed, we can easily interpret religious expression as one of several important modes in which humanity has exercised its imagination to interpret and create a principled and meaningful world. Moreover, this imagination has often served to challenge a deeply ingrained and taken for granted consciousness. The potential and real value of religious thought in this historical moment of materialist triumphalism and moral despair is its very capacity to go beyond the horizons of perceivable possibilities.

I want to make it very clear that I do not present myself as a religious scholar and that my readings and understandings of religious texts are limited and modest. Such understandings do not go beyond the relatively familiar confines of Judaism and Christianity, so I am not able to speak of other rich and influential religious traditions. I say this not only in the interest of honesty and humility, but also as a way of claiming that religious texts are accessible and relevant to lay people and that they should not be the exclusive possession of the highly learned and/or deeply pious. You don't have to be Christian to be moved by the extraordinarily radical views of Jesus nor do you have to be a Talmudic scholar to be struck by the "moral audacity" of the Prophets. The simple point is that religious texts can and do provide educators with valuable insight, imagination, inspiration, and energy above and beyond their particular sectarian and theological significance.

The story of the Biblical patriarch Abraham is a powerful example of the human struggle between conformity and radicalism. Abraham grows up in a culture deeply imbedded in a polytheistic and idol-worshiping spirituality. Indeed, his father is a prosperous and influential member of his community, making his living sculpting and selling religious idols. Abraham himself works in his father's shop but begins to have very serious doubts about the spiritual validity of the very idols that he is selling. Eventually, he comes to feel the presence of God and openly and publicly renounces and ridicules the religion of his father, his family, his culture, and his tradition. There are fierce quarrels with his father (in one episode Abraham literally smashes his father's idols); clashes with neighbors. In another episode he has life-threatening encounters with the furious and alarmed king. So sharp and serious is this break that he decides that he must leave his homeland (the land of Ur) and his family, and he begins a long and fateful trek to other lands in his quest to create a totally new civilization, one resonant with his newly found faith.

To me, this can be read as an heroic story of a struggle against conformity and complacency grounded in deep faith and commitment. Abraham takes enormous risks as he confronts not only the political wrath of the King but faces the alienation of his community and the rejection of his family. It also speaks to possibility grounded in quest, a process of passionate searching that begins in an emerging awareness of greater possibility and more profound meaning than that provided in the existing culture. Moreover, there is in this story an exemplar of the power of human agency that is energized by faith, commitment, and courage. It is, I would maintain, also a story for our time.

In an essay on the Jewish theologian Abraham Heschel's views on religious self-understanding, Byron Sherwin notes that:

"For Heschel, adjustment to a society which 'persists in squandering the material resources of the world on luxuries in a world where more than a billion people go to bed hungry every night' is not something toward which one should aspire. . . . Heschel maintains that the religious endeavor fails in its quest for self-understanding when it claims adjustment as a necessary virtue. Religious self-understanding compels one to emulate Abraham, the father of Western religions. According to Rabbinic tradition, Abraham's distinction was in *not* adjusting but in defying and initiating. Judaism began with Abraham's destroying the idols of his father and his nation. . . . According to Heschel, authentic 'religion begins as a breaking off, as a going away. It continues in acts of non-conformity to idolatry'" (Sherwin, 1982, 19).

According to Nehama Leibowitz, Maimonides' interpretation of the Biblical story of Abraham (as clarified and elaborated by later Rabbinic accounts) includes this summary:

"He [Abraham] had neither teacher nor guide, but wallowed in Ur . . . amongst brutish idolaters, his father and mother and all the people serving the stars, he among them, his mind roving and seeking understanding, till he arrived at the true path and perceived the line of righteousness from his own right reasoning. . . . Forty years old was Abraham when he acknowledged his Creator. Now that he had been granted perception and knowledge he began to debate and argue with his neighbors, protesting that they were not following truth, breaking their idols and publicizing that there was only one God to whom it was meet to serve . . . that all images deserved to be destroyed and broken in pieces to save the people from error as they therefore imagined there was no god but them" (Leibowitz, 1986, 42, 43).

Abraham is not represented in the Bible as a god, but rather as a very human figure beset with limitations, conflicts, and obstacles. His faith and obedience to God extends to his apparent horrifying willingness to sacrifice his beloved son, Isaac. His determination to survive extends to his apparently craven and self-serving willingness to allow his wife, Sarah (whom he passes off as his sister) to enter the royal harem in order to placate an admiring and lascivious king. Despite these troubling acts of caution and passivity, he also displays remarkable independence and courage. Perhaps the most dramatic instance of this comes when Abraham actually confronts God Himself, demanding that He exercise mercy for the condemned and sinful citizens of

Sodom and Gomorrah. In Genesis 18:25, Abraham boldly challenges God's announcement that He is going to wipe out both towns as punishment for their evil ways: "Will You sweep away the innocent along with the guilty? . . . Far be it from You to do such a thing, to bring death upon the innocent as well as the guilty . . . Far be it from You! Shall not the Judge of all the earth deal justly? (Tanakh, 1985)

This is not rebelliousness for its own sake but a protest within a deep commitment to what Abraham knows to be God's will, a protest that is in effect a reaffirmation. The commitment is so steadfast and the faith so enduring, that Abraham is willing to risk all. As Anson Laytner says in his book *Arguing with God: A Jewish Tradition*, "To Abraham . . . it would appear that God stood on the brink of acting unjustly and that therefore He had to be brought around to acting in a more becoming (and godly) manner—an awesome and terrifying task. . . ." Laytner goes on to explain that Abraham derives his right to question God from the Covenantal contract he had entered into with God. "The Covenant, in that it sets forth the concrete and the moral responsibilities of both parties, gives Abraham and his descendants the right to dissent and even protest against any apparent abrogation of its terms by God . . ."(Laytner, 1990, 5).

This adds up to a story of a tradition that recognizes the value of a dynamic of profound challenge, cataclysmic rebellion, and ongoing criticality grounded in faith and commitment. It is a tradition that accepts the inevitability of false consciousness and human weakness at the same time it affirms the human capacity to transcend these limitations. It tells us that no matter how deeply rooted the idolatry, how oppressive the regime, how triumphant the ideology, they all can and must be overcome with human imagination and agency.

I want to briefly cite some modern day examples of this tradition as evidence of its vitality and its relevance to our present tradition. These examples illustrate the way in which religious and political discourse can be integrated, how people with varying backgrounds can converge on fundamental moral principles, and how religious traditions images can inform and strengthen the struggle for human liberation.

The first example comes from the work of Walter Brueggemann, the noted Protestant theologian and scholar of the Hebrew Bible who has written powerfully and eloquently on the prophetic Christian traditions of the quest for personal salvation and social justice. In a recent paper directed at Protestant clergy titled *"Testimony as a Decentered Mode of Preaching,"* Brueggemann addresses the situation of the Church in the context of contemporary times with special reference to postmodern thought. Although he acknowledges that the Church itself has been part of the old political hegemony, he concludes that the church has become intellectually and politically marginalized. He puts it this way:

"It is evident, I take it, that the church is no longer part of the intellectual-ideational hegemony of our culture, for reasons that are complex and obscure. Indeed, one can say that hegemonic power is in some disarray. But as concerns the church, the church has become (in both the United States and in Europe) profoundly disestablished and decentered so that it is no longer able to voice the kind of certitudes that will sustain the hegemony, and increasingly, elements of the church are no longer even willing to try. In a very large sweep, we may say that the church is now faced with a radically *secularized* society, in which the old assumptions of Christendom no longer prevail or command wide-spread and almost automatic acceptance. . . . It is possible to say that as the church has colluded with the old economic, political hegemony, i.e., the *ancien régime*, it was poorly situated to respond to the new cultural, intellectual situation which displaced the *ancien régime*" (Brueggemann, n.d., 6).

He goes on to propose that the church respond to this situation by embracing the metaphor of the Babylonian exile, the time when the Temple had been destroyed and the leaders of Israel had been banished into exile. He says:

"It is my sense that when the preacher proclaims in the baptized community in our present social context, the preacher speaks to *a company of exiles*. . . . Such people are at work seeking to maintain an *alternative identity,* an *alternative vision* of the world, and an *alternative vocation* in a societal context where the main force of culture seek to deny, discredit, or disregard that odd identity. . . . The great problem for exiles is cultural assimilation. The primary threat to those ancient Jews was that members of the community would decide that Jewishness is too demanding, or too dangerous, or too costly, and simply accept Babylonian definitions and modes of reality. . . . As Jews disappeared into the woodwork of Babylon, so Christians now, as never before in the West, disappear into the hegemony of secularism. . . Our task is to see about alternative practices, disciplines, and intentions which may sustain an alternative, subversive, counter-cultural identity" (Brueggemann, 5).

This point of view is echoed in an essay by Paulo Freire titled "Education, Liberation, and the Church" in which he writes from the perspectives of the Latin American struggles for liberation. In this essay Freire distinguishes among different orientations in the church which he describes as "traditional," "modern," and "prophetic." The "traditional church" tends to ignore if not renounce the everyday concerns of life as transient and inherently steeped in sin and impurity; instead, it focuses its attention on the promise of heaven and the dread of hell. Freire sees this orientation as one that ultimately serves the interests of the status quo:

. . . "Thus, seeing the world itself as the antagonist, they [the leaders of the traditional church] attempt the impossible; to renounce the world's mediation in their pilgrimage. By doing so, they hope to reach transcendence without passing by way of the mundane; they want metahistory without experiencing history; they want salvation without knowing liberation. The pain of domination leads them to accept this historical anaesthesia in the hope that it will strengthen them to fight sin and the devil—leaving untouched all the while the real causes of their oppression. . . ." (Freire, 1985, 136)

According to Freire, the "modernizing church" in contrast involves itself in political and social matters but does so in concert with the process of industrialization and modernization.

The modernizing church puts emphasis on being up-to-date, especially in the use of modern modes of mass communication, but Freire maintains that its political orientation is hardly different from that of the traditional church:

"Like the traditionalist churches, of which they are a new version, they are not committed to the oppressed but to the power elite. That is why they defend structural reform over radical transformation of structures; they speak to the humanization of capitalism rather than to its total suppression" (136).

He speaks of a third kind of emerging church, which he describes as "a utopian, prophetic, and hope-filled movement" committed to radical social change. "The prophetic church is no home for the oppressed, alienating them further by denunciations. On the contrary, it invites them to a new Exodus. Nor is the prophetic church one that chooses modernization and thereby does more than stagnate. Christ was no conservative. The prophetic church, like him, must move forward constantly, forever dying and forever being reborn . . ." (139).

Perhaps we might consider revising the metaphor of church and state as indicating less the difference between ecclesiastical tyranny and personal choice and more between what Brueggemann calls assimilation and what Freire refers to as an invitation to a new Exodus.

The public schools do indeed function as powerful instruments of cultural assimilation, much like Freire's modernizing church. They also pose a serious threat to companies of exiles intent on creating an "alternative, subversive counter-cultural identity." The schools do seem to be an important aspect of the modernization process, more intent on institutional reform than prophetic transformation.

Perhaps the principle of separation not only serves the valuable purpose of protecting us from religious dogmatism and conformity but also the more troubling function of shielding us from the searing critique that emerges from religious traditions that demand and provide alternative visions.

Indeed it would seem that a broader analysis of the concept of church would indicate that we have been quite selective in the way we separate church and state. While it is clear that we have more or less successfully resisted the efforts of what Freire calls the "traditional church" to take direct political control of the schools, it is also clear that the traditional church has had and continues to have a remarkable impact on American cultural and social policies on such issues as abortion, gay rights, sex education, and text selection. It is also apparent that the so-called moderate churches and synagogues work comfortably within the basic institutional framework of society and their presence serves as a strong force for continuity and stability, i.e., as part of the cultural dynamic that preserves and legitimates the status quo. For these two traditions, the separation is not a bad trade-off; the forces of traditionalism and modernity get to have an opportunity to significantly affect American life even as they observe constitutional limits.

Moreover, in the context of the present dominant culture, the separation also serves to weaken the impact of the prophetic traditions for it is these traditions that most threaten both the ideological and intellectual status quo. In fact, the prophetic tradition is anathema to a wide spectrum of opinion: to those on the right because it represents a politics of dissent, and to those on the left because it represents a discourse of religion.

Conclusion

My analysis is rooted in the assumption that we live in a time when the dominant culture of materialism, hierarchy, privilege, competition, conquest, and greed has become stronger and more entrenched. This is, partly, because those who are inclined to resist have faltered in their hope and faith in alternative visions. The relatively modest point that I want to make is that as educators we need to attend to that faltering faith, and there are important and substantial resources to be found in certain religious traditions to help in that endeavor.

We cannot be allowed to forgo these resources because of a narrow Constitutional perspective anymore than because of a simplistic understanding of religious traditions. The knee-jerk reaction to the separation clause can, paradoxically enough, deprive us of the intellectual and moral energy required to create a nation where there is liberty and justice for all, one conceived in the notion that all people are created equal. Such commitments are not to be reduced to matters of political theory nor dismissed as banal sentimentalities. Rather they represent the spiritual and moral foundations of our social vision as well as the fundamental agenda of our vocation as educators.

It is true that religious leaders are not always aligned with progressive ideology; nor, for that matter, are leaders in other fields. It is true, for example, that the Catholic Church has very conservative views on a number of gender issues such as birth control and women as clergy. At the same time, the Church has often severely criticized capitalism for its insensitivity to human needs. Pope John Paul II, for example, has said:

"The needs of the poor take priority over the desires of the rich; the rights of workers over the maximization of profits; the preservation of the environment over uncontrolled industrial expansion; production to meet social needs over production for military purposes" (1984, 353).

As a Jew, I am also painfully aware of hyper-orthodox rabbis in Israel whose rigidity, bigotry, and zealotry contribute so much to the dangerous polarization in Israel and the Middle East. However, I am also aware that another orthodox rabbi, Abraham Joshua Heschel, actively participated in the civil rights and antiwar movements on religious grounds. In an essay describing the process of study he undertook before his decision to protest the war in Viet Nam, he had this to say:

"Such discoveries revealed the war as being exceedingly unjust. As a result, my concern to stop the war became *a central religious* concern. . . . Although Jewish tradition enjoins our people to obey scrupulously the decrees issued by the government of the land, whenever a decree is unambiguously immoral, one nevertheless has a duty to disobey it" (1996, 226). When he was asked to respond to President Johnson's dismay that people were questioning Presidential authority so strongly, Heschel replied:

"When the Lord was considering destroying Sodom and Gomorrah, Abraham did not hesitate to challenge the Lord's judgment and to carry on an argument with Him whether His judgment was just. Can it be that the Judge of the entire Universe would fail to act justly? For all the majesty of the office of the President of the United States, he cannot claim greater majesty than God Himself" (226).

Such views, coming as they do from orthodox religious traditions, ought at least to remind us of what we lose when we are separated from a "church" that does not speak a voice of accommodation, resignation, and docility. Who truly benefits from marginalizing voices of political dissent and moral affirmation on the grounds that they are spoken from within religious institutions? It would seem that we ought to celebrate the fact that there are religious leaders who see their task as speaking out with moral and religious fervor on those very issues that seem beyond criticism.

My position can be summarized as follows: we continue to live a life of danger to our basic moral project of creating a community of peace, love, justice, and joy, but the task is further seriously complicated in a time of sociopolitical triumphalism with its concomitant sterility of competing alternatives. I affiliate myself with those who have faith that inevitably historical forces and human genius will once again combine to produce fresh and liberating critiques as well as compelling and energizing alternatives. It is a faith that wavers, however, and is very much in need of support and reassurance that the prime task in this moment is to work to develop the conditions necessary for the restoration of the hope and energy out of which new vitality and imagination will emerge.(My own guess is that these "new ideas" will be a restatement of some traditional ones, but so be it.)

It is in this sense that we face a spiritual more than an intellectual crisis, i.e., a loss of hope, a failure of nerve, a pessimism and despair that saps the will and only inexorably worsens the problem. This is surely *not* to say that we do not also face intellectual barriers but only to posit that the ability to overcome them requires spiritual strength, i.e., the power that comes from internal energy, hope, and animation. The kind of hope and faith I am referring to is not to be confused with romanticism or even optimism; indeed it is what we need in the face of the empirical necessity to reject optimism. In other words, we must face the problem of how to proceed when we know we should but are not clear on direction and pretty sure that if we did know where we should be headed, we wouldn't be able to get there. This is a time when our knowledge tells us that the battle appears to be lost, when it seems senseless to continue, and when, alas, optimism is a delusion. In such despairing times what is urgently required is the kind of hope and energy that is so often powerfully exemplified in our religious traditions. Miraculously enough, such faith seems to have thrived in other times of complacency, if not desperation. I believe that it is our present task to keep this miraculous tradition alive.

References

Ackerman Robert. 1985. *Religion as Criticism*. Amherst, MA: University of Massachusetts Press.

Brueggemann, Walter. 1998. Testimony as a Decentered Mode of Preaching: Unpublished paper.

Friere, Paulo. 1985. *The Politics of Education: Culture, Power, and Liberation* (Westport, CT: Bergin and Garvey.

Heschel, Susanna (ed.). 1996. *Moral Grandeur and Spirituality*. New York: Farrar, Straus, Giroux.

Laytner, Anson. 1990. *Arguing with God: A Jewish Tradition* Northvale. NJ: Jason Aronson, 1990).

Leibowitz, Nehama. 1964. *Studies in Genesis*. Jerusalem: World Zionist Organization.

Origins. vol. 14, no. 22 (1984), 353.

Sherwin, Byron. 1982. *Abraham Joshua Heschel*. Atlanta: John Knox Press.

Tanakh, a New Translation of the Holy Scriptures. 1985. New York: Jewish Publications Society.

Part Four

AN AUTOBIOGRAPHICAL ESSAY

Among the various helpful criticisms that I received on *The Moral and Spiritual Crisis in Education,* none was more telling than the reaction from some of my closest friends and colleagues. They gently but firmly chided me for not being more open and forthcoming about how my personal history was implicated in my work. More particularly, they pointed out that although the book strongly alluded to Jewish thought and traditions, I had not affirmed nor even acknowledged my Jewish identity, which was so clearly reflected in the writing.

I believe that they were absolutely right and have since been more explicit in my writing (and my teaching) about my background and beliefs. Some of this change is reflected in some of the essays in this collection, but the following article is the most systematic effort to situate my professional concerns within my own experiences. As I indicated in my introduction, I was reluctant to include this piece in this book for two reasons. First, the article was written for a book specifically dealing with how various educators have integrated their Jewish traditions with their work. What is central for that book seems marginal, if not parochial, for this book. More importantly, I do not want the article to serve as a distraction from the larger themes of this book. It may very well be that the particulars of my life would be helpful and interesting to those who, for some reason, want to know more about me, but the concerns and issues represented in this book are not mine alone. They involve us all in a struggle that is far more important than the story of any one individual. This is surely not a book about me but a book of my observations on matters that vitally affect our lives and those who will follow us.

However, I include the article as an act of affirmation not only of my background but as a celebration of diversity and subjectivity. More particularly, I see the article as an affirmation of affirmation itself as well as of a particular affirmation of a vision of personal meaning and a just and loving community.

On Being a Jew and
a Boston Braves Fan:
Alone and Afraid in a
World I Never Made

In the Beginning

Much of my family's story is achingly and painfully familiar, part of the narrative of Jewish experience that allows one to use the words routine and tragic in the same sentence. Both my parents were born in the same shtetl in what is now Ukraine, just south of Kiev, and each of them witnessed the murder of a parent by bandits in the chaos and tumult of the Russian civil war. Both fled in terror and made their individual ways as teenagers across Europe by the grace of luck, grit, bribes, some kind people, a network of Jewish agencies, and God knows what else. They eventually arrived in Boston in the early twenties, got married and settled down to a life of poverty, struggle, fear, and grief.

Their life spans coincided with World War I, the Bolshevik revolution, the Red scare, the Depression, the rise of Fascism, the New Deal, World War II, the Holocaust, the Atomic age, the Cold War, McCarthyism, the establishment of the state of Israel, the Korean War, the Civil Rights Movement, the war in Viet Nam, the Watergate scandals, and the assassinations of Archduke Ferdinand, Leon Trotsky, Mohandas Gandhi, John Kennedy, Martin Luther King, and Robert Kennedy.

Politically, they were basically radicals but their commitment to socialism was always delimited by their fear of Stalin and the traditions of virulent Russian anti-Semitism. They adored FDR but were tempted to vote for Norman Thomas, they were strong supporters of the labor movement, and they thought that government was there to protect us from big business. They almost always voted and followed political campaigns with great interest and acumen.

They had read Gogol and Tolstoy in Russian, Sholom Aleichem and the brothers Singer in Yiddish, and Dorothy Parker and Philip Roth in English. They had seen Menashe Skulnik, Maurice Schwartz, and Molly Picon on the stage, in the movies and on television and heard them on the radio, likewise Mary Martin, Helen Hayes, and Paul Newman. They loved Sid Caesar's comic genius, were scornful of Milton Berle's vulgarity, and were much more devoted to *Playhouse 90* than to any sitcom. They never went to a proper school.

They did this in between the frustrating and backbreaking tasks of running a small grocery store, beset with a shrinking clientele and ferocious competition from "the chain stores" and the overwhelming chores that come with parental responsibilities. They had five children (one of whom died from a ruptured appendix at the age of two) each one of whom provided them with opportunities for pride, aggravation, hopes, and disappointments. They had their share of existential crises, marital disputes, major illnesses, and probably less than their share of joys, triumphs, and celebrations.

They were indeed complicated folks, often loving and generous, sometimes mean-spirited and spiteful; always worried and fearful; usually secretive and guarded; capable of genuine gaiety and laughter, and yet ultimately presenting a morose image of themselves as victims, surviving with poignant dignity but struggling to control their demons of terror, fear, and despair. They were very intelligent, even wise; well read; politically sophisticated; sort of open-minded but also wary and skeptical of change. Their attitudes toward their Jewish and American identities were complicated, full of fierce loyalties but laced with ambivalence, ambiguity, and paradox.

They certainly wanted their children to be Jewish, but their modes of acculturation were irregular and unfocused. For one thing, and probably for reasons much more psychological than ideological, they purposefully decided *not* to live in a Jewish neighborhood, which gave us all the opportunity to interact with a predominantly Irish Catholic, working-class community, one which at best aspired to and occasionally reached attitudes of strained toleration toward "kikes." My parents put heavy stress on Yiddishkeit, were only mildly observant although strict on some issues (no mixing of dairy with meat, no pork or shrimp, no school on the Holidays, at least most of the time). Although they were both quite knowledgeable about religious practices and traditions they expressed a skeptical if not cynical attitude towards religious institutions. They were apprehensive, suspicious, and patronizing of *goyim* and contemptuous of assimilating and socially ambitious Jews, whom they called "all-rightniks." They taught us to read Yiddish authors but not the Torah; they discussed/argued political and social but not theological issues with us; and they insisted that we remember and revere our heritage as Jews, even as they disavowed the Jewish God.

I went to Hebrew school four days a week (after public school and on Sundays) and became a bar mitzvah. That was the only formal Jewish education I ever had, and although I learned to read and write Hebrew, it was a very threadbare education at best. And yet I have become convinced that with all the mixed signals and missed opportunities, and all the other craziness in my home, my parents provided me with some critically important and energizing notions that have helped to shape my worldview, one that clearly has a strong Jewish flavor.

In retrospect these Jewish influences that came from my childhood seem to have influenced my professional work more than they did my personal life. (But that's another story.) In some ways my professional foci (citizenship education, critical thinking, clinical supervision, critical pedagogy, moral education), even as they shifted, all seemed to have common resonance with some of the more visible Jewish values. However, this did not become clear to me till I came to write *The Moral and Spiritual Crisis in Education*, the work that best represents my professional concerns and value commitments.

I have to confess that I often felt inspired while I was actually writing this book. By that I emphatically do not mean that the book was ghostwritten by some divine author but rather that I sensed that I had entered a different kind of space, a mysterious space made special and exciting because it seemed to be sacred. I do not believe that I would have been open to this experience had I not just read Abraham Joshua Heschel's monumental and truly inspired work *The Prophets*. When I read it I was afraid I would hyperventilate, so powerful, so profound, and so compelling was it to me. I knew that the paradigm of prophetic thought focusing on a God of history, justice, and mercy who strives in covenant with humanity to create a loving and just community that Heschel so eloquently and passionately describes was and is the one for me. What was so extraordinary was the way Heschel's book was simultaneously familiar and new to me. The substantive elements were all new to me, in truth, up to that point I had zero idea of the significance of the Prophets—who they were, what they did and said, and what they represented. And yet the essential message seemed to be in harmony with my intuitive sense of what constitutes the ultimate meaning and purpose of life. What was annoying to me was that it had taken me so long to find this paradigm. What was mysterious to me was how I had somehow come to resonate with this basic language in spite of my unfamiliarity with the particular literature.

What was also inspirational was that I was struggling with something far more important and worthwhile than my usual limitations and constraints, nothing less than the opportunity to write within that sacred paradigm. How successful or unsuccessful I was in this responsibility is not totally clear to me but one thing did become apparent to me. I had discovered that an essential part of the moral and spiritual grounding of my work had always been there. The exciting thing was that this came to me in such a mysterious way, and the embarrassing thing was that I didn't really know very much about this grounding.

This account only partially explains why the book that eventually emerged, while certainly stressing the centrality of the prophetic tradition, does not speak directly to the Jewish sensibility that permeates it. It took me a long time to fully recognize, as some of my colleagues told me early on, that I had written a Jewish book without saying so. It took me much less time to recognize that if I indeed had written within Jewish traditions, I had done so as an amateur. Hence my agenda became clear. I needed to know a lot more about this grounding, and so I have read and continue to do a lot of reading and studying of traditional Jewish sources. I am finding it to be both exciting and frustrating, both accessible and opaque, simultaneously compelling and remote. I also realized that I needed to be a lot more explicit about my Jewish orientation and have made some tentative and modest steps in that direction in my writing and teaching.

I have taken the time to write about my parents and my personal background partly to highlight the difficulty of factoring out the Jewish dimension of my life from the myriad of other influences and factors, be they psychological, historical, sociological, or characterological in nature. It is easy enough to say that my parents were Jewish, that I grew up in a Jewish home, and that I consider myself to be a Jew. After that it's very hard. Not only is it excruciatingly difficult to explain what I have said about my Jewish background and identity but it is also exceedingly difficult to sort out and explain the enormously complicated dynamics of the matrix of personal, cultural, circumstantial, contingent, and societal events that shape my consciousness. Indeed, it is this complexity that makes this writing assignment so challenging, so difficult, and so risky. Furthermore, when it came time for me to begin to work on the assignment, I realized that my customary professional discourse and writing style were not going to be of much help and more likely would be counterproductive in addressing the questions of the integration of my personal and professional lives.

The task would seem to require serious self-interrogation, a process that I have so far assiduously and successfully neglected and avoided. Indeed, I have been so successful that I've had to think hard about a different approach that would at least enable me to make a good faith effort at writing this essay. This led me to understand that even though until fairly recently I had largely avoided careful, systematic self-examination of my Jewish identity, my Jewish consciousness has surely not evolved randomly, nor is it disconnected from my persona nor from my work. Rather, it is expressed in my attitudes, behaviors, and sensibilities and is lodged in the crowded, messy, and unswept compartments of my interiority.

In order to bring some order to this clutter, I decided to rely on, of all things (you should excuse the expression) my intuition. My intuition told me that I would have to dig deep to find some gems, but that these gems are stored in places that are dear and accessible to me. These places turn out to be the vast treasure of Jewish stories of all varieties, be they legends, tales, jokes, anecdotes, allegories, or midrashim. More particularly, the richest source of self-insight would be those stories that I especially love to read, hear, and tell over and over again. My intuition-driven reasoning is that I can learn a lot from those specific stories precisely because I continue to tell them. Their very persistence in my nervous system indicates that they resonate with my innermost sense of meaning. Therefore, I would like simply to tell a few of these stories and then reflect on their meaning and significance for me.

Before I tell these stories I will need to add a few more bits of autobiographical information that can help to describe and explain the interpretative orientation that I bring to the process. I now believe that one of the most revealing if not formative events of my life was my experience with the Boston Braves during the 1940s. This was a time when there were only sixteen major league baseball teams, and when Boston had franchises in both leagues. One of them was the incomparably more popular and more talented Red Sox; the other, usually referred to as the "hapless Braves," was a team with little or no talent and with few paying customers. As vaunted and revered were the Red Sox as a team of destiny and redemption, the Braves were derided and dismissed as a source of shame and embarrassment. The Red Sox were celebrated, the Braves barely tolerated. Attendance at spiffy Fenway Park would range from twenty to thirty thousand, while the faithful who made their way to dingy Braves Field rarely numbered more than eight or ten thousand. Red Sox fans were braggarts and arrogantly demanding, just as Braves fans were humble and easily satisfied. If the Red Sox failed to finish first in the standings it was considered a miscarriage of justice while it was considered to be a moral triumph if the Braves finished sixth in an eight-team race. I was to become a devoted Braves fan.

How I got to be a Braves fan is fairly clear. One day during summer vacation I walked down to the local park and noticed that a man was passing out cards to other kids. Intrigued, I sidled over and made myself available, hoping that I might be included. It quickly became clear that the man was not discriminating and was pleased to give me or anyone else one of these cards. The card offered the holder free membership in the Boston Braves Knothole Gang, which entitled members to Pavilion admission to any weekday game for the price of thirty-five cents instead of the regular ninety cents. (I didn't know what Pavilion meant except that it was better and more expensive than the sixty-cents bleachers.) That's what led me to what was to be the first of countless visits to shabby, very uncrowded Braves Field.

However, the reason for the constancy of my loyalty in the face of continuous humiliation and disappointment remains elusive although less mysterious than it once was. Although I surely "liked" the Braves, I can't say that I admired them nor was I an adoring fan of any particular player. I can't say that I simply enjoyed going and listening to the games for I became very emotionally involved with whether or not they won (which they usually did not). If they won I would be elated but always aware that the happiness would be of very short duration. When they lost, I would be completely unsurprised but disconsolate nevertheless. I also have to admit that I secretly "hated" the Red Sox and their fans and nothing was sweeter in those scary wartime days than to read the newspaper on a day when the Braves won, the Red Sox lost, the Allies advanced, and the Nazis were repulsed.

I was also mystified by some of my friends who actually chose to root for teams outside of Boston (e.g., the New York Yankees or the St. Louis Cardinals) and appalled by the fact that their choice was based on the undoubted, but to me irrelevant, reality that these were talented and winning teams. Not only did I believe that this was disloyal, but I thought it was a violation of the rules.

It is easy enough to attribute this strong identification, loyalty, and bonding to the developmental processes of early adolescence, but even with greater age and maturity I continued to feel connected and to feel that my well-being was somehow related to the fortunes of the various incarnations of the Braves from Boston to Milwaukee to Atlanta. Moreover, this has also come to be true for all the other Boston sports teams (including the Red Sox, whom I've come to forgive and embrace). The truth is that I still care a lot about how these teams fare, even as I realize how silly and dumb all this is and even more as I realize how well-nigh impossible it is for me to disconnect from these relationships, for try as I might, I cannot be indifferent to the fortunes of these teams.

In some ways the questions and quandaries concerning these connections are similar and parallel to the ones regarding my Jewish identity. Did I choose to be a Braves fan any more or less than I chose to be Jewish? Why is my loyalty to the Braves and Jews independent of anything Jews or Braves believe, do, or say? If the recruiter for the Red Sox Knothole Gang had been at the park a day earlier, would I have become a Red Sox fan? Was my initial bonding to the Braves a matter of obsession? A genuine symbiosis? An instance of self-indulgent pride and chauvinism? Or was it an example of true and profound commitment? Am I Jewish only because of the happenstance of birth, and do I have any more capacity to renounce my Jewish identity than I did to reject my Braves fandom? Did I continue to support the Braves because they were, presumably like my perception of Jews, oppressed, despised, and pitiful? Or was it vice versa? Did I resent the Red Sox because they were a metaphor for the smug, entrenched, and powerful goyim? Perhaps my two major identities were related by dint of their affording me the opportunity to have a unique identity in my neighborhood and/or to be oppositional; perhaps they both represented my status as marginal and minority; perhaps they reflected a concern for justice and mercy for the oppressed, or perhaps they both allowed me to wallow in martyrdom and victimization.

The Stories of My Life

As I have indicated, my plan is to continue this analysis primarily through the use of stories that are dear and compelling to me and that seem to contain important insights into issues of Jewish identity. I have no intention of trying to define, explain, or analyze the concept of story, or the importance of stories to Jewish experience, or even the importance of narrative in a post-modern world. This is because (a) I don't know how to, (b) it's not relevant to my purpose, and besides, (c) it's story time.

The Mother and Her Son the Physicist

The mother of a renowned physicist, proud as she is of her son, feels frustrated that she doesn't really understand what he does, and asks him if he would explain Einstein's theory of relativity to her. The son, the physicist, has mixed feelings about this. He is touched by the gesture but fearful of the difficulty, the inevitable frustration, and the consequences of failure. Nonetheless, he proceeds cautiously and patiently, and miraculously the mother slowly but surely begins to understand more and more until she not only fully comprehends but is able to carry on a sophisticated dialogue with her son on theoretical physics. The son is ecstatic and feels good not only about what his mother has accomplished but also about the implications for science education. The mother is also very proud and happy but it is clear that she remains a bit puzzled and skeptical in spite of her achievement. She decides to share her uncertainty with her son and during a dinner time conversation, as he is summarizing yet again the major elements of Einstein's theory of relativity, she abruptly interrupts him. "Okay, okay," she insists, "I understand the theory fine, but, just tell me one thing, Sonny: Is it good for the Jews?"

This is a very old story and obviously gets subtly changed with the telling, but its shocking punch line has remained the same. There are some interesting and revealing dimensions of the story as told: the relationship between an adoring mother and an achieving son (Jewish jokes rarely speak of achieving daughters); the patient yet anxious son warily trying to please the insatiable demands of a clinging mother; and the paradox and ambiguity concerning the mother's level of intelligence and sophistication. However, the story's power would seem to pivot on the extraordinary reductionism in which sooner or later everything comes to be seen through the vulgar prism of Jewish chauvinism.

I love this story. I find it to be very funny in both its irony and its exaggeration. But I also love it because it has come to mean much more to me than a good gag. For one thing, there is within the story the strong suggestion of the angst and insecurity that is so much part of Jewish experience, for the mother's question could easily be changed to "Is it going to be bad for the Jews?" The concern derives from a consciousness shaped by the requirement to be constantly alert to the possibility of danger including, if not especially, from seemingly benign sources. Paranoid Jew would seem to be a redundant term, and one cannot but identify with the courage of this woman to give voice to the kind of suspicion and wariness that many Jews nervously and embarrassingly feel about the unfamiliar. When we laugh at this woman we are no doubt reflecting our own difficulty in distinguishing absurd from genuine threats since we know that there are plenty of both in the land as we try to simultaneously protect ourselves from looking silly and being victimized. The mother in this story plays it safe; better we should ask, lest we get lulled into a false sense of security by the distractions of family ties and academic thought. In this instance, politics triumphs over concerns for both relationship and scholarship.

It's at this point that the smile weakens, the laughter begins to fade, and the anger and resentment start to appear. We are now back in touch with the reality that a whole people has come to be consigned to the condition of feeling constant and justifiable dread, a condition that speaks to centuries of enduring intolerable injustice, pain, and suffering.

There is additional wisdom here that is obscured by the mother's extreme ethnocentrism, for the story is a powerful statement about the inevitability of subjectivity, partisanship, and perspective. The mother is clearly single-minded in her interests, seemingly obsessively focused, seeing virtually everything solely from the perspective of what contributes to the welfare of Jews. Nowadays philosophers could easily term such phenomena as hermeneutical, while psychologists might call it projection, cultural critics could mark it as an instance of a particular interpretative narrative, ideologues might refer to it as bias, and pundits as spin control. To that extent, the mother's response is prototypically human but, of course, its highly exaggerated form takes it to the level of absurdity and exquisite irony. However, the story does teach us about the relationship between the external and the internal, while providing us with a lesson on the problematics of subjectivity, particularly of the dangers of zealotry and chauvinism.

So what does my fascination with this story tell me about my Jewish identity? The fact that the story is immediately accessible and understandable to me says already that I have a close affinity to some kind of Jewish community. I have to confess that I can both identify with and be repelled by the mother's paranoic obsessiveness and to that extent the story tends to have an alienating effect on me. In spite of this, the story also has within it the roots of quite a number of issues that are at the center of my work. As I've already indicated, the persistence of the fear and dread is so strong and vivid to me that I find it both impossible either to accept or to deny its implicit horror. It is no surprise to me that my teaching and writing is marked by continuous references to the unacceptable presence of enormous unnecessary human suffering and to the assertion that the educational process ought to be seen primarily in its relationship with the struggle for social justice.

This story has also required me to scrutinize my attitudes toward the mother, for even as I am embarrassed by her narrowness, I am moved by her sincerity and earnestness as well as the poignancy of her concerns for a loving relationship with her son and the well-being of the Jewish people. It is surely possible and important to be critical of her attempt to manipulate her son and to distort science but it is also important on a personal level to understand her perspective. We need to celebrate her commitments when we give her the benefit of the doubt, and to at least forgive her parochialism when we can't. The importance of giving the benefit of doubt, of affording understanding and compassion to people, and of searching for moral transcendence in "ordinary people" are themes and values that have intrigued and haunted me as I try to figure out the place of empathy, compassion, and affirmation in my notions of a redemptive education.

More critically, I value the story to the extent that it shows how piety and self-righteousness can mask self-serving, blind, and knee-jerk partisanship. The reaction of the mother in this story is to me a metaphor of a very common attitude among any number of strongly committed folks who so deeply identify with their group or cause that they can get carried away into excessive self-absorption and neurotic xenophobia. Surely this story could be easily adapted to the excesses of other beleaguered groups struggling for recognition and survival. There have been many, many times when I've wanted to tell this story in the context of having to listen to revisionist harangues which place a heretofore neglected group in the number-one spot on the victim list and into the very epicenter of what is most vital in the universe. A sensitivity to political correctness (and worrying about how this would reflect on Jews) usually prevents me, but the devastating punch line is always there waiting only for the set-up: Tell me, at the core of things, is postmodernism (or existentialism, or critical theory) Good for women? For African-Americans? For gays? For the rain forest? or for that matter, the Braves? Just fill in the blanks.

Tell me, is this funny or not? Tell me, Ma, is this part of the Jewish tradition?

The King and the Poisoned Grain

This story is not from the world of jokes but from the realm of Hasidic lore and it is my understanding that it was originally told by Nachman of Bratzlav. However, I have recast the story from the two written versions I have seen and the many I have heard.

In a country long ago and far away, the prime minister comes breathless to the king with disturbing information. "Sire," he says, "I have the most dreadful news to report. The new crop of grain that our people have just completed gathering has been found to contain within it a poison of such power that it makes those who partake of it utterly mad. Since this crop is our only source of food, it is certain that all the men, women, and children of our kingdom will in a very short time become mad." The king is mortified to hear such grievous news and buries his head in his hands, sobbing with great bitterness and pain. "Do not despair, my king," says the prime minister, "for I have other information that surely will ease your pain. There is still some of last year's harvest left in the royal granary. Indeed Sire, there is enough for you and me to carry us through until the next harvest."

The king looks up, dries his tears and speaks softly but firmly to the minister. "No, this will not be done as I do not wish to be a sane ruler of a mad kingdom. Therefore, you and I will both eat of the new crop and we will become mad like everyone else. However, before we eat of the poisonous bread, we will each paint a red dot on our foreheads. In this way, we shall always know and remember that we are mad."

To me this is primarily a story about the importance of confronting and accepting both harsh realities and compelling responsibilities. The king is fully aware of the cruelty and the tragedy of the situation and in this desperate situation, does not grasp for straws and nor does he seek a personal escape hatch. The king's watchful minister also confronts reality head-on and accordingly has performed his bureaucratic

functions well; he has assembled the facts, assessed the available resources, developed options, and has a plan of action. What he lacks,
however, is the king's wisdom and vision that extend beyond political
survival to what is required for a long and difficult struggle for the
kingdom to regain its sanity. What is minimally required is a recognition of the patent suffering that is sure to follow as well as of the
limitations that will face the community in its struggles. Beyond that,
the king knows that the responsibility of leadership rests with full
membership in the community, not just politically but spiritually and
existentially. The denial of the opportunity for special privilege not
only affirms the king's solidarity with and compassion for his people,
but his insight that he must experience and share their suffering if he
is to presume to lead them.

The king is also wise enough to know about denial and the tendency to sentimentalize. He realizes immediately that even the powerful and wise will need to be reminded of what really is, what once was,
and what might yet be. There is in this story a poignant message of
the importance of awareness, memory, and vision and a hint at the
dangers of denial, forgetting, and co-optation. The king is not worried
about preserving the memory of nostalgia but about the preservation
of the memory of lost capacities and aspirations. He seems to fear
that the people will blur what they must face with what they might still
transcend, thus forgetting in their confusion the memory of hope and
possibility. In this story, realism and vision are not contradictory but
complementary, not conflicting but synergistic, not a matter of forced
choice but an opportunity for partnership.

I believe that this aspect of the story helps me to understand why I
have been so wary if not contemptuous of educators who are so optimistic and gushy about the latest research finding, innovation, or
change. I continue to be amazed at the cheerful hubris that surrounds
the claims for the importance of new insights and the possibilities of
the latest educational remedies. Don't they know that things usually
don't work out and that in the long run Murphy triumphs? Don't they
know how devilishly complicated human behavior is and how little we
actually know about it? I guess such alienation and pessimism are part
of the legacy of a Jewish Braves fan.

I also continue to be startled by the way we (I) continue in our
lunatic educational practices, for not only do we persist in engaging in
professionally sanctioned yet morally suspect behaviors, but we are
also active in perpetuating and validating them. It is hard for me to

accept the fact that intelligent and good people do such destructive and corrupting things as grade students, compete for academic honors, participate in selective admissions, and develop merit pay schemes. One popular Jewish response to such determined forgetting, which is often expressed with an exaggerated shrug accompanied with a "Nu, so what can you do?" at least offers some recognition of the seriousness of the situation, but its inherent passivity is troubling. Another Jewish way, as reflected in this story, is the path that I have found to be more productive, and that path is the one of humility and agency in which we definitely act, but in the full awareness of our limitations and restrictions. Consequently, I find myself frequently quoting both in my teaching and writing the wonderful Talmudic adage: "The task is not ours to finish, but neither are we free to take no part in it."

Others see also in this story a major emphasis on the king's iron determination to maintain the Jewish community and his strong bond with the Jewish people, hence the story can be seen as a powerful affirmation of solidarity, community, and peoplehood. The king loves and identifies with these people, it would seem, primarily because he feels very strongly that he is one of them and they are part of him. Hence the very difficult question of distinguishing roots from meaning; to what degree do I value my Jewish roots because I value Jewish traditions and beliefs and to what degree do I treasure Jewish values because I cherish my Jewish roots? This tension between concern for the universal and connection with the particular, although by no means a monopoly of Jews, is perhaps at the center of the struggle represented in this book to integrate Jewish identity (concrete and particular) with the traditions of the Enlightenment (abstract and universal).

There are, in addition, some dimensions to this story that continue to cast dark shadows for me. What are we to make of the king and the kingdom if we are interpret them respectively as metaphors for God and for Israel, as is often the case in Hasidic stories? Is God seeking even closer involvement with His people and/or does He seek to offer hope and support only in times of profound crisis? Is there a suggestion here that the whole world has gone mad and that only God retains the power of choice? Are the people of Israel being asked to accept that madness comes with the territory and that they are destined to a Sisyphean life of struggle to find God's way? Perhaps all God gives us is that red dot and the rest is up to us. Perhaps the story asks us to have faith in the wake of all these uncertainties and fears and in spite of cruel realities and bleak futures.

At times I confess that I could easily interpret the story as telling us that we are indeed already mad but have forgotten by choice or default that we are. As an educator and a Jew, however, I reject that view, as I have come to believe that our most important function is to resist despair and promote hope. I embrace the tradition that insists that it is a sin for a Jew to despair. I accept the wisdom of the red-dotted king in reminding us of our madness, for as upsetting as that acknowledgment might be, it can very well serve as the first step in the struggle for redemption.

In any case, my own work is constantly informed by the issues of the face-off between the forces of harsh reality and the dreams of liberating visions. There surely are compelling reasons to ground an educational program in the task of preparing people to grapple with the world as if it were inhabited with lunatics who occasionally aspire to be sane. I am, however, also attracted to the educational tradition that sees the world as if it were peopled by angels struggling to avoid being evil. I wind up in what I gather to be a characteristically Jewish position of embracing paradox and accepting uncertainty, but nonetheless still insisting on the necessity of human agency. This orientation is brilliantly encapsulated in Reinhold Niebuhr's succinct characterization of the moral significance of the Biblical Prophets as being rooted in their "confidence that life is good in spite of its evil and that it is evil in spite of its good. In such faith both sentimentality and despair are avoided."

The Rabbis and Their Sons
The son of an American rabbi delights his father by deciding that he wishes to follow in his father's footsteps and announces his intention not only to become a rabbi but to go to a yeshiva in Israel for his training. The father is overjoyed and pledges his total and unswerving support. The father's joy is to be short-lived, for just two years into his son's studies he receives a phone call from Israel in the middle of the night.

It is from his son who is in a very agitated state, his voice full of excitement and nervousness. The son has had an extraordinary epiphany and has converted to Christianity! He speaks of a newly found joyous sense of peace and fulfillment, yet is fearful of alienating his parents, yearns for his father's understanding, and begs for his blessing. The father is too shocked and bewildered to respond coherently and asks his son to allow him time to absorb the news.

The father is deeply shaken, racked with guilt, anger, sorrow, and apprehension. He prays, he anguishes with his wife, he reflects, he goes over any number of explanations and while this process helps, he is still tormented by doubt and pain. He says to himself, "I have been an observant and God-fearing Jew and raised my son to be the same, always believing in the goodness and mercy of the Almighty. What have I done to deserve this?"

He is also deeply embarrassed about his son's conversion, and his embarrassment prevents him from sharing his pain and getting help with his anguish. Finally, he summons up his courage and decides to confide in his closest friend, also a rabbi, for whom he has the greatest respect as a wise and pious person. He goes to the friend, tells him the story and asks, "How could it be that such a thing could happen to a pious and observant Jew like me?" The friend listens intently to the story, turns pale, clasps his hands to his face and gasps. He gathers himself together, gives out a long sigh, and answers, "Funny you should ask. I also have a son who likewise went to Israel to become a rabbi and he too became a Christian and I also was too ashamed to tell anyone."

The two friends sit in stunned silence, their pain deepened and their consternation now greatly magnified. When they speak it is with humility and near desperation that they look to each other for some explanation, some way to find meaning in their experiences. They both quickly come to the realization that in such difficult times, only a direct appeal to God Almighty will suffice. Knowing full well the dangers and risks of what they are doing and with great apprehension and reverence, they speak directly to God and beg for some divine inspiration or sign that would provide them with answers to their troubling and heart-breaking questions: "Oh God in heaven, we are two pious Jews who have faithfully and lovingly followed Thy will. We both have sons whom we sent to Israel to become rabbis, and both of them have forsaken their heritage and become Christians. Why did this happen?"

When they finish their prayers and beseechments, there is a hushed and tense silence. The two men, united by their parenthood, vocation, and pain, wait in a state of agitation and anxiety. Soon, there is a rustle in the room followed by the faint rumble of thunder and the appearance of a most pleasing glowing light. Then, much louder thunder and more powerful light, and the unmistakable sound of a voice being cleared. There is the sound of a long sigh followed by a voice that says, "Funny you should ask. I also have a son whom I sent to Israel to become a rabbi and . . ."

Again there is pathos and pain, and again there is irony and mockery, with added dashes of fatalism, victimization, and loss of control. This is a story about good people in bewildered pain and about a God who knows all too well about human anguish. Yet we are left as unsure about His attitude toward it as we are about His ability to do anything about it. However, there are also in this story intimations of struggle, hope, yearning, and aspiration, all aspects of the quintessential human impulse to search for meaning and harmony in the universe and on earth. The story also references the peculiarly Jewish tradition of humans challenging God, insisting on the individual's right to question Him, demanding that God meet His covenantal responsibilities. In addition, the God in this story is not quite as remote and mysterious as other representations. Indeed, this God seems to empathize and even mirror human vulnerabilities. It is this kind of dialectic of divine inspiration and human responsibility that has prodded me to find ways to accommodate revelation, agency, and mystery in my work. To me a proper education needs to make space for the mystery and glory of moral and spiritual imagination, just as it needs to nurture the knowledge, skills, and insights that give those flights of imagination concrete expression.

There are other overtones that connect the story to me, namely the references to America and to Christianity. There is the obvious pride that the fathers feel about their sons' decision to emigrate to Israel, presumably a sign of more profound commitment than even that of rabbis in the Diaspora. At the same time, the fathers have remained in America presumably prospering and thriving so that they have the fruits of freedom, autonomy, and choice. The story reminds me that my life is also informed and shaped for better or worse by my American consciousness and my immersion in a Christian culture.

The connection to Christianity is indicative of the hesitance, ambiguity, and ambivalence that marks my own attitudes toward the tangled and tragic history of Jewish-Christian relations. I certainly bear the pains of anti-Semitism, ranging from the subtleties of innuendo and condescension to the raw experiences of violence and hatred. I share in the anger and bitterness directed at those who would harm and kill Jews in the name of a religion grounded in unconditional love. In addition, I have also suffered from experiencing the disdain and contempt that many Jews have for most Christians. Moreover, I have been drawn to the teachings of the historical Jesus that seem to resonate and complement my notions of what constitutes Jewish ethics, namely a profound commitment to participating in the continuing creation of a world of peace, love, and justice. This affinity has produced significant disapproval over the years not only from my family but from some of my best Jewish friends fearful that I might become an apostate and give aid and comfort to the enemy. I am not at all pleased with this disapproval as it feels constricting and parochial, and it is in such times that I am likely to tell the story of the Mother and the Physicist.

Having said that, I also feel the poignancy of the sons' conversions, not only because of the disappointment for the parents but because the conversions represent a rupture in family tradition and, implicitly, a threat to Jewish survival. I very much value the continuity of family, tradition, and community that is so celebrated by Jews, and can therefore easily empathize with the fathers' anguish. Yet, I certainly very much value and honor modern notions of individual autonomy and choice, evidence of the powerful influences of Enlightenment thought on my life.

Hence, this ambivalence has both political and theoretical implications for me. Politically, it means that I must address the questions of identity; do I identify myself as unambiguously, if not partisanly, Jewish? Is my strategy toward dealing with Christians (as well as with other communities) to be one of competition, coexistence, or ecumenism? Is my strategy toward dealing with Jews on non-Jewish views to be one of mediator, translator, or apologist?

As a professional I need not only to figure out how these matters impinge on my teaching and writing, but I also need to address the compatibility of Jewish and Christian (as well as other) orientations, since my work is vitally concerned with the moral grounding of public education in a multicultural society. I continue to take the position that it is necessary and possible to forge some kind of vital consensus of what might constitute a spiritual and moral basis for an education directed at creating communities of peace, love, justice, and joy within the framework of a diverse and democratic American society. It would seem that this task is both a personal and a professional one in that I need to wrestle with the integration of the various strands that shape my own life as I engage in the larger political and ideological struggles for moral cohesion.

There are, of course, many other stories that are dear to me and many other interpretations of the ones I have told. However, I believe that what I have presented is indicative of much of my thinking on these matters. Writing this essay has enabled me to clarify a number of issues but it has also left me riddled with lots of ambivalence and uncertainty. I find it especially difficult to sort out the effects of my Jewish background and experience from the other influences on my professional life but I have just about decided that this concern is both unanswerable ultimately more interesting than it is important. What I believe is more pertinent to this essay is the question of the degree to which I intentionally and systematically work to frame my professional life within a Jewish tradition.

There are a number of serious obstacles to this connection, not least of which is my inability and reluctance to identify with a particular Jewish tradition. In addition, there are the complicated political, cultural, and institutional problems involved with teaching in a public, secular, nonsectarian university established expressly for the purpose of serving a particular community and its diverse population. There is no question that I am drawn to certain traditions of Jewish learning and prayer that conjure up for me a very appealing fantasy of being in an interpretative community that requires and affirms serious study, reflection, debate, and meditation. However, this fantasy is different from the vision of Enlightenment academic life, for it involves study and dialogue in a shared discourse that is centered on questions of ultimate meaning, cultural practice, and social survival rather than the disparate, multidisciplinary, and poly-dimensional discourses involved in the metaphor of the free marketplace of ideas. I am strongly attracted to a life rooted in grounded study, dialogue, and reflection, but I can also be critical of such a life to the extent that it distracts us from the responsibility to act in and on the world and to the degree that it is enabled through the oppression of others (most notably, women). Still, study is sweet, and to study with a learned and wise companion is sweeter still, especially if the sweetness is an important ingredient in the making of larger meaning. This seems to be a Jewish teaching that is consonant with my professional identity, i.e., the faith that there are communal educational processes that actually do contribute to the creation of a just and loving community, and that function is, in fact, *the* most important purpose of education.

As a faculty member in a modern public university, my task involves working with students from a wide range of orientations and backgrounds. There are certainly intellectual and ideological connections that I share with my students, but they are broader, more procedural than substantive, and in any cases they are not about being

Jewish. Indeed, the discourse of my teaching emerges out of the traditions of Liberalism and the Enlightenment with their emphasis on individual expression, autonomy, openness, and free inquiry. I affirm and support this approach even as I wonder how it would be to study not within the flexible and forgiving framework of permissive liberalism but rather within the stricter parameters of Jewish traditions of study.

As a child of the Enlightenment and a product of American culture, I also find that some extremely important commitments of mine become somewhat problematic within the context of Jewish traditions. My being is in large part defined by commitments to totally inclusive democracy, radical equality, and unconditional love, which are in considerable tension with the hierarchy, sexism, racism, and violence that often permeates Jewish thought. I am frankly impatient with the labored efforts that it takes to find support for these commitments in the Torah, especially when there are other secular or non-Jewish sources where such affirmation is proudly and unequivocally presented.

However, let me quickly add that this ambivalence and hesitation, as real as it is, is incomplete, for I also have come to a place where I can clearly affirm myself as a Jew much beyond the point of doing so by default. What is clear to me is that I very much want to learn more about Jewish thought and experience and to deepen my still-evolving Jewish consciousness. More to the point, this affirmation has significantly manifested itself in my current teaching and writing.

Affirmation

I entered education in part because I believed that greater understanding and knowledge were the keys to making a better world. This notion expanded to the belief that critical rationality in the Socratic tradition of probing skepticism, careful analysis, and precise thinking is the ultimate weapon against prejudice, oppression, and authoritarianism. I still highly value these traditions. Indeed, my teaching style continues to emphasize tough questions that are intended to make students squirm a little and think a lot. (Never mind that the reverse often happens.) Although I have always felt some disquiet about this orientation, it took me a long time to understand that what was unsettling about it was it had no grounding except itself. It seemed to me that either the educators seriously interested in significant social reform were basically saying that it is good to think critically for its own sake or that they were reluctant to be explicit about what they believe to be morally right. It finally dawned on me that what was utterly lacking not only in Education but in all of Academia was moral affirmation, a rather startling omission, particularly for those educators committed to creating a better world.

Again, it is Heschel who speaks to me:

"Socrates taught us that a life without thinking is not worth living. Now, thinking is a noble effort, but the finest thinking may end in futility. . . . The Bible taught us that life without commitment is not worth living; that thinking without roots will bear flowers but no fruit."

My professional work is totally concerned with grounding educational policies and practices not in critical thinking and not in creative expression but in moral commitments. To pursue critical thinking and creative expression for their own sakes is self-indulgent at best and idolatrous at worst. I certainly believe that these processes can be vital resources in the struggle to create a life of meaning but without a framework of meaning they are only neutral techniques capable of enabling good or evil. This makes the affirmation of a framework of meaning the prime requirement of any educational orientation worthy of serious consideration. Once I came to that conclusion, I had no choice but to make my own moral affirmations and framework of meaning as clear as possible, or to use a religious phrase, to profess my faith.

With all this said, I can now make it clearer how in at least two very important ways my Jewish experience is deeply embedded in my professional concerns. Firstly, I am dedicated to moral commitment and to meaning before anything else, before critical thinking, before creativity, before reading, before great literature and art, even before Einstein's theory of relativity. I see the value of education to the extent that it serves the good (I believe that this is what religious Jews call being obedient to God's will); anything else is a bonus. Notions of the good and of the meaningful should provide the criteria for determining the appropriateness of educational policies and practices and for measuring their efficacy. Such a position seems to me to be deeply Jewish since my view is that the most urgent and basic message of Torah is that in spite of a lot of contrary evidence we must operate in the faith that life has meaning, direction, and purpose.

Secondly, to paraphrase Will Herberg: My faith emerges from my affirmation of the history of the Jewish people as my redemptive history, and I have appropriated it as my personal background history, making it the foundation of my existence. If this history is the foundation of my existence then it inevitably is the foundation of the work that serves to define me.

The stories I have told and discussed surely reveal that this faith is constantly being tested by complex and troubling issues, and that a great deal of uncertainty, ambivalence, and ambiguity remain. However, writers like Alasdair MacIntyre have helped me to accept this confusion and move on from there by pointing out the value of identifying with a particular moral tradition and community, as well as the danger, if not impossibility, of pursuing the moral life without such identification. What I find especially helpful is MacIntyre's characterization of a moral community as "an historically extended, socially embodied argument." MacIntyre goes on to say that a critical dimension of such a community involves participants arguing about what should constitute its moral commitments. I fully intend to continue participating in that historically extended, socially embodied argument and to integrate the moral commitments of that living tradition into my work with passion, care, and reverence. The nature of my involvement will probably continue to resemble that of a lover's quarrel, a process of loving affirmation and critical skepticism, occasioned no doubt with moments of indifference, even hostility. As an instance of how this process is going, I cite the following excerpt from a paper I recently wrote on the relationship between education and spirituality, in which I discuss issues related to my Jewish identity. Much of what I say reflects Jewish traditions but I also have to say that I would not be offended if some of it does not; however, I would greatly value critiques of it from any number of Jewish perspectives.

"I affirm traditions that not only recognize that humans are fated to create our world but believes that above all we are called upon to create a world resonant with divine intention—a world of peace, justice, love, community, and joy for all. These are traditions that accept as givens the potentials of human abilities as well as the limits of human fallibilities; they posit our capacity to be generous as well as to be selfish; to be angelic as well as demonic; compassionate as well as cruel; wise as well as foolish. Such traditions revere knowledge but only as it is tempered with the wisdom that advances justice and mercy; a perspective that acknowledges the enormity of the task but dismisses human despair as sinful; and one that represents a consciousness of outrage in the wake of cruelty and injustice but always in the faith that witness, confession, and healing offer the possibilities of transcendence and redemption. What is absolutely crucial to redemption is human responsibility and human agency since these traditions require that we act as God's agents, dedicated to constructing and sustaining communities based on joy, love, peace, and justice."

Epilogue

As I expected, the process of writing this paper has clarified some issues, confused others, and raised brand-new ones for me. Perhaps the issues all come under the heading of the problematics of choice. I did not choose to be a Jew, I do not believe that I can choose not to be a Jew. I am absolutely clear that among other important things, I am a Jew, and I have no problems with any of this. As the adage says, one does not choose to be born or to die, or as George Santayana said, "No one speaks language, everyone speaks a particular language." Or, as the saying goes, everybody has to come from somewhere. Frankly, I don't know if it would be better if I could have chosen or what I would have chosen if I could, but in any case the issue is moot to me.

Of course, I have much more choice about how I express and mani-fest my Jewish identity, and the fact that I have such a lot of choice stems in large part from the happenstance of my living in twentieth-century America. As I navigate between the freedom and autonomy that comes with the territory of the Enlightenment American style and the commitments that come with the territory of Jewish traditions, I struggle with several questions. Is it OK for me to pick and choose the Jewish traditions that are appealing to me and resonant with my work? (I sort of think it is but I need some help with this.) Is it all right to see Jewish sources as, to use Roger Simon's term, fertile grazing areas for finding support for my ideas? Should I define myself as a Jew living in exile or as an American "who happens to be Jewish"? Should I be-come more attached to a particular Jewish tradition and work to de-duce its relevance to American education? Is my work as an educator about encouraging *goyim* to be more Jewish or better informed on Jewish thought, or both, or neither? Perhaps I should accept and even embrace a life of multiple and shifting professional identities, moving from one paradigm and context to another. As a matter of fact, can I just give up fussing over these issues and forget all about this identity thing?

The most complicated question for me personally, however, has to do with my realization that, as with my connection to the Boston

Braves, my deepest and strongest ties are at base irrational. In a very real sense, these bonds have absolutely nothing to do with the content of Jewish history, nor its religious teachings, nor its literature, as much as I love and treasure them. I came to treasure them because I am Jewish; I did not become Jewish because I treasured them. I know this kind of visceral bonding resonates with the consciousness of the physicist's mother, but there it is and I remain very, very puzzled by it all. As far as my work is concerned, would it have had a similar orientation if I were born an Episcopalian? Or if I were a fourth-generation Jew? Or if I were an Israeli? I'm not even sure I need to know.

I end with even more questions than I had when I began, which reminds me of a story.

Two people, one a Jew, the other not, are having a long and heated conversation. One of them, in a moment of frustration, asks, "Why is it that every time I ask a Jew a question, they always answer with another question?" The Jew replies, "So what's wrong with asking questions?"

Afterword

Jeffrey Kane

The true meaning of concrete reality is the creation which is entrusted to me and to every man. In it, the signs of address are given to us.
Martin Buber

As I reflect upon the essays in this volume, I recall a story told by Martin Buber of when he was visited by a young man. He treated the young man with courtesy and spoke with him at length. However, Buber recalls, "I omitted to guess the questions which he did not put" (Buber, p. 13). Soon after, Buber learned of the young man's death. He recounts, "I learned that he had come to me not casually, but borne by destiny, not for chat but for a decision. . . . What do we expect when we are in despair and yet go to a man? Surely a presence by means of which we are told that never the less there is meaning" (Buber, p. 14). Buber realized that despite his efforts to maintain a pleasurable conversation, he was not aware of "the signs of address" when his full presence and nothing less was required.

This was a turning point in Buber's life when he recognized that the highest responsibility he could assume as a human being was in "the every day." He explained, "I possess nothing but the every day out of which I am never taken. The mystery is no longer disclosed, it is escaped or it has made its dwelling here where everything happens as it happens. I know more fullness but each mortal hour's fullness of claim and responsibility."

Buber understood that our ultimate calling and responsibility as human beings is not found in religious practice or behavior guided by ethical reasoning. For him, the most real and pressing aspects of reality are not visible to the physical eye or the rational mind. Some things come only as we encounter the world, open and attentive. Everything is imbued with a meaning and purpose that includes, but goes beyond the functional relationships and even the intellectual connections that can be made through the use of logic. This sense of the meaning and purpose which courses through all things and between them is not developed through abstraction. Abstraction is a process by which we pick phenomena apart focusing on specific characteristics. We use these characteristics to integrate experience into (or to create) systems of thought. These systems provide us with tremendous intellectual flexibility and power, but leave us removed from the experience anything beyond reconstructed fragments.

It is difficult to understand what Buber means by "the signs of address" not because it is so abstract a concept, but rather that it is so immediate and concrete. It constitutes a level of consciousness rather than its content. There is no sorting and classifying of ideas required even as illuminating intellectual insights may follow. The difficulty arises not because great intellectual powers are needed but because understanding of this thought requires an inner awakening, an active imagination to perceive the underlying unity in all things.

In many respects, understanding the address of everyday life is much like appreciating the aesthetic dimension of a piece of music. When listening to a piece of music, a person can focus on the individual note, its pitch, duration, amplitude, etc. However, focusing on the notes, a listener might fail to grasp periods of silence between the notes, and the patterns of relationship between sound and silence carry meaning. Furthermore, no theoretical analysis of the various patterns in the music could convey the aesthetic impulses that shape every note and serve as the creative foundation for the piece as a whole.

In this context, an understanding of music first and foremost requires someone with the imagination and attentiveness to dwell within it. So it is with the call of the moment; so it is with the moral opportunities and responsibilities we have that come to us. It is not enough to think critically; it is not enough to apply reason to the human condition. Here, the reason may follow and refine experience that cannot serve as the well-spring of understanding. In the last analysis, there is only the experience of being human, the humanness of others, and sacredness of all creation.

Herein lies the source of Dr. Purpel's insight and the objectives of his work. The essays in this volume do not so much constitute a collection of theoretical speculation or practical observations. They echo the address that one man hears in the face of concrete reality. The signs of address for Purpel are not reserved for the interaction of individuals. They speak to the humanity in each one of us for the humanity in all of us. Human suffering calls each of us even if it lies beyond our physical sight or the arbitrary borders we use to separate people into classes, races, or nations.

The objective of the essays is not so much to inform readers about educational policies and practices or to demonstrate the intellectual virtues of a critical mind. Even as the essays inform and provoke thinking, they are intended more to awaken the reader to the immediate and pressing moral dimensions of human existence. It is not a book filled with written moral codes or ethical principles. It is one that begins with a sense of the sacredness of life, the mystery of existence, and a heightened sense of moral responsibility. These aspects of being can be understood only as we have the imagination to dwell in the fluid meaning which courses through us and all things.

The message Purpel delivers is not one of inner harmony or universal peace. In fact, he does not direct us to turn inward for understanding. His focus is not on an "inner self" at all but on the relation between self and "the other" or others. As Buber observed, in *I-Thou*, one always lives in relation, never in isolation. We exist as part of the human and larger natural communities. The concept of "self" out of this context of relation to other(s) is a misleading abstraction.

Here, the key question above all else is what each of us is called to do.

For Purpel, the answer is to give voice to outrage, and his goal is to quicken the same outrage in the reader. There is unimaginable and intolerable human suffering in this world at the hands of human beings. There is poverty, hunger, oppression, and injustice. And yet, in our schools and universities human misery goes all but unnoticed. As educators, we all too often focus on providing our students with knowledge and skills, the tools we believe necessary to assume a productive role in a global marketplace. There is little to guide students to develop compassion for those in need or to act to alleviate suffering. As scholars, we conduct our research with clinical detachment where compassion and recognition of human need and responsibility undermine academic accountability. While it may be that schools have never focused on heightening moral consciousness or that academe since the days of the Enlightenment has separated knowledge from personal expression of faith, Purpel insists that the time has come for change.

Since the days of Descartes, we have held to a model of knowledge unfettered by personal belief or bias. In varied forms, the principle has long been that knowledge as opposed to opinion requires clear public observation and the use of precise reasoning. The personal preferences or inclinations of a knower would introduce variables into knowledge that would not be public or open to explicit, critical review. There is great benefit in this model as it guards against the institutionalization of personal bias, the proliferation of error, and the imposition of dogma.

However, many philosophers and scientists, including Michael Polanyi, Gregory Bateson, and Fritzjaf Capra, have revealed that this Western model of knowledge is deeply flawed and that, in fact, it has not accounted for the growth of our scientific understanding. Personal intuition, aesthetic sensibility, and an active imagination play a central role in inquiry and discovery even as they are a subject to critical analysis. Although Purpel does not concentrate his efforts on the refinement of a personally grounded epistemology in science, there is a growing recognition of the need for personal affirmation in science and in modern intellectual life. He understands that an affirmation of our moral and spiritual responsibilities as human beings opens the possibilities for dangerous social error. However, he would rather assume the risks heightening the level of our humanity than avoid them at its expense. Personal insight need not be personal bias. It can be an expression of what is deepest and most essential in all of us. It may be as Ralph Waldo Emerson asserted in "The Oversoul," our humanness is defined not by what separates but rather by what unites us. "We are all inlets to the great All." Affirmation, in this sense, is a personal act with a universal source. Purpel would have us raise ourselves to meet the concrete reality that requires our response rather than limit the world to conform with our narrow conceptions of knowledge.

It is time to affirm basic beliefs and commitments that cannot be explained fully by reason or experiment. It is time to affirm that it is an abomination for us to deny or ignore injustice, oppression, abuse, hunger, and poverty. It is time to declare that each of us shares a responsibility for human suffering and for its alleviation. The essays contained in this volume are quite distinctive in this regard. They employ clear and precise reasoning but do so always in a context which transcends rational analysis alone. Purpel draws upon his own Judaic heritage as a source of inspiration for his deepest convictions. It is in Judaism that he finds others who burn with the same passion and outrage. For him, the Prophets rather than the great literary figures of the Enlightenment speak to what is most essential and true. However, there are other sources of religious insight that apart from ritual and dogma understand the call of the moment and we need to act with compassion. Each reader is asked to search his or her own traditions in search of guidance on how to live with a sense of moral urgency and moral agency. The critical manner of thought we have developed in the West over the past four centuries is an invaluable but insufficient basis for understanding. It needs to be balanced with an immediate and concrete sense that there is meaning, sanctity, and purpose to human life.

In this broad context, it is easy for our passions to lead us to the mistaken conclusion that extraordinary action is necessary, that we must assume Herculean moral tasks. However, the surest path to exhaustion, defeat, and cynicism is, as Purpel explains, lack of humility: a lack of recognition of indeed how limited we are and how much there is to do. Each of us is asked to respond to the human suffering with the full presence of person Buber recognized as required in his meeting with student. With Joshua Heschel, Purpel reminds us, the rabbis of old explained, "Whoever destroys a single soul should be considered the same as one who has destroyed the whole world. And whoever saves a single soul is to be considered the same as one who has saved the whole world" (Heschel, p. 14).

Notes

Buber, Martin. 1971. *Between Man and Man.* New York: The Macmillan Company.

Heschel, Abraham J. 1962. *The Prophets.* New York: Harper & Row.

Studies in the Postmodern Theory of Education

General Editors
Joe L. Kincheloe & Shirley R. Steinberg

Counterpoints publishes the most compelling and imaginative books being written in education today. Grounded on the theoretical advances in criticalism, feminism and postmodernism in the last two decades of the twentieth century, Counterpoints engages the meaning of these innovations in various forms of educational expression. Committed to the proposition that theoretical literature should be accessible to a variety of audiences, the series insists that its authors avoid esoteric and jargonistic languages that transform educational scholarship into an elite discourse for the initiated. Scholarly work matters only to the degree it affects consciousness and practice at multiple sites. Counterpoints' editorial policy is based on these principles and the ability of scholars to break new ground, to open new conversations, to go where educators have never gone before.

For additional information about this series or for the submission of manuscripts, please contact:

Joe L. Kincheloe & Shirley R. Steinberg
637 West Foster Avenue
State College, PA 16801